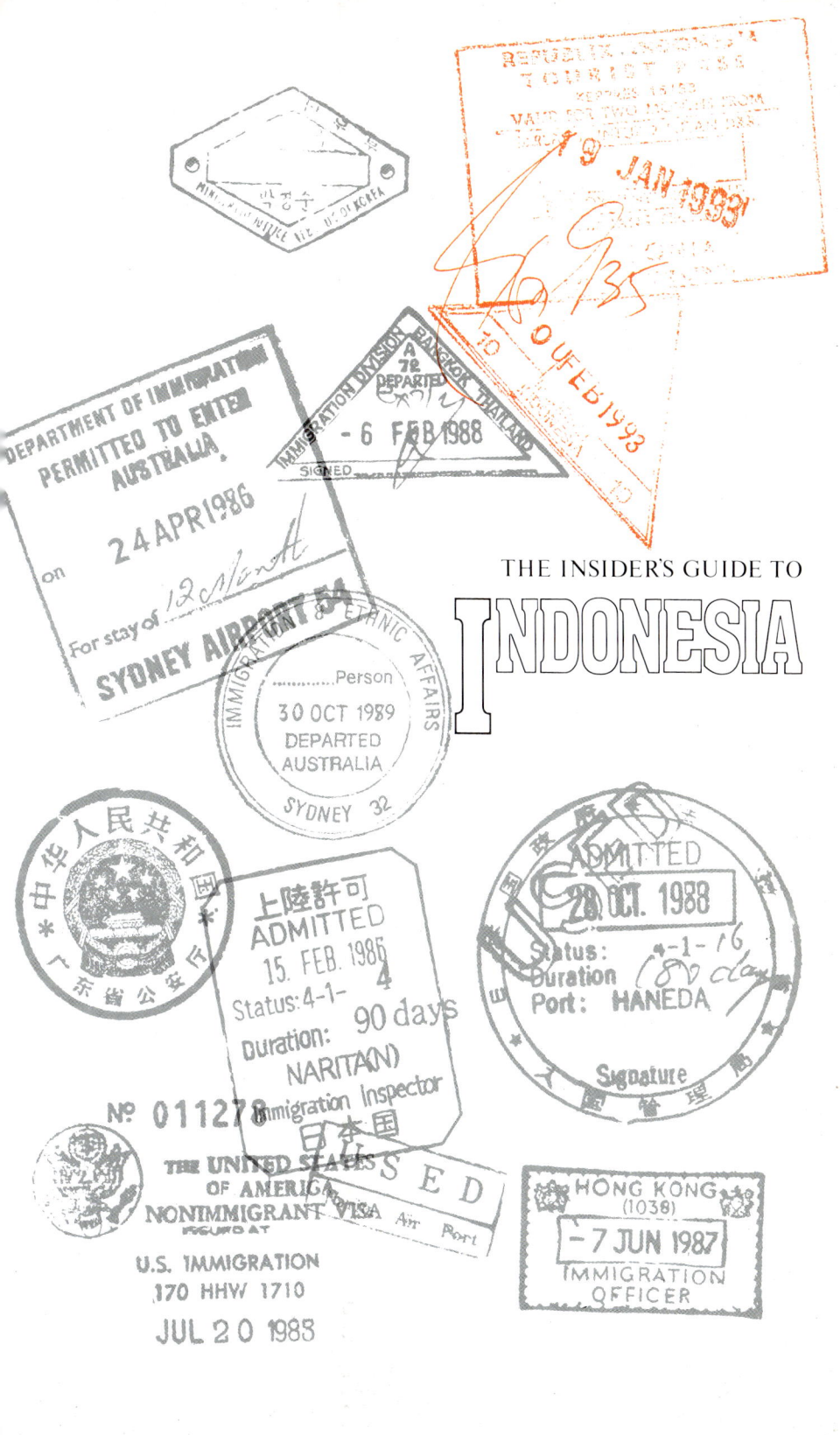

THE INSIDER'S GUIDE TO

INDONESIA

THE INSIDER'S GUIDES

AUSTRALIA • BALI • CALIFORNIA • CANADA • CHINA • EASTERN CANADA • FLORIDA • HAWAII •
HONG KONG • INDIA • INDOCHINA • INDONESIA • JAPAN • KENYA • KOREA • NEPAL •
NEW ENGLAND • NEW ZEALAND • MALAYSIA AND SINGAPORE • MEXICO •
PORTUGAL • RUSSIA • SPAIN • THAILAND • TURKEY • WESTERN CANADA

The Insider's Guide to Indonesia
First Published 1993
Moorland Publishing Co Ltd
Moor Farm Road, Airfield Estate, Ashbourne, DE61HD, England
by arrangement with Novo Editions, S.A.
53 rue Beaudouin, 27700 Les Andelys, France
Telefax: (33) 32 54 54 50

© 1993 Novo Editions, S.A.

ISBN: 0 86190 253 X

Created, edited and produced by Novo Editions, S.A.
Editor in Chief: Allan Amsel
Original design concept: Hon Bing-wah
Picture editor and designer: Chan Sio Man
Text and artwork composed and information updated
using Ventura Publisher software

Printed by Samhwa Printing Company Limited, Seoul, Korea

THE INSIDER'S GUIDE TO

INDONESIA

By David DeVoss

Photographed by Nik Wheeler

MPC

Contents

BURMA   THAILAND   KAMPUCHEA   VIETNAM

INDONESIA

SOUTH CHINA
SEA

STRAIT OF MALACCA

Banda Aceh
ACEH
Mt Leuser
3381▲   Belawan
GUNUNG   Medan
LEUSER N.P.   Prapat
SIMEULUE
Gunung   Lake
Sitoli   Toba
NIAS
Teluk
Dalam
BATU ARCH.   Bukittinggi
Padang
SIBERUT
SUMATRA
SIPORA   JAMBI   Jambi
PAGAIA UTARA
MENTAWAI ISLANDS   Musi   Palembang
PAGAIA   Bengkulu
SALATAN
BENGKULU   LAMPUNG
Bandar Lampung   Panjang
KRAKATAU   Anyer   Banten
Bogor   Jakarta
UJONG   Bandung
KULON   Borobudur
N.P.   Yogyakarta
JAVA

MALAYSIA

SINGAPORE   BINTAN
BATAM   Tanjung Pinang
RIAU
Pekanbaru

NATUNA SEA

BUNGURAN
UTARA
ISL.

BRUNEI

MALAYSIA

KALIMANTAN
WEST
KALIMANTAN
Pontianak
CENTRAL
KALIMANTAN   Tenggarong
Arot   Barito   SOUTH
Kahayan   KALIM.
Sampit   Banjarmasin
Kumai
Bay   Cape
BELITUNG   Puting

BANGKA

JAVA SEA

Cirebon   Semarang   MADURA
Mt Lawu   Surabaya   BALI SEA
3030   Malang   Ampenan
Denpasar   Mataram
BALI   LOMBOK   S

NUS

INDIAN

OCEAN

Introduction

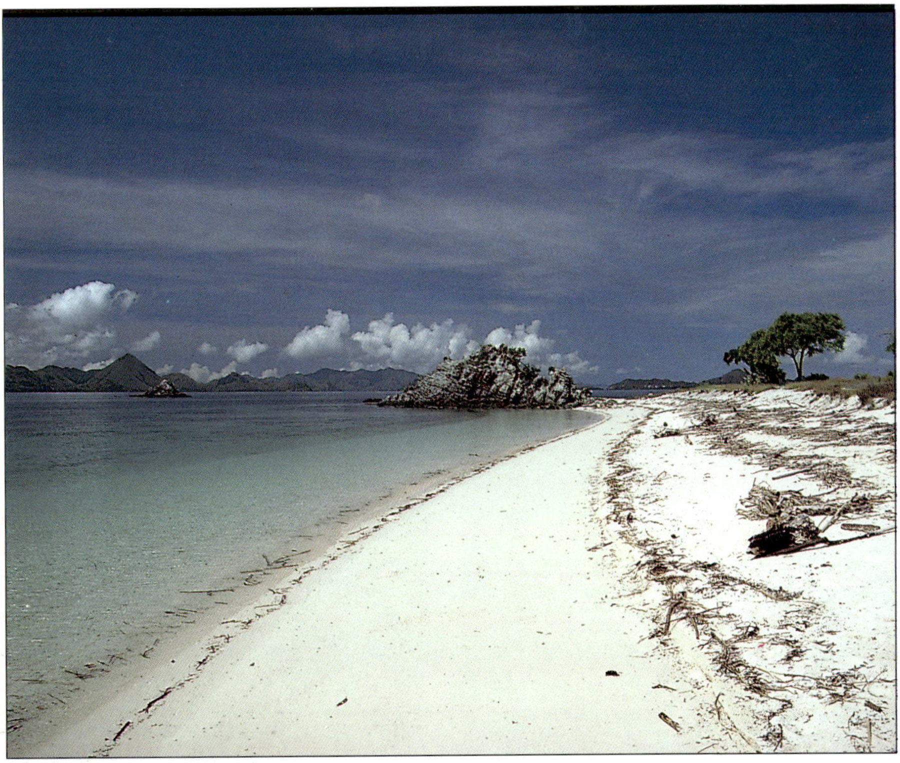

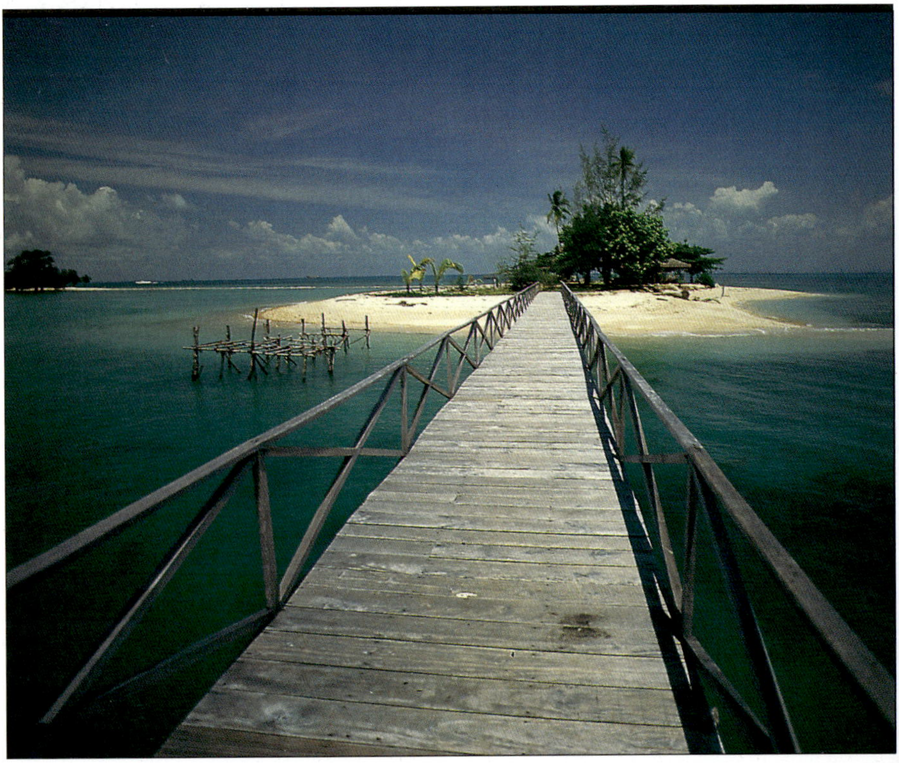

FOR hundreds of years the exotic islands of Indonesia have fired the imaginations of foreigners. Hindu traders in the second century were astonished by the variety of foods, the profusion of spices and the gentleness of natives like those on Bali, who now refer to their home as the "Isle of the Gods." Already possessing everything they needed, the Spice Islanders proved to be difficult trading partners. Finally, the Chinese, desperate for the islands' pepper, nutmeg and cloves, agreed to pay in gold, and used Song Dynasty porcelain as supplemental ballast on the long trip south from the Center of the World.

The infusion of riches only added to the islands' exotic allure. Marco Polo, who swung through the archipelago in the thirteenth century on his return voyage to Italy, described the region as the wealthiest place on earth. "The quantity of gold collected there exceeds all calculation and belief," he noted. Arabs arriving two centuries earlier had planted the seed of Islam at the northern tip of Sumatra, then proceeded to ship spices back to Damascus. Competition among the European nations to secure a portion of the lucrative spice trade prompted the inadvertent discovery of the New World by Columbus in 1492. In his 1939 travel classic, *Inside Asia*, John Gunther's impressions of the country were remarkably similar to those of Marco Polo seven centuries before. "The dominant fact about the islands is that, like Croesus and John D. Rockefeller, they are rich," he wrote. "They are the Big Loot of Asia."

The days of sailing galleons into Indonesia and filling them with loot are over. Today adventurers come to explore the ruins of lost civilizations, or hike through stone age villages where pigs are the principal medium of exchange or watch maidens in gold-embroidered bodices seductively dance in front of elaborately carved temples beneath the full moon.

Indonesia today has 192 million people making it the world's fourth most populous country. Its 13,667 islands stretch more than 5,160 km (3,200 miles) along the equator, a distance equal to that from San Francisco to Bermuda. Half of New Guinea, the world's second largest island (after Greenland) belongs to Indonesia, as does three-quarters of Borneo, the world's third largest island. Sumatra, which ranks sixth in size, is as big as California.

Yet for all its size and wealth, vast areas of Indonesia remain largely undeveloped wilderness. More than 1,600 of the world's 9,000 species of birds are native to Indonesia. At least 40,000 species of plants and trees, ten percent of all the existing in the world, are found here. There are 3,000 kinds of trees in the rain forests of Sumatra and Kalimantan (the Indonesian name for its portion of Borneo), which alone boasts twice as many species of trees as all of Africa. There are

more than 300 nature reserves, national parks and protected forest areas. Indeed, 6.5 percent of the country's total land area (of over two million square kilometers) must remain pristine by law.

Indonesia is a land of volcanoes: towering, jungle-covered peaks that both enrich and destroy. Of the 500 volcanoes in Indonesia, 128 remain active. Yet the overriding rhythm of the nation is set by wind and water, not rock and fire. From November to March the west monsoon brings torrential rain to Sumatra, Java and the Lesser

ABOVE: Palms bend with the trade winds at Aceh Beach in Northern Sumatra. OPPOSITE: Island hideaways: Fida Daru Island, near Flores TOP and No Man's Island, Batam, BOTTOM.

Sunda islands. For the remainder of the year the eastern monsoon buffets the country with dry air parched by the heat of the Australian deserts.

EARLY KINGDOMS

The first great Indonesian kingdom, **Srivijaya**, rose to prominence in the seventh century in South Sumatra. A Buddhist kingdom in which nobles were taught Indian Pallava script by monks invited from India, Srivijaya's power resulted from its location on the Malacca Strait. Srivijaya's rulers were expansionist by inclination, and soon their realm included ports along the Malay Peninsula and parts of modern Thailand. By the tenth century an impressive triangle trade linked Sumatra with India and China. Gold, porcelain and silk would be traded by the emperor of China for rhinoceros horn, cloves, cardamom and camphor wood. To India and beyond Srivijaya kings would dispatch cloves, aloe, ivory and sandalwood.

As Srivijaya prospered, it ran up against the equally powerful Hindu kingdom of **Mataram** on the plains of Central Java near present day Yogyakarta. The leaders of Mataram were not worldly sophisticates like their peers from the Sumatran coast. Their kingdom was inland and agricultural.

The Mataram empire eventually fell when the Buddhist **Sailendra Dynasty** allied itself with Srivijaya's remaining rulers. The new Buddhist empire celebrated its power in 850 with the construction of Borobudur in Central Java. Yet within a few years of the completion of the world's greatest Buddhist temple, the Sailendra princes were overthrown by survivors of the Hindu kingdom of Mataram, who commemorated their triumph with the temple complex of Prambanan.

By the end of the thirteenth century the Hindu-Buddhist empires of Central Java, and the crumbling remnants of Srivijaya on the Sumatran coast, were gradually being replaced by the **Majapahit Kingdom**. Founded in East Java in 1293 the Majapahit empire only lasted one hundred years, but many Indonesian historians consider it to be their country's greatest epoch because of the kingdom's enlightened leadership. Majapahit leaders such

as Gajah Mada and Hayam Wuruk sought to extend their influence through the force of art and ideas, not violent conquest. But the Majapahit's greatest legacy, however, undoubtedly was its incorporation of Hindu thoughts, words and symbols into a unified Indonesian culture.

ARRIVAL OF ISLAM

Arab traders began arriving in Sumatra even before the birth of Mohammed in 570 A.D. As trade between India, Melaka and China grew, so did their influence. By the end of the fifteenth century most of the area around modern Banda Aceh had converted to Islam and proselytizing imams were hard at work

in Java and Sulawesi. With the Portuguese capture of Melaka in 1511, Islamic traders began moving to Indonesia in even larger numbers. In 1477, the people of Demak accepted Islam *en masse*. Cirebon and other Javanese cities quickly followed.

Though rajahs and sultans had great power over the life of the people, Islam from the outset was considered an egalitarian religion, a faith in which all people were equal before Allah and his prophet Mohammed. Islam not only allowed Indonesians to escape the Hindu caste system but also provided a unifying force against Christian colonialists.

As the spice trade increased, so did the spread of Islam. Never was it proffered at the point of a sword. Animist Dyaks who rejected the religion because of its prohibition against their favorite food, pork, survived unchanged after the wave of Islam passed. Ironically, the greatest change probably occurred to Islam itself, which gained millions of converts by pragmatically adapting itself to the disparate cultures and beliefs of the archipelago.

PRECURSORS OF COLONIALISM

In most parts of the world the advance of European civilization was preceded by the cross and the sword. In Southeast Asia, Europe's advance guard was financed not

Stone sentinels loom over Borobudur on the island of Java.

by the church or the crown but by merchant trading houses anxious, nay desperate, to monopolize the lucrative trade in spices. It is no exaggeration to assert that everything which transpired in the archipelago from the sixteenth to the eighteenth centuries stemmed from the scramble for cloves, nutmeg, cinnamon and pepper.

The first European (after Marco Polo) to arrive in Indonesia was Alfonso d'Albuquerque. A Portuguese adventurer fresh from his victory over Melaka, Albuquerque's goal was to locate the Moluccas and

then organize the spice trade out of Tidore and Ternate.

Unlike the French with their *mission civilitresse* or the English, who were determined that Britannia should rule the waves, the Portuguese did not try to subjugate alien societies. Their goal was simply to establish defensible trading bases — colonies similar to Melaka, Macao and Goa — through which natural resources and trade wares could be funneled back to Lisbon.

Because they did not attempt to hold large amounts of territory or install their own officialdom, the Portuguese often were dismissed as a relatively harmless force, no better or worse that the usual sort of brigands that roamed the South China Sea. In 1570, however, the Portuguese decided to venture outside their armed fort and play palace games of intrigue. Imagining they would receive better terms from his successor, they assassinated the sultan of Ternate. Too late, the overextended and woefully outnumbered Portuguese garrison realized their miscalculation. Instead of meekly accepting the fait accompli, the people of Ternate violently rose up and threw the Portuguese off the island.

The Portuguese may have proven themselves inept colonialists, but they hung on in Indonesia longer than any other European nation. It was not until 1975 when the Indonesian army invaded and forcibly annexed the colony of East Timor that Lisbon's flag finally was lowered officially.

By the beginning of the seventeenth century Portugal's presence was waning rapidly, but Holland's control of the islands was by no means certain. For a time it appeared that it might be the British who would eventually get the upper hand. Wherever the Dutch East India Company (*Vereenigde Oost-Indische Compagnie or* V.O.C. for short*)* had a trading post, so did the British East India Company. The Dutch finally succeeded in pushing the British back to Malaya, but in 1811, when Holland was occupied by France in the Napoleonic Wars, Britain returned in the person of Sir Stamford Raffles.

The renowned father of Singapore immediately set to work and within five years he had started a trading post at Bengkulu, unearthed the overgrown temple of Borobudur, chronicled the cannibalistic proclivities of Lake Toba's Batak tribesmen and discovered an enormous insect-eating flower 100 cm in diameter that a delighted London Zoological Society named *"Rafflesia"* in his honor.

Impressed by Indonesia's natural resources, Raffles urged Whitehall to hang on to the archipelago, but in 1816 he was overruled and eight years later Britain, in return for Dutch possessions in Malaya and India, formally recognized Dutch sovereignty over the East Indies.

COLONIALISM UNDER THE DUTCH

Three and a half centuries of Dutch colonial rule began inauspiciously in 1596 when Dutch captain Cornelius de Houtman limped into the West Java port of Banten. For Houtman it had been an arduous voyage in which

---

ABOVE: Indonesians have worshipped in mosques similar to that at Sumenep on the island of Madura for nearly 500 years. OPPOSITE: A sultan's guard at Yogyakarta.

more than half of his 250 man crew had died. That he had found Java at all was something of an accomplishment. The location of the East Indies was a secret. Portuguese were the only Europeans who knew how to sail to the fabled spice islands, and they jealously guarded their charts and rudders. Houtman's dismay vanished when after returning home he discovered that his cargo of pepper and cloves brought a handsome profit.

To maximize their effort and prevent needless competition among themselves

cloves on Ternate. By the end of the decade Coen had exterminated most of the people on Banda and controlled nutmeg as well.

From its base in Batavia (today's Jakarta), the V.O.C. expanded its sphere of influence, capturing Melaka (1641), Makassar (1667) and south Sumatra. By the end of the seventeenth century the V.O.C. had eliminated the threat from the Portuguese, Spanish and British and had established a trade route extending half way round the world.

Because the V.O.C. goal was high commodity prices, not increased productivity, it

Dutch merchant companies joined together in 1602 to form the *Vereenigde Oost-Indische Compagnie* (United East India Company). The V.O.C. had extraordinary powers and functioned as an independent government that raised an army, signed foreign treaties and administered justice on behalf of the Netherlands government.

The commander of the V.O.C. in the Indies was Jan Pieterszoon Coen, and under his direction "Jan Compagnie" quickly set about monopolizing the spice trade. In 1607, after defeating the Portuguese at Tidore, the V.O.C obtained exclusive rights to all the

often burned existing plantations and destroyed surplus amounts of cloves, nutmeg and cinnamon. The policy caused tremendous human suffering, but revolts were kept to a minimum because of the V.O.C.'s adroit manipulation of competing sultanates. The culmination of Holland's "divide and conquer" policy came in 1755 when the V.O.C. divided the old Mataram kingdom so that the sultans of Yogyakarta and Solo could scheme among themselves instead of uniting to oust the Dutch.

Despite its initial success, the V.O.C. found itself in trouble by the middle of the eighteenth century. Unsuccessful wars and the increase in British sea power brought an end to monopolies and secure trade routes. As

Spirits of Dutch planters silently wander the nutmeg groves surrounding Fort Belgica on Banda Neira.

the V.O.C. became more isolated, corruption increased. Import duties and local production taxes were diverted by company employees. In 1799 the V.O.C. declared bankruptcy and was taken over by the Dutch colonial service.

Dutch civil servants sent to Batavia quickly learned that the V.O.C. vast empire was not what it seemed. Beyond Java, Makassar and selected Sumatran enclaves, the Indies were mostly in the hands of Indonesians. Not only were the islands not producing revenue, they actually were a drain on the Netherlands, which itself was fast approaching bankruptcy following the partition of Belgium in 1830.

The response to the demand for more revenue was the Culture System in which all of Java and Sumatra, save for the ungovernable northern tip around Aceh, were turned into state-owned plantations. Instead of growing rice to feed the population, Indonesia's most fertile land was used to grow cash crops like coffee, cotton and indigo that would bring good prices in Europe. Along with increased taxes the Culture System made colonialism profitable again, but the abuses so enraged Dutch liberals that they began to push in parliament for a series of reforms known as the Ethical Policy.

Essentially, the Ethical Policy aimed to create a system that was both humane and profitable. After two centuries of neglect, Dutch politicians reasoned that if they improved the economic well being of Indonesians, the Indonesians themselves would become an enormous market. For the first time, starting in about 1910, Indonesian children were brought to Holland for advanced education. But the Ethical Policy was too little too late. Many children of the elite who were brought to Holland and exposed to the ideas of Kraal Marx became revolutionaries. As for the great bulk of people, little changed. At the start of the war, only 630 Indonesians out of a population of 68 million had graduated from high school.

RISE OF NATIONALISM

Despite three centuries of rule, the Dutch never fully subdued Indonesia. More than 15,000 Dutch soldiers died putting down a Central Java rebellion by Mataram Prince Diponegoro in 1825. The Acehnese fought the Dutch to a stand-off in a bitter *perang sabil* "holy war" that lasted 70 years. The Bugis battled the Dutch on and off for nearly 200 years. Indeed, it wasn't until 1905 that peace finally came to South Sulawesi.

By the early decades of the twentieth century it was clear that, despite Holland's Ethical Policy, colonialism couldn't last forever in Indonesia. In 1909 the Islamic Organization, or *Sarekat Islam*, provided a forum where Indonesians both urban and rural found common cause against the Dutch. In 1914 the *Perserikatan Kommunist Indonesia* began to organize quietly. Begun in Bandung in 1927, the Indonesian Nationalist Party, *Partai Nasional Indonesia,* soon became the largest and most outspoken voice for independence primarily because of its leader, a young engineer named Sukarno. Sukarno saw himself as the Gandhi of Indonesia, a man who would gain full independence through the use of civil disobedience.

Unfortunately, for Sukarno, the rise of the PNI coincided with the world-wide depression of the 1930s. With commodity prices falling the Dutch refused to consider reform and responded to the nationalist sentiment by sending the main leaders into internal exile.

In January 1942 Japanese troops landed on Borneo and the Celebes. The following month they invaded Sumatra. By mid-March Batavia had fallen and the retreat was on. Unable to contain the onslaught, Dutch soldiers, planters, civilian officials and families boarded transports bound for safer harbors.

Initially, Indonesians welcomed the Japanese as fellow Asian liberators and in the early months the Japanese military supported nationalist movements and talked of granting independence. But before long Tokyo's true intentions became clear. In fervently Islamic Aceh people were forced to begin the day by bowing east toward Tokyo instead of west toward Mecca.

Resentment against the Japanese was kept to a minimum, however, by nationalists like Sukarno and Mohammed Hatta, who were allowed to carry on their political activities and form groups like the Volunteer Army of Defenders, a civil defense militia that provided a foundation for the independence struggle to come.

In the waning months of the war the Japanese gave their consent to a conference in which Sukarno outlined his vision for the new Indonesia. In addition to the island groups historically considered part of the country, Sukarno's boundaries encompassed Netherlands New Guinea, Sarawak, Brunei and North Borneo plus the entire Malay peninsula. The Japanese, who had no power to further Sukarno's ambitions or prevent their own collapse, demurred, as did the British and Australian military leaders who temporarily occupied the country at the end of the war.

STRUGGLES FOR INDEPENDENCE

In 1946 Dutch troops began to filter back into Indonesia, but the country to which they returned was not the one they had left in 1942. Medan and Palembang on Sumatra had to be bombed before they could be reoccupied. Nationalists in Bandung burned most of the city rather than turn it back to the Dutch intact. Heavy fighting destroyed much of Surabaya and Yogyakarta had to be strafed by Dutch fighters to make it safe for troops to enter. Dutch troops eventually regained control of all major towns, but the rural byways and paddy fields remained in the hands of nationalists who rallied the peasantry with cries of *Merdeka* (Freedom).

The cries may have fallen on deaf ears in the Hague, but at the United Nations and in Washington the combination of Dutch intransigence and Indonesian persistence became an annoying embarrassment. Disturbed that the amount Holland was spending on the war was approaching the sum it was receiving from the United States under the Marshall Plan, Washington threatened to curtail aid and join the Netherlands' adversaries in the United Nations. Confronted with a war they did not have the means to win, the Dutch finally capitulated and on December 27, 1949 Indonesia proclaimed its independence.

CHAOS AND DEMOCRACY

The new nation of Indonesia began to unravel within weeks of its declaration of Independence. The Minahasans of North Sulawesi wanted nothing to do with the new country. Neither did the Ambonese, who had fought alongside the Dutch. Despite Sukarno's guiding concept of *pancasila*, under which democracy would be forged from Islam, tribal *adat* (custom) and patriotic nationalism, communists, radical Moslems and disgruntled minorities all wanted their regions to succeed.

Sukarno's response was an oxymoronic concept called "Guided Democracy" in which the country's democratically-elected parliament was suspended in 1956 and decision-making power was given to administrators picked by Sukarno.

In 1958 armed rebellions against Sukarno's centralized administration flared briefly in West Sumatra and North Sulawesi. Army troops crushed the rebels, then, in 1962, fulfilled Sukarno's lust for *lebensraum* by successfully annexing Netherlands New Guinea.

Sukarno's sheer audacity completely offended Western leaders. Sukarno kept mistresses openly and bragged about his sexual prowess. He even had portraits of his amorous conquests hung in the Hotel Indonesia (where they continue to decorate guest rooms to this day). The West could laugh at Sukarno's peccadilloes, but it could not forgive his flirtation with Maoism, and in 1965, following a botched communist coup, it stood by silently as the Indonesian army methodically eliminated hundreds of thousands of suspected communists and Sukarno supporters. The general who led the 1965 anti-Communist purge, Suharto, remains in charge of the country today.

OPPOSITE: Flag bedecked pier at Jakarta Bay.

Java

SUMATRA
Bandar Lampung
Panjang

J A V A   S E

Sunda Strait
Banten   Jakarta
Anyer

KRAKATAU

Labuhan   Bogor
Mt Pangrango
UJONG KULON   2763
NATIONAL PARK   2743
Mt Gede

WEST JAVA   JAVA

Cirebon   Tegal

Bandung

Tasikmalaya

Ujunggenteng

Pameungpeuk   Cilacap

N

I N D

124 miles
200 km

JAVA is the cradle of Indonesian civilization. Though it comprises only seven percent of the country's total land area, it provides every other part of the country — the "outer islands" with political, economic and Social direction. Bali may. have become Indonesia's leading tourist destination, but the nation's heart and soul, along with 65 percent of the total population, reside in Java.

Though Java contains Indonesia's most modern and prosperous cities, the island is a study in contrasts. It is, beyond question, the most fertile stretch of earth of this planet, yet its population lives on the brink of Malthusian calamity. It is 80 percent rural, yet still manages to be one of the most densely populated places in Asia. It is the center of power for the world's largest Islamic nation, yet people value Buddhist tranquillity and spend long tropical nights retelling epic Hindu legends.

Though all of the residents of the Island respond to the term "Javanese," the island actually is home to five distinct sociological groups, three of which have a significant impact on the culture. Traditional Javanese

live in the central and eastern portions of the island and comprise the bulk of the population. Heirs to an extremely sophisticated culture and language, they continue to prize the Brahman refinements introduced centuries ago by Hindu mystics. For Javanese, the *kratons* (Sultans' palaces) of Yogyakarta and Solo are not dusty anachronisms, but a reflection of the values still cherished by society.

West Java is home to the island's Sundanese, the island's second largest group which practices a purer form of Islam. The island of Madura, along with an adjoining slice of Java north of Surabaya is populated by Madurese. Unlike the Javanese, who consider displays of emotion uncivilized, the less prosperous Madurese are hot-tempered practitioners of *pencak silat*, a particularly lethal form of hand-to-hand combat.

Though each group exhibits a distinct personality and approach to Islam, all perceive themselves to be part of a social hierarchy that values courtesy, self control and the wisdom that comes with age. Deference and good manners are essential on

Java since there's scarcely any room to run amok. Indeed, the island is so crowded that each year thousands of impoverished peasants voluntarily petition for resettlement under the *transmigrasi* program started by the Dutch.

Two-thirds of the world's active volcanoes are located on Jave, but the tumultuous natural forces at work on the island have not inhibited a refined appreciation of the arts and music. In Central Java, *wayang kulit* shadow plays repeatedly are presented in village *kampungs*, while in the West Sundanese gather to see *wayang golek* puppets perform similar stories. As a result, travelers who venture beyond Jakarta are never far from the exotic chime of *gamelan* orchestras whose music has been described as the sound of "moonlight and flowing water."

The delights of Java are tempered, of course, by the archipelago's most serious social problems. But despite the poverty, noise and traffic Java remains a sensual delight; a place where the smell of cloves, the wonder of ancient temples and the caress of a batik sarong all come together.

JAKARTA

For many travelers a vacation to Indonesia begins in Jakarta, a sprawling metropolis of 10,000,000 that covers two and a half times the entire land area of Singapore.

After several decades of tremendous growth, Indonesia's capital can seem overpowering. The streets meander like those in a rural village, constantly changing names and numbering systems. The traffic is unrelenting, especially at rush hour. Some visitors closet themselves in resort hotels, surrounded by tennis courts, jogging paths, nightly barbecues and shopping arcades. But they miss discovering a city that has modern skyscrapers, excellent museums and more colonial architecture than any other capital in the region.

The first thing to realize is that even Indonesians barely tolerate the heat and noise of the city. The second is that NOBODY WALKS. It's simply too hot for such nonsense. That said, you should make a list of things you want to see, rent an air-conditioned car (chauffeur-driven, of course) or taxi by the day or hour and go exploring. Because Indonesia is an OPEC oil producer, transportation here is amazingly cheap. Nobody rides buses if they can afford a taxi. So find a good driver, bargain for a fair price and begin an adventure that can't be equaled elsewhere in Asia.

BACKGROUND

Early in the seventeenth century, Dutch and British merchants peacefully established outposts along the Java Sea coast. The situation changed radically a few years later in

expanded, so did the city. A suburb named Weltevreden was built at the end of the eighteenth century to house the more affluent citizens. As Batavia grew its canals turned out to be a mixed blessing. They were ideal for social and commercial transportation, but also served as a refuse dump for the city's waste. Accordingly, they stank, and from 1730 to 1830 frequent outbursts of malarial plague gave Batavia the reputation of being "the graveyard of the Orient."

Building construction during the early nineteenth century under the direction of

1629 when Sultan Agung of the Mataram Dynasty in Yogyakarta attacked Dutch fortifications protecting the garrison they called Batavia. Dutch governor general Jan Pieterszoon Coen arrived from the Moluccas the following year. He routed Agung, burned the city the Javanese called Jayakarta and established a system of colonial administration that would endure for the next three centuries.

Under the determined and occasionally ruthless leadership of Coen, the Dutch set out to build an "Amsterdam of the tropics." A geometric matrix of streets and canals named after Dutch cities and provinces was laid out. Houses, warehouses, churches, a court and a *stadhuis* were built. As business

Dutch Governor Daendals centered on Weltevreden. Konigsplein, now Merdeka Square, was completed in 1818; Waterlooplein, now Lapangan Banten Square opposite the Borobudur Hotel, in 1826. In 1839 the Immanuel Church in front of the Gambir Railway Station went up. It was followed in 1848 by the Supreme Court, now the Ceramics Museum. During this same period a new Dutch Governor's residence was built that today serves as the National Palace or *Istana Negara*. The opening of the Suez Canal in 1883 prompted the construction of a new port at Tanjung Priok.

By the early twentieth century the hub of the city was the *Konigsplein*, an area now known as *Medan Merdeka*. All of the white stolid government buildings and museums along Jalan Medan Merdeka Barat and Medan Merdeka Utara once housed departments of the Dutch East Indies. In the decades between the wars, the city expanded south along Jalan Thamrin. The effect of all the building around the Weltevreden area was to move the heart of the city away from Old Batavia, today referred to as Jakarta Kota.

GENERAL INFORMATION

The head office of the Department of Tourism,

Post and Telecommunications is at Jalan Kebon Sirih 36, Jakarta 10110. ((21) 372646, fax: (21) 375409.

For more detailed information concerning regions that require special permission to visit write the Directorate General of Tourism at P.O. Box 409, Jalan Kramat Raya N° 81, Jakarta 31045 or call (21) 310-3117. Faxes sent to (21) 310-1146 will reach the Directorate.

For maps, routine assistance and general directions once you arrive in Jakarta check with the Kanwil V Depparpostel Dki Jakarta (Regional Office of Tourism, Post and Telecommunications) or the Diparda Dki Jakarta (Provincial Tourist Service). Both are located in Jakarta Selatan on Jalan K.H. Abdurrohim at the corner of Jalan Gatot Subroto. If

((21) 511742, 511816 or 512-0223 are busy, try 511073. These two offices have background information for the entire island of Java as well as Jakarta. They also have up to date listings of festivals and special events that might be occurring during your visit.

If you're unsure whether to fly, drive or take a train to your next destination, these offices can provide schedules, fares and excellent advice. Do not rely on the airlines for objective information. Garuda, Merpati and Bouraq are fiercely competitive. The last thing Garuda will admit is that there is a

cheaper, more convenient Bouraq flight leaving earlier.

WHAT TO SEE

Jakarta's size and traffic congestion make it vital to plan sightseeing in advance. Fortunately, this is easily done since the city already is divided into sectors. Just about everything a visitor to Jakarta will want to see is located along a North-South axis extending from Sunda Kelapa on the Java Sea

OPPOSITE: An old Batavia drawbridge spanning the Kali Besar still serves modern commuters.
ABOVE: Elaborate Portuguese graves and a watchtower built by the Dutch East India Company bespeak Java's rich colonial heritage.

to Taman Mini Indonesia and the highway to Bogor in the south.

Secondary points of reference are provided by the Indonesian capital's many statues. President Sukarno used to say that "only a great nation honors it heroes." With the help of Soviet artists, who during the 1950's were actively exporting "Socialist Heroism" statuary, Sukarno sprinkled monuments throughout Jakarta. Today, they have become points of reference — "Jalan Blora is two blocks south of the Welcome Statue" — that not only help people pinpoint destinations, but also commemorate revolutionary martyrs, historical events and Javanese mythology.

Hanoman, the King of Monkeys from the *Ramayana*, is incarnated as **God of the Wind** atop a curving pedestal in the traffic circle on Jalan Gatot Subroto.

Several monuments honor the fight for independence. The large figure of a man breaking his chains in Lapangan Banteng in front of the Borobudur Hotel commemorates the **Liberation of Irian Jaya**. The statue of a woman giving rice to a peasant soldier at Menteng Prapatan in front of the Hyatt Aryaduta is known as the **Farmer Statue**.

In the center of Merdeka Square is **Monas**, the *Monumen Nasional*, a 137 m tall marble column topped by a flame covered with 35 kg of pure gold. The base of the monument houses 48 dioramas of Indonesia's struggle for independence. A one minute elevator ride to the top of Monas brings a spectacular view of the entire city, the mountains rising in the south and the thousand islands extending far to the north across the Java Sea.

The **Welcome Statue** in front of the Hotel Indonesia was built for the 1962 Asian Games. It shows a young boy and girl extending their arms in a gesture of greeting. Located in a traffic circle at the entrance to Kebayoran district at the end of Jalan Jend. Sudirman is the **Youth Spirit Monument** which shows a muscular young man carrying the "torch of development."

Because of their alien style and disproportionate size, Sukarno monuments are subject to spoofing. The Youth Spirit Monument usually is referred to as "pizza man" or "the mad waiter" since the torch of development resembles a pizza flambe. The Welcome Statue is known as Hansel and Gretel.

Jakarta Kota

Old Batavia is the logical place to begin exploring Indonesia's capital since Jakarta was born along the banks of the Ciliwung River. Sunda Kelapa, where the Ciliwung enters the Java Sea, was the main port for the Hindu Kingdom of Sunda, the capital of which was near Bogor. The Muslim leader Fatahillah Khan captured Kelapa in 1527, forced the population to accept Islam and renamed the city Jayakarta, which means "Complete Victory." In 1619 the newly-appointed Dutch Governor General Jan Pieterszoon Coen marshaled his forces, destroyed Jayakarta and claimed what remained for the Dutch East India Company or *Vereenigde Oost-Indische Compagnie (V.O.C.)*.

The area settled by Coen begins at the end of Jalan Pintu Besar Selatan, itself an extension of Jalan Gajah Mada, and extends northward to the sea. Heading north, Jalan Pintu Besar Selatan turns into Jalan Pintu Besar Utara. It passes the **Kota Railway Station** on the right and the **Bank Exspor Impor Indonesia** on the left, one of the area's best restored examples of early colonial architecture.

Within a block or so past the bank is **Taman Fatahillah** the V.O.C's administrative center that ironically is named after another foreign conqueror, Fatahillah Khan. In the center of the cobblestone square is a polluted fountain that two centuries ago was the area's main source of clean water. Before being executed prisoners kept in the basement dungeons of the *Stadhuis* were allowed a final drink from the fountain.

Built in 1627, the Stadhuis is supposed to be the **Jakarta Museum**, but the building is in appalling condition and is nearly devoid of furniture. It nevertheless is worth visiting to see the Sukarno-era murals that show porcine Dutch colonials hobnobbing at a rijstafel with posturing Javanese nobles. Before leaving be sure to crawl inside one of the dungeon cells where Javanese revolutionaries were kept chained. Entry is Rp 200. Open daily from 9 am to 2 pm except on Mondays: Friday to 11 am; Saturday to 1 pm; Sunday to 3 pm.

Bugis schooners from the Celebes and beyond make the port of Sunda Kelapa a favorite of photographers.

On the opposite side of the square sits the old Portuguese cannon **Si Jagur**. Local folklore claims that just sitting on its barrel will restore fertility to women.

On the west side of the square is the **Wayang Museum**, an old Dutch Church (Jan Pieterszoon Coen is buried here) that now houses Indonesia's best collection of puppets. Wayang puppet shows were used to arouse Indonesian peasants against the Dutch during the revolution. Every Sunday at 10 am a free puppet show complete with *gamelan* orchestra is presented on the second

floor of the museum. Entry is Rp 200. Tuesday to Thursday, 9 am to 3 pm; Friday 9 am to 2 pm; Saturday and Sunday 9 am to 12:30 pm. Closed Monday.

Directly across from the Wayang Museum on the east side of the plaza is the **Art and Ceramics Museum**. The collection of paintings housed in this, the old *Raad van Justitie*, is limited, but interesting. Don't miss the wing housing the Adam Malik collection of Chinese ceramics on the second floor up a spiral wrought iron staircase. His collection includes rare Ming and Song celadon. Entry is Rp 200. Both collections open Tuesday to Saturday 9:30 am to 3 pm; Sunday 9:30 am to 4 pm. Closed on Monday.

After inspecting Taman Fatahillah's two museums, head back to Jalan Pintu Besar Utara and go north to the old bridge over the

Kali Besar (grand canal). This point was originally the mouth of the Ciliwung River and where Jan Pieterszoon Coen built the first Dutch fort, Kasteel Batavia. The remains of the fort are long gone, but the **watchtower** on Jalan Ikan remains, just like it was in the days when the Dutch military used it to guard against invaders. Entry is Rp 100, Rp 300 if carrying a camera.

From the watchtower you'll see a large number of sail-powered schooners called *pinisi* that still ply the archipelago's shallow-draught ports. Get a closer look at the boats by entering **Sunda Kelapa Harbor**. Entry is Rp 500 per person plus Rp 120 for your car or taxi. The *pinisi* bring timber from Kalimantan and return with rice, cement and consumer goods. Ask permission and most captains will allow you to pay a brief visit on their boat. For an even better photo, bargain with one of the old boatmen along the dock for a trip around the harbor on one of their sampans. The going price, after spirited bargaining is $2. The trip will take you around the original warehouses where the Dutch stored pepper to the breakwater where locals fish.

After a long morning in Old Batavia the best place for lunch, and a radical change of pace, is to head west to **Ancol Park** on the shore of the Java Sea. The park is huge, divided into a Disneyland-type theme park called **Dunia Fantasi** and an art market called **Pasar Seni**. Entry into the park is Rp 800 per person plus Rp 1,000 per car. Pasar Seni has several outdoor restaurants.

Dunia Fantasi, worth an entire day should you want to see the entire park, is divided into different thematic areas: a wild west section representing North America, an English Tudor house symbolizing Great Britain. After paying to get into Ancol, Dunia Fantasi is an additional Rp 600 on weekdays, Rp 800 on Saturdays and Rp 1,200 on Sundays.

Jakarta Merdeka

Merdeka Square, the old Dutch *Konigsplein*, is the center of modern Jakarta. Most of the major government ministries, the office of President Suharto, the national oil company Pertamina and the National Museum are located in this area.

Learn how to build and sail a Buginese *pinisi* schooner at Sunda Kelapa's Museum Bahari.
OPPOSITE, TOP: Jakarta's sprawling expanse makes it one of Asia's largest cities.
OPPOSITE, BOTTOM: The Kota Railway Station, Jakarta's largest, is a scene of perpetual confusion.

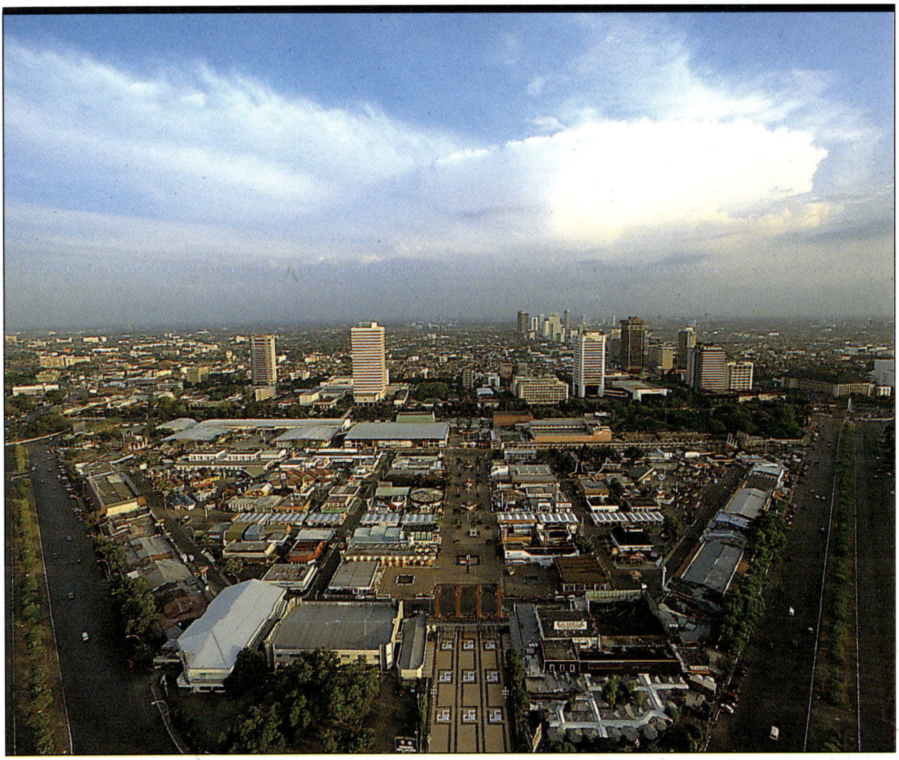

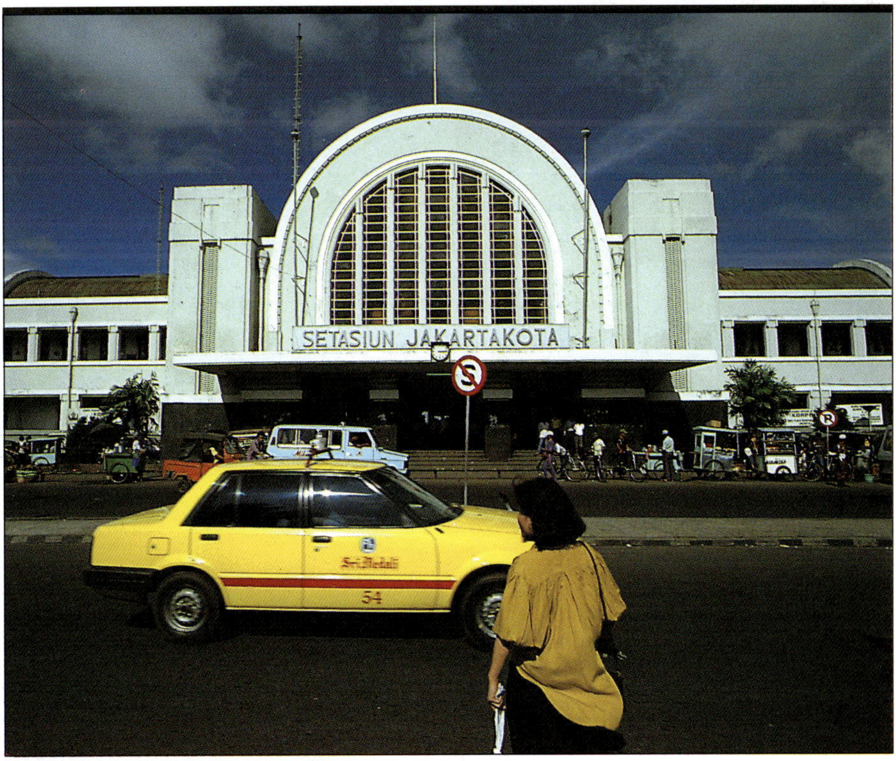
SETASIUN JAKARTAKOTA
54

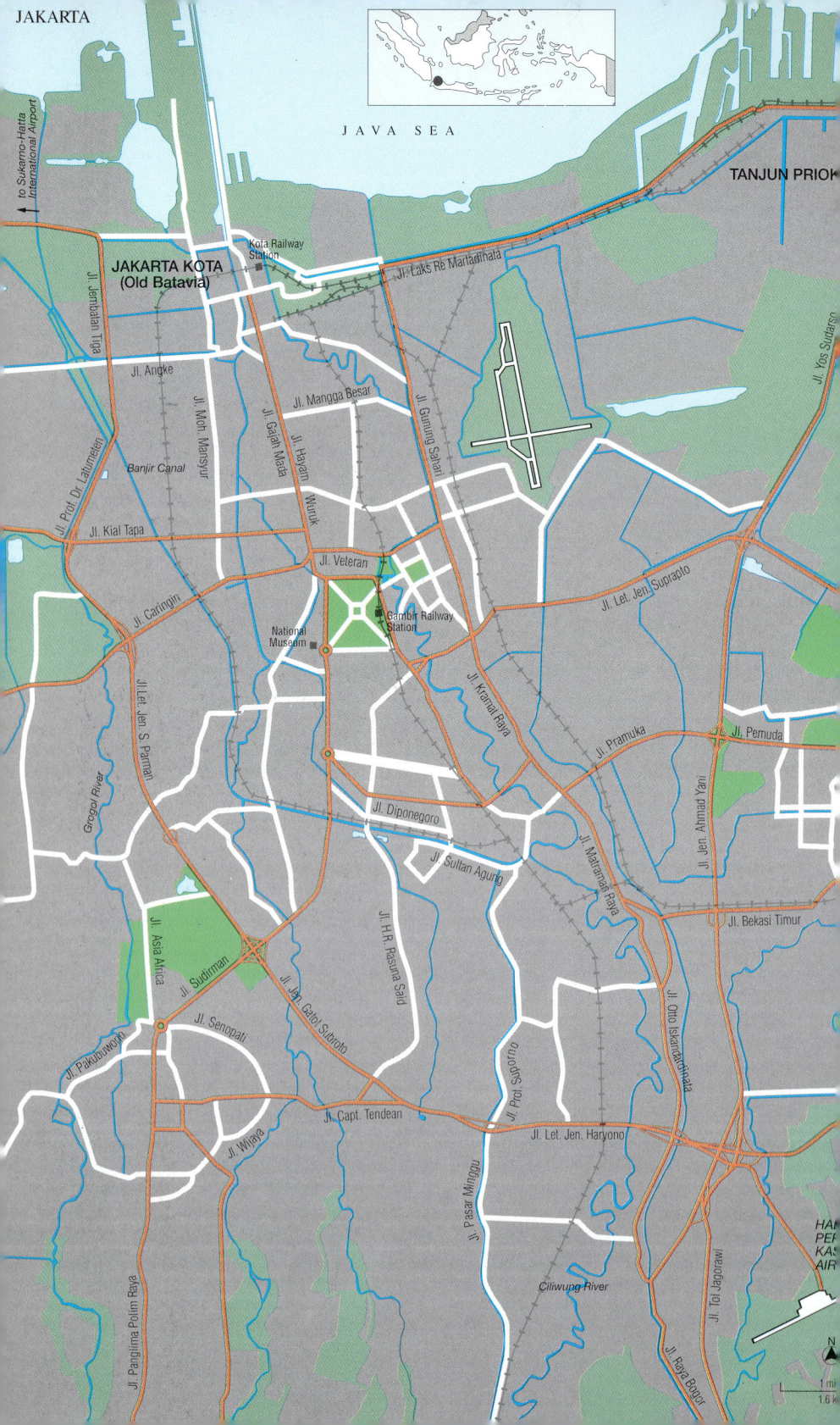

The Monas Statue

The **National Monument** is a 137 m-high marble obelisk which "burns" with an eternal flame made of bronze that is gilded with 35 kg of pure gold. The top of the column sports an observation deck that costs Rp 1,500 to visit. At the tower's base is the **Museum of National History** that traces Indonesia's revolutionary struggle in 48 dioramas. The museum and tower are open daily from 9 am to 5 pm except the last Monday of each month. Entry fee for the museum is Rp 300. If you find yourself at Monas during lunch time, stop at the **Sari Krung** across the street, an open-air Sundanese restaurant.

Merdeka Palace

Completed in 1879 for Dutch Governors General who considered the adjacent Istana Negara too small, this white colonial building on Jalan Merdeka Utara originally was known as Konigsplein Palace. It was seldom used by the Dutch governors, who preferred the climate in Bogor. President Suharto also prefers to live and work elsewhere, but uses the Palace for important state occasions.

Istana Negara

Behind Merdeka Palace on Jalan Veteran is the slightly older Presidential Palace built for a Dutch businessman. This is a separate palace in which state functions are often held. Between the two palaces is the State Guest House, **Wisma Negara**, where foreign dignitaries stay.

National Museum

Founded 200 years ago as the Batavia Society for Arts and Sciences, this five-section museum on Jalan Mederka Barat has a Hindu-Buddhist wing with stone carvings from the seventh through fifteenth centuries, a pre-history room with skulls, weapons and cooking utensils and an ethnographic department with displays from all of the archipelago's island groups. There also is a Ceramics room featuring Chinese, Thai and Vietnamese porcelain and a heavily-guarded treasure room with jeweled statues, solid gold krises and gilded amulets. Open daily except for Monday from 8 am to 3 pm. On Friday the museum closes at noon. Entry fee is Rp 300. On Sunday morning the museum stages a Javanese or Sundanese *gamelan* performance between 9:30 and 10:30 am.

Java Man

One of the National Museum's most valued treasures is the skull of Java Man. In 1890 Dutch military physician Eugene Dubois, an amateur paleoanthropologist assigned to Central Java, discovered the fossilized jawbone of a primate possessing definite human characteristics. Could it be the "missing link" between apes and *Homo erectus* written about by Charles Darwin? Christian groups op-

posed to the theory of evolution denounced Dubois, arguing that there was no link to discover. But similar fossils discovered outside Peking in 1921 vindicated Dubois' "Java Man."

Several museums claim to have the skull unearthed by Dubois. There is a Java Man here at the National Museum. Another rests at the Sangiran site outside Surakarta where Dubois' dig was located. The geological Museum in Bandung claims to have the original, but when pressed for some proof of authenticity the curator confides that the original is locked in a laboratory at Bandung's Institute of Technology.

For a bird's eye view of the Dutch mansions around Medan Merdeka ride the lift to the top of the National Monument.

All these museums, plus several others, claim to have the original. In reality, they're all probably telling the truth since any skull found on the island has to have belonged at one time or another to a Java Man.

Memory Lane

Walking in Jakarta can be unpleasant because of the heat, humidity and general traffic noise. But there are two tree-lined avenues — Jalan Imam Bonjol and Jalan Diponegoro — that can only be appreciated from the unhurried perspective of a pedestrian. Heading east from the Welcome Statue, Imam Bonjol (which quickly changes names to Diponegoro) cuts through the trendy residential section of Batavia the Dutch developed between the two world wars. The homes are textbook examples of Dutch colonial architecture that now serve as diplomatic residences.

Jakarta Selatan

The southern portion of Jakarta is the newest part of the city. Much of the area consists of upscale residential and shopping in Kebayoran and Bloc M. Although there are few historical points of interest, there are two locations relatively close together that can fill an interesting day.

Armed Forces (Satria Mandala) Museum

Anyone interested in military history should visit this museum on Jalan Gatot Subroto N° 14 which originally was the family mansion of Dewi Sukarno, wife of Indonesia's first President. Scores of dioramas focus on the military struggle for independence from 1945 to 1949. Entire floors are devoted to displays of small arms. Outside there are field artillery, tanks and fighter planes parked about landscaped gardens. Entry is Rp 250 per person. Open daily except Mondays from 9 am to 3:30 pm.

Taman Mini Indonesia

Nineteen kilometers (12 miles) south of the center of Jakarta just off the toll expressway to Bogor is the Taman Mini "Indonesia in Miniature" recreation park built by Pres. Suharto's wife, Madam Tien. At Taman Mini you can see and enter traditional housing from each of Indonesia's 27 provinces such as the Redang longhouses of the Kalimantan Dyaks and the saddle-shaped Toraja houses of South Sulawesi. There are miniature replicas of Central Java's Borobudur and Prambanan, plus a bird park orchid garden. There is even a building built in the shape of a Komodo Dragon. Open daily from 9 am to 6 pm. Children enter for Rp 250, and accompanying adults are charged Rp 150. It costs Rp 1,500 to bring a car on the grounds.

English-speaking guides can be hired for Rp 5,000 per hour if you call ahead to the park's protocol office.

WHERE TO STAY

Unlike other OPEC countries, Indonesia has prospered despite the decline in oil prices because of expanding revenues from tourism. This year more than 2.5 million tourists will visit Indonesia. In Jakarta the hotel business is booming, and over 2,000 new rooms have been added to the city's lodgings since the Visit Indonesia Year in 1991. This relieved a shortage; it did not create a glut, so don't expect prices to fall. Nevertheless, Jakarta offers some of the most reasonably priced accommodation

Most of Jakarta's leading stores can be found at the Blok M Plaza.

in Southeast Asia. The basic room rates listed below are subject to an additional 15.5 percent government tax and service charge.

Expensive

Located on nine hectares (23 acres) in the heart of Jakarta, the **Borobudur Inter-Continental** on Jalan Lapangan Banteng has 860 rooms, all of them equipped with IDD telephones, minibar refrigerators and televisions that show satellite channels and in-house movies. Though singles can cost $190, most of the newly-renovated rooms facing the garden (the National Mosque with its early-rising muezzin is on the other side) range from $230 to $275 for a one-bedroom Executive Suite.

Besides its location, the Borobudur's biggest advantage is its garden which contains an Olympic-size swimming pool (where Lady Di swam one hour every morning during the Prince of Wales' 1989 visit), eight tennis courts (two of them inside), eight squash and badminton courts, a jogging trail and miniature golf course plus a track for roller skating.

Among the hotel's 1,500 employees are a number who speak Japanese. There is also a Japanese room service menu. The breakfast buffet offers a wide range of western and Indonesian food at $10 a person. From 3:30 to 6 pm the Pendopo Lobby Lounge offers an English high tea. Going out on the town? The hotel will supply a baby-sitter for $15 an hour. ((21) 370333, 380-5555, fax (21) 380-9595.

With a staff of more than 1,700, the 617-room **Jakarta Hilton** on Jalan Jend. Gatot Subroto is a mini city. Fifty gardeners manicure its 14 hectares (35 acres). More than 40 ball boys man the 14 tennis courts. One jungle path leads to a pizzeria, another ends up at a Japanese restaurant. The Hilton's "shopping arcade" consists of 20 shops located in a Balinese village built around a man-made lake.

Many expatriate families move in and never leave. Indeed, the Hilton built two 30-story apartment buildings on its perimeter several years ago for long-staying guests. You can join them on Saturday for the "Mexican Ole" buffet or on Sunday for the "Hilton Hoe-down," a barbecue where Indonesian employees dress up like dude ranch cowboys and croon country-western ballads. Both cost $18 per person; children under 12 receive a 50 percent discount. Guests also enjoy access to the Executive Club, a members-only sports and social club frequented by some of the capital's most prominent citizens.

The Hilton has five floors reserved for non-smokers, special rooms designed for the handicapped and several Executive Lady Traveler floors on which many of the rooms come with floral wallpaper, women's magazines and personalized service from a Guest Relations officer.

A double room with minibar, IDD and cable television in the main hotel costs $180. In the Garden Tower a double goes for $215. Suites range from $225 to $1,800 for the Tower penthouse.

A final tip: Instead of ordering the complimentary beer or soft drink on arrival, ask for a *sunda kelapa*, a blend of markisa, orange, lime and pineapple juice available at the Kudus Bar. ((21) 570-3600, fax (21) 583091.

Located at Jalan Prapatan Nº44-48 on the banks of the Ciliwung River next door to Jakarta's Petroleum Club and not far from the Gambir railway station, the **Aryaduta Jakarta** has 340 completely renovated rooms priced at $180 in the main wing and $195 in the newer Ambassador wing. In addition to the standard amenities, all rooms have electric hair dryers and safety deposit boxes. Persons staying in a Regency Club room, which costs $220, receive a complimentary breakfast plus free cocktails and snacks in the afternoon at the Regency Lounge on the 16th floor.

The Aryaduta has a variety of excellent restaurants. The Teratai Cafe off the lobby has a reasonably-priced menu and a buffet lunch for $20. At 4 pm there is an afternoon tea in the Ambassador Lounge with finger sandwiches, Viennese pastries and scones with clotted cream. ((21) 386-1234, fax (21) 380-9900.

Opened in 1979, the 27-story Mandarin Oriental Jakarta is strategically located on Jalan M.H. Thamrin in the center of Jakarta's business and financial district. The massive Plaza Indonesia shopping enter plus the IBM and Unilever headquarters are within easy walking distance. So are the British, German and Japanese embassies. Many of its 462 rooms recently underwent a $2 million renovation. In addition to minibars, cable television and IDD phones, they now have card keys and in-room safety deposit boxes.

The Mandarin Oriental makes up for its lack of a garden area with exceptional service. On arriving at the hotel every guest is greeted with a pot of hot tea and a basket of fruit. Persons staying in Executive Deluxe rooms on the 18th floor (where a housekeeper is available to help unpack and a butler will gladly sew on loose buttons) in addition receive a bottle of champagne (or Black Label scotch if they're Japanese), and a nightly snack of chocolate or cookies. There is also a 24-hour Business Center with secretaries skilled in four word processing programs plus Lotus and Quattro.

A deluxe room at the Mandarin Oriental costs from $180 whether you're one or two people. A similar room with a personal valet costs an additional $10. The Mandarin also has one and two bedroom suites that range from $400 to $500. ((21) 321307, fax (21) 324669.

The **Grand Hyatt Jakarta** in Jalan M.H. Thamrin is designed to dazzle and coddle business travelers with a well-conceived range of a services and facilities. All rooms are spacious and well-appointed, and the recreational deck on level five includes three hectares of gardens, tennis and squash courts, an 800 m jogging track, a Jacuzzi and a 43 m pool with a swim-up bar. Eateries and bars, with entertainment, beckon at every level the four floor atrium. Standard room rates are $260. $290 gets you a room in the six top Regency Club executive floors with breakfast, early evening cocktails and all day tea and coffee service included. Suites start at $500. There is no charge for children under 18 sharing their parents room. ((21) 310-7400 or 310-7410, fax (21) 334321.

Built in 1974, the **Sahid Jaya** at Jalan Jend. Sudirman N° 86 is the flagship of Indonesia's largest privately-owned hotel chain. More than two-thirds of the 744 rooms can be found in the recently opened Sahid Jaya Tower. Both connecting buildings have no-smoking floors and the same level of service, but the Tower probably is the better place to stay since now it's the old building's turn for renovation. Tower rooms

come with king size beds, a weighing scale, hair dryers, a well-lit desk for working, and cable television that carries UPI news bulletins 24 hours a day.

In the new 20-story tower a deluxe room costs $150 a night, while suites start at $180. In the older 18-story hotel a superior room is $125. ((21) 570-4444, fax (21) 583168.

The French flavored **Méridien Jakarta** is in the the business and shopping district at Jalan Jend. Sudirman Kav 18-20 . Opened in 1992 the hotel has 265 rooms, with rates for a double at $180 and $210 for a room on the executive floor. ((21) 571-1414, fax (21) 571-1633.

Moderate

The 440 room **Horison** on Jalan Pantai Indah overlooks the Java Sea and nearby Ancol Park. Though the ocean view is romantic, the water is murky and guests are advised to remain in the pool. A resort hotel out of Jakarta's mainstream largely catering to group tours from Taiwan and Hong Kong, the Horison does not pretend to be a business hotel. A giggling doorman bangs a gong every time guests enter or leave the hotel. Outside there is a fleet of antique roadsters renting for $15 an hour for those who want to drive through Ancol Park.

Rooms facing Ancol's golf course are priced at $140. An ocean view costs $170. ((21) 680008, fax (21) 684044.

Hotel Indonesia on Jalan M.H. Thamrin was built in 1962 by President Sukarno who needed an international hotel for athletes invited to the Asian Games. In 1965, Indonesia's "Year of Living Dangerously," it was the eye of the storm from which journalists filed on rioting sweeping the city. Though the hotel has expanded several times and today has 650 rooms, Sukarno's influence still dominates the art deco interior. The huge mural in the Ramayana restaurant was conceived by Sukarno; copies of his favorite painting — a sultry nude brunette — still hang above the beds in many of the rooms. The hotel is being extensively renovated, so prices probably will increase in 1993. For the time being, however, a standard room costs $105 while remodeled deluxe rooms go for $120. The hotel has a pool and several tennis courts, but the main attraction is the

Wednesday and Saturday nights cultural show and buffet which costs $17.50 per person. If you need a baby-sitter the hotel can provide one for $11 an hour. ((21) 322606, fax (21) 321508.

The 500 room **Sari Pan Pacific** on Jalan M.H. Thamrin (((21) 323707, fax (21) 323650), has the best disco in Jakarta in the Pitstop, and probably the best deli, Sari Delices, which sells everything from air-dried chorizo to cappuccino chocolate cake. The Fiesta coffee shop has a nightly rijstafel for $14 a person. The Sari Pacific offers Executive and Super Executive rooms. The former costs $135 for two people, while the latter goes for $140. The hotel offers free transport to Soekarno-Hatta Airport.

Adjacent to the Hotel Indonesia on Jalan M.H. Thamrin, the **Wisata** has 165 rooms. There are no IDD phones or cable television, but each room does have a small refrigerator stocked with soft drinks. On Mondays a classical Javanese orchestra plays at the Rebana coffee shop's $7 luncheon buffet. From 5 to 7 pm drinks are half price at the Jampang Bar. A standard room costs $105 for two, $140 if it is a remodeled deluxe room. P.O. Box 2457, Jakarta Pusat 10230; ((21) 320308, fax (21) 324597.

The **Cikini Sofyan** at Jalan Cikini Raya N° 79 is a clean, casual hotel of 115 rooms within walking distance of dozens of antique stores on Jalans Surabaya, Kebon Sirah and Cikini Raya, rooms with twin beds range in price from $37 to $71. Don't worry about walking around this part of Jakarta at night. Because President Suharto's home only three kilometers away, there's no shortage of police patrols. ((21) 320695, fax (21) 310-0432.

Built in 1969, the **Kartika Plaza** at Jalan M.H. Thamrin N° 10 is a few steps south of the Welcome Statue that anchors Jakarta's main intersection. Its 275 rooms are in the process of renovation, so ask for the full range of prices before making a reservation. Standard rooms facing Jalan Thamrin start at $85; those on the pool side of the hotel cost $125. The hotel has no restaurants of note, but its Shila Bar offers the best Happy Hour deal in town: half price drinks every day from 2 to 5 pm. P.O. Box 2081, Jakarta Pusat; ((21) 321008, fax (21) 322547.

Set in Kebayoran Baru southwest of Jakarta, the 100-room **Kemang** on Jalan Kemang Raya charges $70 for a single. A double goes for $80 and suites are $100. The coffee house specializes in fondue. P.O. Box 163, Jakarta Selatan; ((21) 799-3208, fax (21) 799-3492, 799-3620.

The **Menteng II** on Jalan Cikini Raya N° 105 falls into the category of "basic accommodation," but for $53 for a single and $58 for a double what can you expect. Though small and Spartan, the rooms are clean and quiet. Not so the hotel's Tigakuda nightclub, open from 10 pm to 2 am with a cover charge of $4.50. The Menteng II's sister hotel, the **Menteng I**, is located several blocks away at Jalan Gondangdia Lama. Its late night disco, the Hotman, is even wilder than the Tigakuda. ((21) 325208, fax (21) 310-4151 (for either hotel).

Inexpensive

Comfortable lodging in Jakarta does not have to be expensive. Indeed, many experienced travelers prefer the smaller guest houses, or "home stays," along Jalan Raden Saleh in the fashionable neighborhood of Menteng.

Yannie on Jalan Raden Saleh N° 35 is a 15 room guest house run by two English-speaking sisters — Ghardini, a dentist, and Yulia, an architect. The $25 charge for an air-conditioned room includes a continental breakfast. ((21) 320012, fax (21) 327005.

A basic room at the **Karya II Hotel** on Jalan Raden Saleh N° 37 costs $25 to $30. Deluxe rooms with television (no cable) and refrigerator are $36. Breakfast included. ((21) 325078, 310-1380.

WHERE TO EAT

The **Art & Curio** at Jalan Menteng Raya N° 29 (((21) 322879) is a very simple, old-time, semi-open-air European cafe down by the railroad tracks in the Menteng area where a three course meal runs around $16. After dining wander through the adjoining curio shop. Open Tuesday through Sunday for lunch and dinner. Closed Monday. Cash only.

Bakmi Gajah Mada at Jalan M.H. Thamrin N° 21 (((21) 310-2258 and 310-2259) makes even diehard meat and potato eaters fall in love with basic Indonesian cuisine. *Nasi* *goreng* costs only $2.50 here and coconut-flavored chicken soup sells for $1 a bowl. Two other Gajah Mada restaurants at Jalan Gajah Mada N° 92 and Jalan Melawai Raya N° 3 serve Jakarta's craving for noodles. All three are always packed. There are no reservations or maitre d's at either location. When you see people finishing their meal, go stand behind them and grab the chairs when they get up. All three Bakmi Gajah Madas are open for lunch from 10 am to 3 pm, and at night from 4:30 pm to 10:30 pm. Cash only.

The George and Dragon at Jalan Teluk Betung N° 32 is an English pub and curry house that's nestled between the Hotel Indonesia and Kartika Plaza not far from the Welcome Statue. After work it's a favorite hangout for expats. At night the crowd moves from the bar to the tables for delicious grilled fish, salads and Indian curry. A sumptuous dinner costs only $10. Open from 10 am to midnight, Sundays 4 pm to midnight. ℂ (21) 325625.

When Jakartans are in the mood for fried chicken they head to the Kebayaron area of Jakarta Selatan where two of Java's most famous restaurateurs, **Ibu Umi** and **Nyonya Suharti**, provide simple yet tasty meals for around $7.50 a person. Chicken comes in whole or half portions, with side dishes averaging only $0.50. Ibu Umi is at Jalan Supomo Manggarai N° 14, ℂ (21) 829-4752. Suharti is at Jalan Kapt. Tendean N° 13 in Jakarta Selatan, ℂ (21) 514595. Both are open daily 10 am to 10 pm. No reservations; no credit cards.

Jakarta has a number of fine Korean restaurants all within walking distance of the Welcome Statue. The fanciest is the **Korea Tower Club** on the 30th floor of the Bank Bumi Daya Plaza, Jalan Imam Bonjol N° 61, ℂ (21) 330311. Open daily from 11:30 am to 3 pm and from 6 pm until 10:30 pm, it offers a panoramic view of the city, as well as excellent *bulgogi* (Korean barbecue) diners for $13.

The nearby **Korea Garden** at Jalan Teluk Betung N° 33, ℂ (21) 310-4501 provides standard Korean fare in a relaxed garden setting. Luncheon reservations required. Try the ginseng chicken soup. Diners average around $12.

Two doors away from the Korea Garden is the **Shilla International Restaurant**, Jalan Teluk Betung N° 35, ℂ (21) 324012, which specializes in Korean barbecue and Japa-

nese food. A bulgogi dinner here costs $7.00; ribs with all the side dishes cost $9.

Memories in the Wisma Indocement building on Jalan Jend. Sudirman Kav. N° 70-71 (ℂ (21) 578-1009) is a new restaurant in a new building, but once inside the front door diners immediately feel as if they've arrived in colonial Batavia. The Baruna bar, where you can knock back an oude genever for $4, resembles a gentleman's bar aboard an old Holland-America cruise ship. The menu, which lists a nightly rijstafel for $12, is heavy with Dutch dishes like Belgian en-

dives with ham, cheese sauce and mashed potatoes for $15.50. Manager Klaus Kamp, 64, began importing Dutch steak when Memories opened in 1986. "The steak led to Dutch peas, then *matjes* herring. When my sister came to Jakarta I told her to get in the kitchen and make meatballs like our mother used to make." Six times a week Kamp wanders through the antique shops along Jalan Surabaya. The treasures he finds are on display and for sale. Dinner with appetizer and coffee is $28. If you just want a salad for dinner, Memories has the city's best salad bar at $6. Dinner served daily from 7 to 11 pm. Lunch every day but Sunday from noon to 3 pm.

Tucked away on busy Jalan A.H. Agus Salim, **Natrabu** (ℂ (21) 335668) is one of the best places in Jakarta to try *padang* food. The moment you sit down 12 dishes are brought to your table along with rice by waiters dressed in traditional Sumatran garb. The spinach-like dish consists of young tapioca leaves; that wrinkled slice of beef is cow lung. Try a bit of everything (and pay for every dish) or stick to dishes like shrimp satay and beef simmered in coconut cream. $6.50 per person if you eat everything.

Club Noordwijk at Jalan Juanda N° 5A (C (21) 353909) offers home style Dutch Indonesian cooking in a tranquil Old Batavia

Bar is enlivened by colorful Balinese masks and Javanese paintings. The menu is studded with items like Beluga caviar and Tournedos Rossini, but more moderately priced fare is available. Ginger-flavored frog leg fillets seasoned with peppercorns cost $7, as does the fresh marinated tuna steak. If there's a brief wait for a table, ask Nyoman (the maitre d') to show you the antiques upstairs. The Oasis is the only restaurant in Jakarta (and perhaps the world) where a 12-course rijstafel still is served by a dozen beautiful maidens. Warning: the

setting. Dutch street organ music and dancing nightly. Open daily except Sundays. Lunch: noon to 3 pm. Dinner: 6 to 11 pm. Dinner for two runs about $35.

In 1928 **The Oasis** at Jalan Raden Saleh Raya N° 47 was built as a private residence in Raffles period style by a Dutch millionaire. During World War II the last Governor General of the Dutch East Indies made the house his unofficial residence when Japanese bombing made him feel uneasy in Konigsplein Palace. After the war the building became the residence of the United States Naval attaché, who had the annual Marine Ball in the garden. The main dining room is decorated with gold-embroidered sarongs from Sumatra. The adjacent Topeng

band in the Sumatra Room can be a bit loud, so ask for a table on the Garden Terrace. Open daily for lunch and dinner. Reservations essential. C (21) 325397 and 327818.

Pare'gu at Jalan Sunan Kalijaga N° 64 in Blok M is the best Vietnamese restaurant in Indonesia. Dinner for two: $15.50. Open daily 11:30 am to 2:30 pm. and 6:30 to 10 pm. C (21) 717114 and 774892.

Near the Horison Hotel and Ancol Park, the **Phinisi** (C (21) 690-0947) is a floating seafood restaurant at Pantai Marina in the Java Sea. Enjoy grilled fish on the top deck or go

Exotic savory snacks at affordable prices OPPOSITE and colorful fruit and beverage hawkers ABOVE make Indonesia's outdoor markets extremely popular.

below for Chinese and Thai food. Moderately priced. Open daily from 11 am until 2:30 pm and from 5:30 to 10:30 pm.

The **Ponderosa Steak House** at Jalan Jend. Sudirman N° 2 in the Arthaloka Building has great steaks, Mexican food, basic Italian dishes and a huge salad bar. Dinner for two is about $22. There are two additional Ponderosas, one up Jalan Sudirman in the Widjojo Center and the other in the Centerpoint Building, Jalan Jend. Gatot Subroto N° 35-36. The latter are open daily from 11 am until 10:30 pm. The Arthaloka site is closed Sundays. ((21) 583280.

An outdoor garden restaurant on Jalan Silang Monas Tenggara with artificial waterfalls serving typical Sundanese food, **Sari Kuring** ((21) 352972) serves mainly grilled fish, (that you eat with your right hand) but there are other items on the menu like shrimp satay at $0.35 a stick and grilled lobster for $7. End the meal with young coconut meat with ice or a peanut milkshake. Also try a glass of markisa fruit juice from Northern Sumatra. Open daily for lunch and dinner.

Feast for hours on excellent food and pay only pennies at the **Satay House Senayan** at Jalan Kebon Sirih N° 31-A. A bowl of Madurese beef soup costs $1.75, *gado gado* salad is $1.40 and *nasi goreng* is $1.90. Satay costs from $2 to $3 depending on whether you order chicken, mutton or beef. Daily 10 am to 10 pm. ((21) 326238.

The **Toba Rotisserie** on the third floor of the Borobudur Hotel is the place to go for elegant European dining. Cost for two with appetizer, entree and dessert: $130. Open for lunch on weekdays, dinner every night. ((21) 370333.

WHERE TO SHOP

There are three types of shopping areas in Jakarta. The first are air-conditioned shopping plazas where original and fake designer collections are mixed with ready-to-wear batik and *wayang golek* puppets. Here prices are fixed and major credit cards are accepted.

The second category consists of pasars where gold can be bought by the gram, fabrics by the meter and where curios compete for space with baby prams and electric fans.

Though many items bear price tags, discounts are granted if you are the least bit insistent.

Travelers with a sense of adventure will want to head straight for the city's antique shops where bargaining is de rigueur. These shops are scattered about the city near enclaves of expatriate homes and in hotels. Here travelers checks are accepted only grudgingly and the use of a credit card depends on the amount of the purchase. Prices drop dramatically, however, at the merest hint of hard cash.

Note: Women staying in Jakarta for more than several days should stop by the **American Women's Association** on Jalan Sinabung N° 11-20 in Kebayoran Baru to purchase a copy of the organization's 200-page *Shopper's Guide*. The book has locations, hours of operation and helpful comments on just about everything one can do, see or buy in Jakarta. The AWA also sells a fact-filled book called *Introducing Indonesia* for Rp 15,000 that provides excellent background on Indonesian customs, history and culture. The book is intended for expat wives planning to settle in Jakarta, but its travel section has succinct descriptions of hotels, restaurants and shopping areas throughout the country you may find interesting.

Shopping in Style

Ratu Plaza on Jalan Sudirman is the type of shopping mall you expect to find in Singapore or suburban Los Angeles. A "Beam me up, Scotty" elevator sheathed in glass carries shoppers to one of the mall's six floors. On the third floor Matahari sells trendy fashions made in Hong Kong or Singapore. There is a theater on the sixth floor, a Japanese restaurant on the fifth and a burger stand at ground level. Interspersed are jewelry shops and designer boutiques.

are the standard by which competing outlets set their prices.

Bargain Centers

Glodok Plaza in the middle of China Town is difficult to get to because of the traffic clogging Jalans Gajah Mada and Hayam Wuruk, but the wait is worth it if you're in the market for computer or electrical products. Bargaining is essential here, but don't be too insistent when it comes to computer software. Prices are higher now that Indonesia enforces anti-piracy laws.

The **Keris Gallery** on Jalan Cokroaminoto is Jakarta's newest and flashiest galleria. This is an excellent destination for shoppers interested in jewelry since the various stores offer a variety of designer, costume and traditional native styles. There is also a generous selection of designer batik stores, some of which sponsor midday fashion shows.

Two **Sarinah Department Stores** on Jalan Thamrin and in Kebayoran Baru are priority stops since each offers a good selection of handicrafts and batik at reasonable prices. Both stores have batik boutiques with original creations by famous batik designers such as Irwin Tirta and Poppy Dharsono. This is an excellent place to begin your comparison shopping since prices charged by Sarinah

Just east of the old Portuguese Church and across the street from Jakarta's Kota Station railway yard is the **Manga Dua Shopping Center** on Jalan Manga Dua Raya. Most of the merchandise here consists of Chinese lanterns, basic kitchenware and AA bras sized for the Javanese bosom, but you should go anyway, especially on Sunday, to take in the scene of thousands of Jakartans out enjoying their middle class buying power. Divided into numerous blocks, sections and floors, Manga Dua is not a place to get separated. Hundreds of shops line a

OPPOSITE: Curios from throughout the archipelago are brought to Jakarta. ABOVE: Some of the best antiques can be found in the stalls along Jalan Surabaya.

maze of crowded aisles, so hang on to your children.

Antiques

For hundreds of years Indonesia has been a crossroads for traders from throughout Asia. Indians, Turks and Chinese all brought treasures to trade for spices. Portuguese, Dutch and British who came as colonists brought household goods. Once settled in the archipelago, they commissioned the building of houses full of furniture. Today, everything they left behind (and faked imitations) is for sale side by side with native handicrafts.

Jalan Surabaya in Menteng is the first stop for any antique hunter. On this street, open-front antique shops extend for more than a half mile. Each store has its specialty. Some offer Buddha heads in bronze or sandstone, Dyak artwork, Russian samovars or Dutch hanging lamps. Others sell maritime navigational instruments, Japanese swords, old coins or porcelain from sunken ships. Bargaining is essential and all transactions are in cash. Be sure to say hello to Erwin Rosyady at stall 172, the Jakarta representative for **Masters Voice Service** antiques who has an astounding collection of 1920's Victrolas that come with original Caruso recordings. Memed Kusmana at **U.D. Sahabat** in stall 162 is the man to see for lenses and brass. Specifically, antique chronometers, old telephones and Ernst Leitz microscopes.

After exploring Jalan Surabaya, move on to Jalan Kebon Sirih Timur. **Amadeus** on Jalan Kebon Sirih Timur. N° 50, ℂ (21) 324664, specializes in primitive art from Irian Jaya and the Lake Toba area of Sumatra. here are also stores on Jalan Majapahit.

Bahni Art Shop, Jalan Kebon Sirih Timur N° 6, ℂ (21) 324094, has an eclectic assortment of merchandise ranging from German clocks to antique telephones. Most of the store is given over to Chinese porcelain. Chinese ceramics were brought to Java during the height of the spice trade. Much of what one finds today is "kitchen Ming," roughly made porcelain that was used as ballast for ships carrying tea, coffee and other spices. Open Monday to Saturday 9 am to 6 pm.

Buyung Art Shop at Jalan Kebon Sirih Timur N° 20 has a wide selection of primitive art as does **New Ganesha** at Jalan Kebon

Sirih Timur N° 5A and **Uji Dornis Art & Curio** at Jalan Kebon Sirih Timur N° 20A. Primitive art does not necessarily mean old, of course. Much of what is available is of recent vintage, items produced by the country's stone age tribes.

Ndalem, Jalan Kebon Sirih Timur N° 8½, ℂ (21) 310-4064, sells aged batik and stone carvings. Its Buddha figures range from $500 to $5,000. Open daily from 9 am to 6 pm.

Sriwijaya at Jalan Kebon Sirih Timur N° 158, ℂ (21) 325501, has a large assortment of Dutch lamps and antique terra cotta roof

tiles from Palembang, South Sumatra. There are also Batak-carved buffalo horns from Northern Sumatra.

Jalan Bangka Raya, Jalan Kemang Bangka and Jalan Ciputat Raya also have their share of antique stores due largely to the nearby expatriate housing in Menteng. Be on the lookout for Huanghuali rosewood chairs from China. Ming Dynasty furniture is rapidly appreciating in value because the Huanghuali species of hardwood is extinct.

Art

Jakarta has hundreds of art galleries featuring traditional and batik painting. One of the nicest places to browse is **Pasar Seni** in Ancol Park. Built atop a reclaimed swamp, this immaculately clean park allows artists, restaurateurs and strolling musicians to mingle under the stars beside the Java Sea. **Gita Ramayana**, ((21) 685571, features batik paintings that can be paid for with all credit cards. **Sanggar Bali**, ((21) 850-2876, has Balinese paintings and wood carvings produced in Ubud and Mas.

Batik

Central Java offers the best buys on batik, but if Jakarta is your only stop **Batik Berdikari**, ((21) 548-2814, on Jalan Mesjid Pal VII,

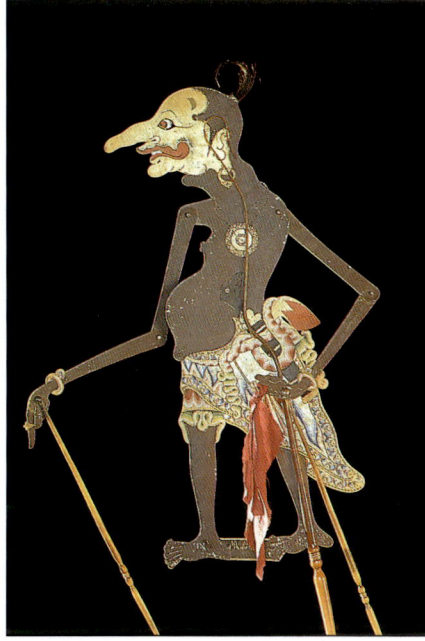

N° 7B Palmerah is a worthwhile stop. Here you can see the creative process unfold in addition to purchasing hand made silk and cotton garments. Be sure to bring a camera to photograph the 40 employees waxing, dying and washing fabric out back. Located in West Jakarta, the factory is open daily from 9 am to 5 pm.

Beauty

While in Jakarta take advantage of the low labor costs and visit one of the many barber and beauty salons. The **Elizabeth Arden Facial Salon**, ((21) 730170, on Jalan Iskandarsyah N° 1½, 5th floor, Sarinah Jaya in Bloc M specializes in facials, manicures, pedicures and waxing. Open daily 9:30 to 8:30 pm.

Also a favorite with expatriate wives is the **Estee Lauder Make-Up Salon**, ((21) 713632, on Jalan Paletehan N° 1/32-33 in Bloc M. Facials here rely on Estee Lauder cosmetics. As with Elizabeth Arden, all Estee Lauder employees speak English. Open Monday through Saturday from 8:30 am to 5 pm.

Rounding out the big three is the **House of Revlon**, ((21) 511568, 512013, on Jalan H.R. Rasuna Said, Kav. N° 10, Gedung Bina Mulia. Open 9 am to 7 pm, Monday through Saturday.

The House of Beauty, ((21) 340798, on Jalan Jambu N° 50 is a real Indonesian beauty salon. It costs less and has more atmosphere than the three expat handouts, but the command of English is less. Still, this is a very professional salon offering facials with imported or local products. You can also get a traditional Javanese massage. Daily 8 am to 5 pm.

Though most Jakarta beauty salons provide unisex service, men usually prefer to get their hair cut and manicure at **Rudy Hadisuwarno**, ((21) 325002, on the 3rd floor of the Jakarta Mandarin on Jalan Thamrin. Hadisuwarno is a well-known hairdresser who has studied in England, France and Japan and many of his employees have overseas experience. United States diplomats get their trims from Chacha or Okky. Open 9 am to 6 pm. Monday through Saturday and 9 am to 4 pm on Sunday.

Handicrafts

Jakarta Handicraft Center, Jalan Pekalongan N° 12A, ((21) 338157, has a variety of wood carvings, rattan baskets, brass and copper artifacts and Sumatran textiles. Open 9 am to 6:30 pm, Sunday 10 am to 4 pm.

WHERE TO RELAX

One might expect the capital of the world's largest Muslim nation to have a rather subdued nightlife. Fortunately, that is not the case with Jakarta. Though it lacks the raucous excess of Bangkok and Manila, there is plenty to do and see after the sun goes down.

OPPOSITE: *Wayang golek* puppets dressed in colorful batik are carved in Western Java.
ABOVE LEFT: *Wayang kulit* shadow puppets are a Central Java favorite.

Although government offices and most private businesses begin their work day at 8 am, Jakarta is not an early-to-bed town. Discos don't really begin to fill until after 10:30 pm. Many sidewalk food vendors around the National Monument stay busy serving *nasi goreng* and *satay* long past midnight to Jakartans enjoying the (relatively) cool night air.

The reason Jakartans can literally burn the midnight oil and still make it to work the next morning is because they pace themselves throughout the hot tropical day, and take a brief nap after returning home from work. Resting from 5 pm to 6:30 pm is a good idea for you, too, if you hope to enjoy most of the attractions listed below.

Cultural Performances and Comedy

Though Yogyakarta is considered the center of Javanese culture, Jakarta has much to offer in the way of classical dancing and puppet shows. For *wayang orang* and *ketoprak* (Javanese dance dramas, visit the **Bhatara Theater** on Jalan Kalilio. *Wayang orang* is performed nightly from 8:15 pm to midnight, except on Monday and Tuesday. *Wayang kulit* and *wayang golek* are staged alternately at the National Museum every Sunday evening starting at 8 pm.

Interested in Sundanese folk drama? Then catch the "Miss Tjitjih Show," a West Java-style opera-cum-passion play presented nightly at 7 pm and again at 9 pm at Jalan Kabel Pendek in **Cempaka Baru**. If comedy is more your liking, and you have access to an interpreter, don't miss the so called Srimulat Show, staged nightly from 8 pm to 11 pm at **Taman Ria Senayan**. Even if you lack an interpreter pass by anyway since there's plenty of slapstick to enjoy.

There is always something happening at **Taman Ismail Marzuki** (TIM), Jakarta's largest cultural center. For the daily listing of events look at the "Around Town" part of the *Indonesian Observer* or the "What's on in Jakarta Today" section of the *Indonesian Times*.

Bars and Discotheques

Pub crawling can be an expensive proposition because of the high taxes on imported liquor. Fortunately, sticking with beer is no sacrifice. Bintang, San Miguel and Anker are all excellent. Bintang, in fact, was developed under the supervision of the former *brewmeister* of Heineken in Holland.

Early in the evening (before 10 pm) most of the activity is centered in the major hotels. The **Tavern Pub** in the Aryaduta is popular with local expats and visiting businessmen because of its *tapas* and cold beer. Also a local favorite is the **George and Dragon** at Jalan Teluk Betung N° 32 next to the Kartika Plaza hotel. Directly across Jalan Thamrin from the Kartika Plaza is a small lane awash in neon called Jalan Blora. The jumble of country-western bars and Chinese nightclubs make it seem an exciting place, but the interior of these bars belies the promise outside, and it's best to avoid the entire street.

Many flight crews who regularly visit Jakarta frequent the **Jaya Pub**, an upstairs bar behind the Jaya Building at Jalan M.H. Thamrin N° 12. There is a piano behind the bar and singers after 10 pm. If things aren't happening at the Jaya, simply walk across Jalan Thamrin to the **Green Pub** behind the Jakarta Theater building.

For the hyperactive the place to be in Jakarta is the **Ebony Videotheque**, Jalan H.R. Rasuna Said in the Kuningan Plaza, ((21) 513700. The Ebony is a posh, two-floor discotheque with an enormous video screen on which flicker old movies. If you really want a memorable experience, begin the evening at **Casablanca**, a true supper club next door to the Ebony at Jalan Rasuna Said N° C11-14, ((21) 514800. Have the hotel concierge call to see what type of entertainment is featured at the Casablanca, then hit both places with one cab ride.

The **Hotmen Bar Diskotik** in the Menteng I Hotel, (see page 37) ((274) 325208, swarms with young women and Middle Eastern businessmen on the prowl. The booths are dark, the air is smoky. If you're willing to pay the $4 cover to view this visual reconnoiter, then go for a brief visit. But if you really want to dance, listen to decent music or meet somebody who knows more English than "What you name?," pay the $4.50 cover and enter the **Tanamur**, Jalan Tanah Abang Timur N° 14, ((21) 353947 around 11 pm. The selection of music here is as good as the sound system, and, despite the frenetic activity, you can actually have a conversation with the people you meet.

HOW TO GET THERE

All international flights into and out of Jakarta used the Soekarno-Hatta International Airport. All departing flights, whether international or inside Indonesia, require a departure tax be paid in rupiah. Check with your hotel concierge before leaving for the airport or call the airline to confirm the current amount of the tax.

Some internal flights continue to leave from Jakarta's two secondary airports, Kemayoran and Halim.

WEST JAVA

The province of West Java is surprisingly beautiful and easily accessible due to modern, divided highways built over the past 15 years. Only minutes outside Jakarta the roads begin to climb and the foothills of the highlands begin to emerge. Bamboo forests and tea plantations accent miles of terraced ricefields.

ALONG THE COAST

Along the western and southern coastlines, West Java has excellent beaches that look out on the Sunda Strait and the massive volcano **Krakatau**, which shook the entire world when it first erupted in August 1883. The actual volcano was destroyed in the explosion, but a new crater known as **Anak Krakatau** (son of Krakatau) can be visited by boat. Make sure, however, the volcano is safe to visit since from time to time it still emits dangerous fumes. This area also has West Java's **Ujung Kulon Nature Reserve**, the last refuge of the near-extinct one-horned Java rhino. Starting point for both attractions is the sleepy fishing village of **Anyer**.

WHERE TO STAY

The **Anyer Beach Motel** on Jalan Raya Karang Bolong, ((21) 310-6440, has 62 bungalow-style rooms that cost from $42 to $55. Slightly more expensive is the nearby **Mam-**bruk **Quality Resort** ((254) 81601, fax (254) 81723 which has luxurious villas and lanais right on the beach next to a grass volleyball court, swimming pool and soccer field.

SOUTH COAST

On the southeast corner of Barat province is **Pangandaran**, a fishing village and beach resort. Situated on a peninsula, the village has a safe side and a dangerous one. And plenty of inexpensive seafood. It also is near a second excellent game reserve, the **Pananjung Pangandaran**, where a variety of civet cats, monkeys, pythons and deer can be seen within a teak forest.

West Java's southern coastline is cloaked in mystery and superstition. It is the home of the mythical goddess Nyi Loro Kidul, the Queen of the South Seas. The south coast's major resort, the Samudra Beach Hotel, keeps room 318 permanently empty for the goddess' occasional visits. The room attracts pilgrims from throughout the country who believe Nyi Loro Kidul's blessing can protect them on crossings of her treacherous seas.

THE THOUSAND ISLANDS

One marine attraction near to Jakarta that is often overlooked is **Pulau Seribu** or "the thousand islands" which lie in the Java Sea's Bay of Jakarta. Actually, there are 600 islands and many of them are privately owned or uninhabited, but 128 islands do have tourist facilities and are within a one to two hour boat ride of Jakarta. Some of the islands, such as **Pulau Putri**, **Pulau Ayer** and **Pulau Antuk** are fairly well developed with cottages, restaurants and nightclubs. Others, like **Pulau Melinjo**, have only basic amenities. All the islands are composed of coral (you'll want to swim in tennis shoes, so remember to buy a cheap pair in Jakarta) and offer excellent snorkeling. Motor boats and hovercraft leave from the Jaya Ancol marina near the Horison Hotel or from Tanjung Priok. Make reservations through a Jakarta travel agent who can direct you to a thatched jungle

OVERLEAF: West Java's Ujung Kulon reserve is the only place endangered Indonesian rhinos can still be found.

hut, a bamboo house on stilts at the edge of the ocean or a traditional resort hotel. Scuba and snorkeling packages are available.

NORTH COAST

The northern coast of West Java is much more settled having been subject to outside influence for centuries. Once the site of a mighty kingdom, **Cirebon** still has two palaces, or *kratons*, where its sultans live. Neither **Kasepuhan** nor **Kanoman** palace has changed much over the past 700 years. Both have museums containing ancient *krises*, court jewelry and costumes. Of special interest are the walls of Kasepuhan Kraton which are embedded with Chinese ceramic plates used by Chinese traders as ballast since their ocean junks lacked deep keels.

WESTERN HIGHLANDS

Most of West Java's population lives in the mountains where the volcanic soil and fast running rivers have provided the base for civilizations extending back to the fifth century. While Chinese, Indian and Arab trader were picking up spices, ivory and rhino horns at the north coast ports of Banten, Sunda Kelapa and Cirebon, the Hindu kingdom of Pajajaran, which extended from Bogor to beyond Bandung, thrived in isolation. The arrival of Islam in the sixteenth century marked the end of Pajajaran. The Muslim rulers soon were joined by Dutch officials of the Dutch East Indies Company, who took long weekends in the highlands to escape the heat of Batavia.

In 1810 the Dutch Governor General Daendels built the Great Post Road, a 1,000 km-(620 miles)-long highway stretching the entire length of the island. The road is still used today and serves as one of Bandung's main streets.

BOGOR

A beautifully landscaped four-lane divided highway links Jakarta with Bogor, a mountain town that was the summer residence of the Dutch Governors General. The Dutch loved the **Summer Palace**, naming it *Buitenzorg*, or "free of care." So did Stamford Raf-

fles, who ruled Indonesia from 1811 to 1816 during the "British Interregnum."

"I have now from my window the prospect of the most delightfully picturesque scenery," he wrote, "a valley filled with rice with a romantic little village at the beginning of a stream which rushes down by twenty torrents and roars booming over rocks innumerable; in the background a magnificent range of mountains, wooded to the top and capped in clouds."

By the middle of the nineteenth century the palace, rebuilt following an earthquake in 1834, had become the Governor General's primary residence. Today it is used by the government as a guest house for state visitors, who, once settled in, find themselves surrounded by president Sukarno's collec-

tion of 375 paintings and statues, most of which highlight the nude female torso. A marble staircase leads up to a crescent-shaped Throne Room with Corinthian pillars. There also is a hidden room for meditation in which Saudi King Ibn Saud once closeted himself.

The palace is not normally open to the public, but a written request sent two weeks in advance to the Istana Negara Head of Protocol on Jalan Veteran in Jakarta may open the doors.

The main attraction in Bogor is the **Botanical Garden**, or Kebun Raya, 91 hectares (225 acres) of orchids and other tropical plants growing on the former palace grounds of the old Hindu kingdom of Pajajaran. Laid out by German botanist C.G.L. Reinwardt and

two assistants from England's Kew Gardens in 1817, the gardens contain over 15,000 species of trees and plants. Asia's first oil palm, brought by the Dutch from West Africa in 1848, is still growing here alongside 400 other species of palm. There are nutmeg trees from the Moluccas, Sumatran pines, black orchids from Kalimantan and the world's largest flower, the *Rafflesia*, which blooms in October. The garden is open daily from 8 am to 5 pm, Rp 1,200 per person to enter.

Before leaving Bogor, make a quick stop at **Bengkel Gong**, the Gong House at Jalan Pancasan N° 17 ☏ (251) 27390. Open from

Buried under volcanic ash following the eruption of Krakatau, the Ujung Kulon nature reserve in west Java now boasts a variety of jungle wildlife.

8 am to 3 pm every day except Friday, this shop has the added advantage of having its "factory" across the street. The rough instruments are heated in a bed of coals, then beaten while red hot until the metal — a mixture of copper, tin and brass — yields exactly the right pitch.

Apexindo Tours (℡ (21) 370108, 376598) on the third floor of the Borobudur Hotel offers five-hour excursions to Bogor. The price is $60 for one person, but can drop to $20 or less if four or more people go. **Satriavi Tours** on Jalan Prapatan N° 32 (℡ (21) 380-

3944) has a six hour tour that costs $25 if four or more people are in the van.

PUNCAK PASS

Outside Bogor the divided toll road climbs steeply past terraced fields of tapioca and hedges sculpted into the shapes of animals. Beds of daffodils compete for space with Pagoda Bushes, whose orange flowers are shaped like tiny temples. At the top of Puncak Pass there are spectacular views of 2,763-m (9,066-ft) Mt. Pangrango and the smaller Mt. Gede. There are also several large tea plantations that welcome visitors and are regular stops on tours to Puncak Pass.

Where to Stay

There are several hotels in the Puncak area, the largest being the **Puncak Pass Hotel** ℡ (255) 2503, fax (255) 2504, a Dutch resort built in 1928 that is midway between Jakarta and Bandung. Built on the side of the mountain, Puncak's 45 rooms have magnificent views and fireplaces, which you'll need at

night. (Note: If you plan to overnight at Puncak buy a sweater in Jakarta at one of the Chinese markets in Glodok.) Rooms with a single double bed cost $60. Those with two beds are $78. All room prices are discounted 25 percent on weekdays. Dinner for two at the hotel's European restaurant averages $15. On cold nights ask Mr. Hasanudin, the hotel's bartender for the past 15 years, to bring you an Irish Coffee or Cafe Royal. An equally nice restaurant, **Rindu Alam**, serving *padang* food is one kilometer down the road.

A bit further along the highway in the village of **Cipanas** there are numerous small hotels and homestays. The village is known for its hot springs and for its colorful roadside stands that sell fresh fruit, vegetables and flowers. Cipanas also has some astounding nurseries, which sell, among other exotic flora, bonsaied tea bushes.

Just before Cipanas, a right turn onto a small road leads to the **Cibodas Botanical Gardens**. After walking through the gardens you can climb the 2,743-m (9,000-ft) Mt. Gede. From the peak on a clear day you can see all the way to Jakarta.

BANDUNG

Known as the "flower city" of Indonesia, Bandung sits in a huge mountain valley surrounded by volcanic peaks. In the late nineteenth century it was established by the Dutch who found the temperate climate conducive to growing cool weather crops such as vegetables, coffee, quinine and tea. Planters lived on their isolated farms during the week, coming into Bandung on the weekends for supplies and recreation. Because of the stylish relaxed lifestyle and the cosmopolitan cafe society that developed, it soon became known as the "Paris of the East." Most of the fine hotels, houses and government buildings still surviving were built during the Art Deco period from 1920 to 1940. Bandung ranks second only to Miami, Florida as having the largest concentration of tropical art deco architecture in the world.

Background

As you wander about Bandung you'll notice the marked difference between the

northernandsouthernpartsofthecity.After
World War II, Allied forces supporting the
resumption of Dutch colonial rule pres-
sured the Indonesian army to withdraw
from their positions south of the railroad
track and return Bandung to the Dutch. The
independence army under Indonesian General Nasution complied, but not before torch-
ing the entire southern half of the town.
North of the railroad tracks "Kampong
Blanda" — the area where the Dutch army
was headquartered and most colonialists
lived — looks much like it did over a half

What to See

Bandung has 27 institutes of higher education. The M.I.T. or Cal Tech of Indonesia is the
Institut Teknologi Bandung (ITB), a school
that is as prestigious as it is photogenic. The
Minangkabau-style peaked roofs of its aca-
demic buildings are complemented by prom-
enades shaded by bougainvillea. This may
be the best place in the country to talk with
Indonesia's brightest university students in
a relaxed setting.

Bandung was a planned recreational community designed by the Netherlands East

century ago. Lined with mahogany trees,
Old Holland Road, now called Jalan Cipa-
ganti, is pure visual history that should
be savored either before or after a leisurely
inspection of the Savoy Homann Hotel,
perhaps the world's best example — along
with the Bumi Siliwangi in the nearby
town of Lembang — of tropical art deco
architecture.

General Information

Located at Jalan K.H. Hasan Mustafa N° 22,
the Regional Office of Tourism, Post and
Telecommunications for West Java (Kanwil
VI Depparpostel Jawa Barat) has free maps
and suggestions about affordable local tours.
((22) 81490.

Indies Institute of Architects. As you drive
through the city you'll notice that all the
main streets and housing areas look out on
or lead to one of the surrounding volcanoes.
Behind **St. Peter's Cathedral** just north of
the railroad tracks is the former headquarters of the Dutch Army. Between St. Peter's
and ITB is the **Gedung Sate**, a building completed in 1920 when Bandung was being
considered as the East Indies new capital.
The top spire of the building, now the capital
of West Java, is a "skewer with six meats," a

OPPOSITE: Puncak Pass east of Bandung is the only
spot on Java where travelers wear sweaters and
sleep under blankets. ABOVE: The "flower city" of
Bandung is a showcase for art deco architecture.

spike with six rings representing the six million guilders spent on construction.

Just down the street from the Gedung Sate not far from the Bumi Asih hotel is the **Geological Museum of Bandung** at Jalan Diponegoro N° 73, ((22) 73205, 73208. The museum has skeletons of prehistoric elephants and rhinos plus a 156 kg meteor which fell on Java in 1884 and one of the many skulls of the original Java Man.

Sundanese are known for their music made with the *angklung*, a percussion instrument made of bamboo pipes which when

shaken produce a mellow tone similar to that of a xylophone. *Angklung* concerts are performed at several places around Bandung, the most famous of which is **Pak Ujo's Angklung Show** in the village of Padasuka. Here every afternoon at 3:30 pm about 30 local children play Javanese and Western tunes. $3 per person.

Where to Stay
Bandung is a city where you definitely need a reservation, especially on weekends when Jakartans drive up for the cooler temperatures. In addition to the room rate expressed in United States dollars or rupiah, there is an additional 21 percent service charge and government tax.

Just south of the railroad tracks at Jalan Merdeka N° 2, the **Panghegar Hotel's** Panyawangan Revolving Restaurant has Bandung's best view. Stop for a sunset cocktail at 5 pm and you'll easily see the effect of the

Bandung's Savoy Homann may be Java's most beautiful hotel.

1946 decision to burn the southern half of the city. A deluxe room with a north looking view costs $50. Suites range from $80 to $120. If you've hired a car in Jakarta, the hotel has rooms for drivers that cost $18. On Wednesday and Saturday nights at 7:30 pm attend the Sundanese buffet and cultural show ($9 per person) in the Pasundan dining room. ((22) 432286, 432287, 432295, 57751, fax (22) 431583.

The **Papandayan** on Jalan Gatot Subroto N° 83 has no-smoking rooms, special rooms for female travelers and an executive floor with complimentary breakfast plus afternoon tea and cocktails. The Papandayan has a kennel for people traveling with pets and a full range of athletic facilities. On weekends the hotel really comes alive with a Saturday night buffet followed by a Sunday brunch, both priced at $9. Deluxe rooms cost $75, with the same room on the executive floor going for $90. Add $10 for double occupancy. ((22) 310799, fax (22) 310988.

The **Grand Hotel Preanger** at Jalan Asia Afrika N° 81 is a 62-year old 53-room art deco hotel that recently was enlarged with the addition of a 157-room high-rise. The architect tried to duplicate the atmosphere of the original building, but to capture the true feel of pre-war Bandung ask for one of the old rooms in the Asia Afrika wing (they have "Brieven" on the mail slot). Singles or double start at $100. Studio suites are $140. ((22) 430682, 431631, fax (22) 430034.

When Dutch architect A.F. Albers was commissioned to take down the old Homann Hotel and put up a new modern one in 1939, he designed a pleasure palace meant to remind colonial plantation owners and visiting bureaucrats of what was in those days the epitome of good living — a luxury cruise ship. In so doing, Albers built what art historians say is a Tropical Art Deco masterpiece, the **Savoy Homann** on Jalan Asia Afrika N° 112. The long building with its central bridge and rising funnel has corridors that resemble the deck of a ship. Clever stepbacks or recessions in the facade provide the building with a unique rhythm as if it were rising and falling over ocean waves. Zhou Enlai, Norodom Sihanouk and Jawaharlal Nehru stayed here while attending the 1955 Asia-Africa conference (that became the nonaligned movement) across the street. Charlie Chaplin and Mary Pickford also hung out at the Homann during the 1920's. Completely renovated in 1989, all 157 rooms have balconies. Sixteen of the old Dutch suites have been preserved in their original condition with teak wainscoting, ceilings and Dutch glass doors dividing the bedroom from the sitting room. Double rooms range from $63 to $94 with junior suites costing $100.

The Savoy dining room serves a nightly rijstafel for $12 per person. A jazz band at the Garden Bar keeps the Savoy stompin' late into the night. ((22) 432244, 430083, fax (22) 431583.

Opened in late 1990, the **Sheraton Inn** at Jalan Ir. H. Juanda N° 390 has 105 rooms. Rates are from $80 to $100, single or double occupancy. Suites start at $150. ((22) 210303, fax (22) 210301.

Travelers searching for a more intimate place to stay should consider the **Bumi Asih**, (Jalan Cilamaya N° 1; ((22) 50419, fax (22) 433208) a Dutch-style hotel across from the Gedung Sate in beautiful north Bandung. Built in 1934, all of the 27 rooms come with high ceilings and verandahs with rattan recliners. Rooms start at $27 and go up to $50. The Bumi Asih also has a small restaurant offering a variety of Indonesian, Dutch and German dishes for around $2.50 each.

Where to Eat
Less spicy than most Indonesian fare, Sunda food relies on fresh vegetables, fruit and fish. *Ikan mas* (gold fish) is a popular Sunda specialty that is served fried (*ikan mas goreng*) or steamed with spices (*ikan mas pepes*) and served with a sour vegetable soup (*sayur asam*).

Babakan Siliwangi at Jalan Siliwangi N° 7, ((22) 81394 specializes in gold fish which diners can personally select from terraced ponds. Covered by a roof but otherwise open to the elements, tables look out beyond the fish ponds to a vest pocket rice field. Left overs get tossed to the gold fish, which can fight like piranhas when scraps are at stake. Dinners cost around $8. Open daily 9 am to 10 pm.

Just around the corner from the Savoy Homann and the Grand Hotel Preanger, the **Braga Restaurant** on Jalan Braga N° 58, ((22) 50519, is a brasserie with a pastry chef who

began his apprenticeship when Indonesia still belonged to the Dutch. This bakery and restaurant is one of the city's oldest and finest restaurants, but it looks new because of a complete renovation. It has a large menu containing European and Szechwan dishes. Dinner for two is $16 with a side salad and appetizer. Open daily from 9 am to 11 pm.

Bandung's best Chinese restaurant is the **Queen International** on Jalan Dalem Kaum N° 79, ((22) 51561. Open daily from 10 am to 11 pm, it specializes in Cantonese food. Dinner for two $14.

Where to Shop
A large fashion industry has developed in Bandung, which produces 60 percent of Indonesia's textiles. Jeans and all kinds of denim accessories along with tee shirts and belts are sold at bargain prices along a colorful street known as **Cihampelas**. Shop after shop vies for attention with whimsical facades. One features a taxi crashing through the roof, while another has Indian totem poles. Jeans cost $14. Cotton shirts sell for $11. Stores are open from 10 am to 9 pm.

Shoes also are a bargain here. **Jalan Cibaduyut**, seven kilometers (four miles) south of the railroad track, is an entire street with more than 50 open-fronted shops full of leather, snakeskin and crocodile shoes. The variety here is tremendous and the prices are low. If you like a style that's not in your size and can afford to wait for three or four days, then the stores will have shoes made to order to your size. Handmade men's shoes are $50 a pair, women's shoes cost $11.

For modern sterling silver jewelry visit **Runa Jewelry workshop** on Jalan Gegerkalong Hilir N° 64, ((22) 83503. Runa also sells pottery from the nearby village of Plered, batik and *wayang golek* puppets.

In the case of *wayang golek* puppets it's possible in Bandung to go to the source, 47-year old Aming Sutisna, the best puppet maker in West Java who lives at Jalan Moh. Ramdan N° 4. It takes six days to make a puppet, the time about equally divided between carving and painting the soft *albassia* wood. For the Sutisna family, puppets are literally a cottage industry. Aming's workshop is the kitchen, his wife Aos Utari makes all the puppets' clothes. Sutisna's puppets start at $40, more than Jakarta's Sarinah department store charges, but the carving is much more detailed. Open every day, all the time for cash transactions.

Where to Relax

Nearly 40 percent of Bandung's 2.2 million people are students, and many of them can be found late at night at the **La Dreampalace**, ((22) 433970 a discotheque on the second floor of the Asia Afrika Plaza next to the post office. One of this disco's two dance floors is on springs, which tests your balance as well as your rhythm. Open nightly 9 pm to 2 am Weekend cover charge is $6.

On the same floor of Asia Afrika Plaza more sedentary entertainment can be found at the **Laser Karaoke** ((22) 432351, a video sing along pub with a private room for families who want to sing together. Open daily 7 pm to 2 am. All credit cards.

People who play golf should definitely bring their clubs to Bandung. The city has three excellent courses while a fourth in Lembang, which has an altitude twice that of Bandung, is probably the most beautiful in the country. The 18-hole **Dago Golf Course** at the top end of Jalan Juanda is beautifully laid out in hilly countryside. The **Bandung Giri Gahana Golf and Country Club** at Jatinangor some 40 minutes from Bandung is unanimously considered the best in Indonesia. The 9-hole **Panorama Panghegar Golf Course**, near Lembang, is best known for its beauty.

How to Get There

Merpati and Bouraq airlines both have several daily 30 minute flights to Bandung from Halim Airport in Jakarta. Sempati has two daily flights from Soekarno-Hatta. Roundtrip fare is about $60. Sempati has two daily flights from Soekarno Hatta. The cheapest way to get to the city is by a "48/48" taxi which charges $6 per person for a four hour one way ride. "48/48" taxis leave Jakarta about every five minutes from their depot next to the Satriavi Tours office on Jalan Prapatan. Rail travel between Jakarta and Bandung is fast and convenient. The *Parahyangan* train travels six times a day in both

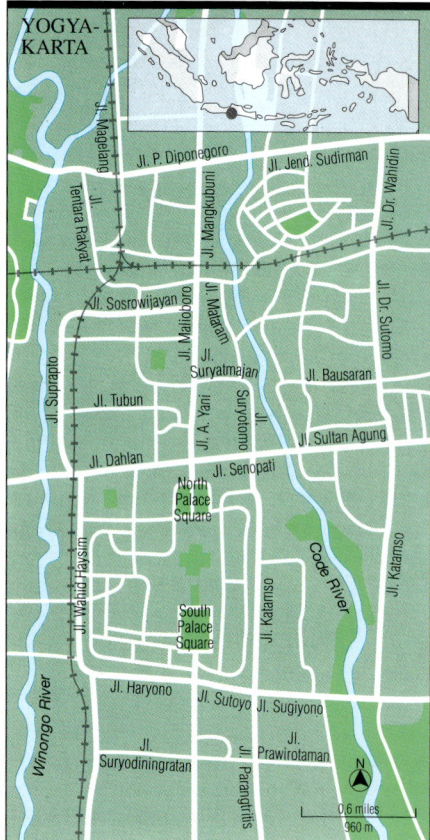

directions. First and executive class coaches are air-conditioned. In Bandung the railway station number is ((22) 50367. Trains stop at each of Jakarta's three stations: Gambir ((21) 362982, 352981; Kota ((21) 678515 and Jatinegara ((21) 819-2231. There is also an express train to Cirebon called the *Gunung Jati,* that leaves Jakarta Kota Station three times a day.

In Bandung, metered cabs operate like those in Jakarta. Bandung taxis can be hired for $4 an hour for service inside the city.

YOGYAKARTA

Central Java is the cultural cradle of Indonesia. Together with the special administrative area of Yogyakarta, it accounts for more than 30 percent of Java's population. Most of the region's creative energy radiates from the Yogyakarta–Surakarta (Solo) corridor where earlier civilizations flourished on the rich volcanic soil. Indeed, the history of Indonesia,

OPPOSITE: The Taman Sari "Water Castle" west of the *kraton* of Yogyakarta evokes an image of bygone splendor.

from the coming of Islam to the arrival of Independence, turns largely on actions taken by the sultans and kings of Central Java.

In no other Indonesian city does the past so intimately overlap the present as it does in Yogyakarta, a "special autonomous region" of 2,945 sq km (1,137 sq miles) and a population of 3,100,000. The sultan's palace or *kraton* is still the heart of the city, and comes alive every Sunday when a *gamelan* orchestra and Javanese dancers perform. The Sivaistic temple complex of Prambanan and Buddhist Borobudur, acclaimed as one of the seven wonders of the world, are impressive today as they were back in the tenth and ninth centuries when each embodied the grandeur and sophistication of the Mataram and Sailendra dynasties. Carefully restored with help from UNESCO, these and other temple complexes reflect the vitality of Central Java's modern culture which makes Yogya second only to Bali as a preferred tourist destination.

GENERAL INFORMATION

The regional tourism office is just beyond the Kilometer 7 post on Jalan Adi Sucipto, ((274) 5150. The Provincial Tourism Agency is in central Yogyakarta at Jalan Malioboro N° 14-16, ((274) 3543.

WHAT TO SEE

There are two places you must visit. One is **Borobudur** about an hour's drive northwest town. The best time to visit is at sunrise or either early or late in the day since the massive stone temple absorbs the midday heat. The second imperative is **Prambanan**. Just northeast of the city on the highway to Solo, Prambanan can be an afternoon trip, following a morning at Borobudur and lunch back in Yogya. Alternatively, you can stop at Prambanan on the way to Solo.

Borobudur

After uncovering the ruins of Borobudur in 1814, Stamford Raffles wrote: "The interior of Java contains temples that, as works

Built four centuries before the great cathedrals at Chartres and Reims, Borobudur is the world's most imposing Buddhist monument.

of labor and art, dwarf to nothing all our wonders and admiration at the pyramids of Egypt." Raffles might be even more impressed today now that Borobudur has been rebuilt with the aid of $60 million in UNESCO funds.

The largest Buddhist shrine in the world, Borobudur was built between 778 and 856 AD, 300 years before Angkor Wat and 200 years before Notre Dame. Seen from the air, the temple forms a mandala; from the ground it is shaped like a bell-shaped dome or stupa, and covers the top of a steep hill like a mantle. The elaborately-carved galleries ascend in ten levels, corresponding to the divisions within the Mahayana Buddhist universe. The first visible level (the temple's original base no longer is visible) depicts the delights of human life and the punishments that await sinners. Then comes five levels of diminishing size that are surmounted by three more circular and concentric terraces that support 72 miniature, perforated stupas, each of which contains a meditating Buddha. A total of 2,700 carved stone panels on the balustrades about the monument relate the Buddha's teaching and depict scenes from his life, so that climbing Borobudur is a religious journey. Open daily from 6 am to 5 p.m. with an entry fee of Rp 500.

If time permits, visit **Candi Mendut**, a temple with intricately carved panels just 1,100 m (1,200 yards) to the east of Borobudur. The reliefs here, largest of any Indonesian temple, are breathtaking in their beauty and show everything from child-eating ogres to mythological money trees.

Prambanan

Just off the Solo highway on the opposite side of Yogyakarta from Borobudur sits Prambanan, a Hindu temple with three shrines dedicated to Shiva, Vishnu and Brahma. Each of these shrines is accompanied by smaller ones for their riding animals: the bull Nandi for Shiva the destroyer, the swan Hansa for Brahma the guardian and the mythical bird Garuda for Vishnu the creator. Prambanan is open daily from 7 am to 5 pm and costs Rp 500 to enter.

From May through October during the full moon the *Ramayana* ballet is performed from 7 to 9 pm over a period of four nights in Prambanan's outer courtyard.

After a visit to Prambanan, walk through the rice paddies to the nearby **Sewu** and **Plaosan** temples which have not been restored but remain in good condition.

Kalasan Temple

Across the Solo highway from Prambanan is the Kalasin Temple, a beautifully ornamented temple built in the shape of a Greek Cross. Open daily from sunrise to sunset. There is no entry free but a donation of Rp 150 is appreciated.

Five hundred and fifty meters (600 yards)

northeast of Kalasan is the **Sari Temple**, a two-story structure formerly used by monks as a sanctuary where they could live, meditate and instruct their followers on the way of the Buddha.

Sambi Sari Temple

One the way back to Yogyakarta, stop at the tenth century Sambi Sari Temple. The fully restored structure is about six meters (21 ft) below ground level, which indicates the amount of volcanic ash released when

OPPOSITE: Built around 900 AD, Prambanan celebrates the Hindu dieties of Brahma, Shiva and Vishnu. ABOVE: Bas-relief carvings at Prambanan provide a backdrop to performances of the *Ramayana* each summer.

Mt. Merapi erupted in 1006. Ash from Merapi that dwarfed Sambi Sari buried Borobudur for close to a millineum.

Kraton Ngayogyakarta Hadiningrat

Back inside Yogyakarta your first stop should be the 235-year old Kraton Ngayogyakarta Hadiningrat, the residence of Central Java's sultans. Open daily except Friday from 8:30 am to 1 pm (entry Rp 600) the *kraton* is divided into seven parts. Inside the front gate is a large Pendopo-style pavilion supported by four central pillars representing fire, wind, earth and water. The beams of the ceiling are arranged like beams of the sun.

Beyond the main entry, which is guarded by two large statues, is the area where the sultan's main business was conducted. The first sight is an 800-year old *gamelan*, plus other artifacts used in official ceremonies. The *kraton* also is the residence of the present sultan, Hamengku Buwono IX. Don't leave before seeing the Picture Gallery. Sultans VII and VIII are photographed in Dutch military uniforms. Notice that in a photograph made with the Dutch Governor General all the family members of Sultan VII have their military tunics unbuttoned. The reason: Indonesia's climate is far to hot for blue serge.

Just beyond the **Bird Market** on Jalan Polowijan is the **Taman Sari**, or "beautiful park," a recreational Water Palace for past sultans and their families. Now a ruin, it exists as a reminder of luxuries Central Java's sultans once enjoyed. The top rim of the main bathing pool is an excellent place for photography with unobstructed views of the *kraton*.

The Road to Imogiri

Several small roads head south out of Yogyakarta toward the beach, but Java's entire southern coast has dangerous rip tides and should be avoided. The drive to this rugged, remote coast however, is beautiful. The road to Imogiri cuts through rice paddies and fields of sugar cane. Stands of banana and papaya trees sprout in front of houses along the roadway. A tidy little town with small brick houses, **Imogiri** is the resting place of Central Java's kings and sultans. The famous Mataram Sultan Agung is buried there, as are most of the succeeding princes of Yogyakarta and Surakarta. The 345 steps leading up to the tombs are worn thin in many

places for Imogiri is a destination for Moslem pilgrims. The tomb-filled courtyards atop the hill are open only on Monday and Friday afternoons. Be sure to carry a pocketful of Rp 100 notes since numerous "donations" are required. On the way back to Yogya, turn west about five kilometers (three miles) before the city limit to visit Bagong Kussudiardjo's Dance Training Center

Bagong Kussudiardjo's Dance Training Center

Established in 1978 by the 63-year old classical artist, dancer and composer, the Center is a boarding school for students studying music, Javanese dance and batik painting. There is a batik art gallery in which student paintings are sold, but the real reason to visit is in order to watch the dance practice from 8 to 11 am and from 4 to 6 pm every day. There are three large studios and during those hours each is filled with young Indonesians from every part of the country dancing to the accompaniment of a *gamelan* orchestra

The dances, dramas and puppet shows of Java and Bali are based on the *Mahabharata* and the *Ramayana*, Hindu epics brought to Java by traders more than 15 centuries ago. Incorporated into the traditional *wayang kulit* performances, the plots and characters remain essentially unchanged despite the passage of time. The two classics, tales of good versus evil in which the forces of darkness inevitably are defeated, never grow old because the actors, dancers and puppeteers offer slight plot twists and different interpretations at each performance.

In the *Ramayana Ballet*, Prince Rama, the legal heir to the throne of Ayodhya, is banished to the forest along with his wife Sita and his brother Laksamana. While wandering through the forest, Sita is observed by evil King Rahwana who, smitten by her beauty, sends a golden deer to lure her away. Rama and Laksamana chase the deer, leaving Sita in a magic circle for protection. Rahwana then appears disguised as a Brahmin priest begging for food. Sita leaves the circle in order to help him and is immediately carried off to the island of Alengka (Ceylon) by Rahwana. Determined to save

Virtue always triumphs when Yogyakarta theater groups perform the *Ramayana* Ballet.

Sita, Rama enlists the aid of the Monkey King, Hanoman, who builds a bridge to Rahwana's kingdom. A terrible battle ensues and in due time Rama's forces prevail. He returns to Ayodhya with Sita to begin a reign still remembered as the Golden Age.

The *Mahabharata*, the longest poem in the world, is the story of a great war fought by Indo-Aryans in Northern India in the fourteenth century BC. The "Epic of the Bharata Nation," or *Mahabharata*, is seven times the length of the *Illiad* and *Odyssey* combined. It tells the tale of the great war between rival

branches of the Bharata tribe, the Kauravas and the Pandavas. It begins when Pandu, King of Hastinapura whose five sons are called the Pandavas, dies and is succeeded by his brother Dhristarastra, who has 100 sons known as the Kuravas. A rivalry develops and the Pandavas go into voluntary exile. Friction continues, however, and eventually a war breaks out. The most famous part of the epic is when the charioteer Krishna explains to the Pandava warrior Arjuna that his soul is immortal, so he should not be reluctant to go into battle. Whoever dies honorably, Krishna insists, will be reborn. The Pandavas finally win the 13-year war, but not before great heroes from both sides display bravery and compassion.

WHERE TO STAY

Built on the grounds of a Sultan's palace between the airport and downtown, the completely redecorated 257-room **Ambarrukmo** on Jalan Adisucipto is Yogyakarta's biggest hotel. The Borobudur restaurant on

the seventh floor offers classical dances with dinner on most nights. Every afternoon a *gamelan* orchestra plays in the lobby. A standard room costs $75, $85 for two people. Experienced travelers, however, spend $10 more a day and take superior rooms which look out over the pool toward Yogyakarta's Merapi volcano. ((274) 88488, fax (274) 88933.

Located in the heart of Yogya, the **Natour Garuda** at Jalan Malioboro N° 60 has been the focus of history since its construction in 1911. The elegant glass-domed port cochere and the two enormous chandeliers in the lobby date from the Dutch epoch. During World War II it was home to Japanese army officers. Following the Japanese occupation, its Presidential Suite became the headquarters of the Indonesian independence movement. About half of the hotel's 240 rooms, however, date from 1981 when the Garuda underwent extensive renovation.

The Garuda caters to package tours, most of them from Holland and Japan, so reservations are essential. Standard rooms in the new part of the hotel cost $110 but couples with a sense of history and love of high ceilings may wish to stay in one of the colonial suites which cost $135 to $200 depending on the size. ((274) 66353, fax (274) 63074.

Just down Jalan Malioboro from the Garuda, the 140-room **Mutiara** is in the center of the downtown shopping area. Standard rooms fronting on Yogya's main street cost $40 based on double occupancy. Spend $12 more for a quieter room in the south wing. ((274) 4531 & 5173, fax (274) 61201.

The **Sahid Garden Hotel** on Jalan Babarsari ((274) 87088, fax (274) 63183) has 64 motel type rooms, and an additional 80 in a nine-floor high-rise. A high-rise double goes for $70, a comparable room at ground level costs $50. A family suite in the motel goes for $80. This hotel is on the outskirts of town, so you'll need to rent a car.

Yogyakarta is known for its guest houses, most of which have swimming pools and landscaped gardens. The Yogyakarta Tourist Information Center at Jalan Malioboro N° 14-16, ((274) 3543 can check for available space, but it's probably easier to ask a travel agency in Jakarta to make an advance reservation.

The **Airlangga** on Jalan Prawirotaman N° 6-8 has 35 rooms in a garden setting with a nice pool and two restaurants with live entertainment. Single rooms are $32. Doubles cost $34. Breakfast included. ((274) 3344, 88727, telex 25376 AIR.

The **Duta Guest House** at Jalan Prawirotaman N° 20-26 ((274) 5064 offers a garden setting with 22 rooms built over and around fish ponds. Air conditioned singles range from $22 to $25, doubles from $25 to $27. Rooms with a fan are $5 cheaper. Price includes breakfast, an evening snack and tea. The ten rooms in the new building are the nicest. Parents with children ask for room 39. Yogya has several guest houses named Duta so make sure you arrive at the address above.

WHERE TO EAT

Gita Buana on Jalan Adisucipto N° 169, ((274) 87164, has a huge very reasonably priced menu containing everything from Russian borscht and burgers to prawns in brandy sauce and fried crab rolls. Dishes vary in price between $3 to $6. Cool off with a champagne punch and try the almond pancakes for dessert. Open daily 9 am to 3 pm. and from 6 pm to 10 pm.

Hanoman's Forest Garden Restaurant at Jalan Prawirotaman N° 9, ((274) 55153, has western and Indonesian food. Dinner for two costs around $6. Hanoman also has puppet shows and Javanese dancing starting at 7:30 pm each night. There is a cover charge for the floor show.

There's nothing especially elegant about **Nyonya Suharti**, Jalan Adisucipto N° 208, ((274) 5522, but Javanese seldom pass through Yogya without stopping for some of the island's best *ayam goreng*. A whole fried chicken accompanied by a bowl of chicken soup, vegetable salad, a spicy dish of *sambal* and a large Bintang beer, the feast comes to less than $10.00. Open seven days a week from 10 am to 10 pm.

Located west of the railroad station, **Pesta Perak** at Jalan Tentara Rakyat Mataram N° 8, ((274) 86255, offers the city's most extensive Indonesian buffet. Innovatively designed so that most of the tables are near fern grottos and fish ponds, Pesta Perak offers thirty different dishes heaped in steaming tureens.

Palavers are constantly being refilled by a staff dressed in traditional Javanese outfits. At night there is a *gamelan* orchestra. Though officially open from 9 am until 10 pm, remember that nap time is from 3 to 4 pm.

Next door to the Ambarrukmo Hotel on Jalan Adisucipto is one of Yogya's newer Japanese restaurants (and karaoke bar) **Yaski No Ki**. One can eat traditional Japanese dishes from 10 am to midnight in one of the restaurant's tatami rooms, or just come for snacks and drinks at the karaoke bar which is open from 7 pm. to 1 am.

WHERE TO SHOP

Yogyakarta is arguably the best city in Indonesia for shopping. It is often, and quite rightly, called the "city of batik" because of its factories that turn out the colorful material using traditional means of hand waxing and hand stamping. Yogya also is famed for its leather craft. Nearly all of Indonesia's *wayang kulit* puppets are made here.

Also made locally is the Indonesian *kris*, a dagger with a pistol-like grip that is believed to possess mystical powers. Imbued with the soul of its most valiant owner, a magical *kris*, so the story goes, must taste blood before it will return to its scabbard.

Some of the finest *krises* were made during the Majapahit and Mataram dynasties. Although the scabbard and handle are often elaborately decorated, the blade is the most

OPPOSITE: Yogyakarta's Garuda Hotel became Japanese Army headquarters during World War II. ABOVE: Batik paintings come in both abstract and traditional styles.

valuable part. The best blades are forged from nickel-rich iron that is repeatedly rolled and hammered until the blade contains layers of iron and steel. When dipped in a solution of arsenic, the nickel-rich iron turns white causing various patterns to emerge. The double edged blade can be straight or wavy; the latter design said to be the best for penetrating the rib cage.

Krises are worn on formal occasions in Central Java and are part of the uniform worn by attendants in the *kratons* of Yogyakarta and Solo.

Yogyakarta has a large selection of attractively priced antiques, and the best place to start looking is the **Sapto Hudoyo Gallery** at Kilometer 9 on the Solo Highway; ((274) 62443. This may well be the most beautiful antique store in Southeast Asia. Arrayed about an elegant Javanese villa, the objects are displayed with an interior designers sense of style. Can't figure out what you would ever do with a *wayang golok* puppet? Hudoyo shows how an exterior light source can make them come alive. Balinese bells hang beside Dutch lamps. There is a large selection of Irian statues, one of which is topped with an actual human skull. Prices here can go as high as $10,000, but Sapto Hudoyo is worth a visit even if you can't

afford the merchandise. Open everyday from 8 am to 5 pm.

Not very far from Sapto Hudoyo on Jalan Babarsari N° 1-3 is **Kendedes Antique Artshop**, ((274) 86498. This shop specializes in European furniture, crystal and Chinese wedding beds with gilded canopies. Open daily 8 am to 5 pm.

Asikin Antiques is located inside the old city walls near the *kraton*. There are actually two locations: one at Jalan Langenastran Lor N° 3B and the other one block away at Suryoputran PBII/12C; ((274) 63151. This store features stone carvings and antique roof tiles from Sumatra. Open daily.

A few blocks from Jalan Prawirotaman where Yogya's best guest houses are located is Jalan Tirtodipuran, a quiet lane full of batik shops and antique stores. **Ancient Arts** at Jalan Tirtodipuran N° 50 has a good selection of roof tiles shaped like roosters, squirrels and Naga snakes. Open daily 9 am to 5 pm. Closed Friday afternoons.

A few doors down the street is the **Dieng Art Shop**. This store sells Dutch lamps, Chinese lacquer ware and antique *wayang golok* puppets. Open daily from 8 am to 9 pm.

Across the street from Dieng Art is **Griya Kriyasta Nugraha**; ((274) 25198. This self-styled "arts and crafts house" sells a variety of primitive statues and stone carvings, all of them new. Decorative art here is not valuable, but neither is it expensive. Open daily.

Jalan Taman Garuda is known for bamboo and rattan, which are made into lampshades, fruit baskets and decorative shopping bags.

Central Java is the best place in Indonesia to buy **batik**. The word is an amalgam of several Indonesian words: *tik*, or small, *bitik*, to draw, and *titik*, point or dot. Hence the word batik means "to draw something very small and detailed." The processing of batik is an intricate, classical art form. There are scores of different motifs, each of which has a special meaning. Plants and animals, for example, are symbols of prosperity. More than 60 percent of the "batik" sold in Central Java is an imitation in which classical designs are printed on textile by a machine. Imitation batik, which can be very attractive, costs much less than the real thing because it covers only one side of the material.

Genuine batik must be made with wax by hand. The wax can be "drawn" on the material with a copper tool called a canting or stamped on with a copper chop. When the wax hardens, it is dye-resistant, so the unwaxed parts of the cloth can be dyed. The process is repeated over and over again, depending on the pattern and the number of colors desired, by boiling the hardened wax off the cloth and applying a new wax pattern.

One of the best places to buy real batik, in addition to seeing the actual process take

paintings for as much as $4,000. There is a selection of dresses, blouses, batik purses and men's shirts, but Amri's heart clearly is in painting.

Kuwat Soemihardjo on Jalan Mangkuyudan N° 15A, ((274) 3061, sells genuine batik sarongs that have up to nine colors. The $250 asking price stems from the fact that each sarong takes more than three months to make. Open daily 9 am to 9 pm.

Imam Batik Workshop, Jalan Dagen N° 76B, is an artist collective run by law student Imam Nuryanto. Open from 8 am to

place, is **Batik Plentong** on Jalan Tirtodipuran N° 48; ((274) 2777. Open daily from 8:30 am to 6:30 pm, Plentong's owner, Judantoro, is happy to go through the batik process step by step and allow photography of women using their *cantings*.

Ardiyanto Batik, Jalan Taman Garuda; ((274) 5485 sells bedspreads, napkins and table cloths in pastel blues and greens. All items are real batik. Wall hangings measuring about one yard square sell for $100. Open daily 9 am to 9 pm.

Amri Yahya, Jalan Gampingan N° 67; ((274) 5135, is one of Indonesia's leading batik artists. Open Tuesday through Sunday from 9 am to 5 pm, Amri's gallery, a converted Javanese house, sells innovative, modern

10 pm, the gallery has a good assortment of batik paintings in all styles and price levels.

Extremely popular with Westerners traveling through Yogyakarta are the brief and practical classes in batik painting offered by Hadjir Digdodarmodjo, 60, a high school art teacher completely fluent in English. Taught in Hadjir's home, which is located adjacent to the entrance of the Taman Sari "Water Palace," the three and five-day courses run from 2 to 6 pm and cost only $4 a day. Students learn how to apply wax with the canting pen and copper stamp and various

OPPOSITE: Song birds purchased near Yogyakarta's *kraton* bring good luck when released from their cage. ABOVE: Indonesia's finest batik comes from open-air "factories" in Central Java.

techniques for making their own waxes and dyes. The daily fee includes all materials.

Souvenir shops throughout Yogya sell wooden *topeng* masks. Originally, the masks were made of gold and were placed over the face of a corpse as a symbol of eternal life. Later, dancers would use a *topeng* in hopes of recapturing the spirit of the famous person the mask resembled. Many of the shops along Jalan Malioboro sell *topengs* resembling animals or historical characters. Masks also can be found in the shop of **Pak Warno Waskito** in the village of **Karantil** south of Yogya.

9 am to 6 pm; ask the owner, Mrs. Yuni, to show you her chimpanzee.

Persons searching for **earthenware and ceramics** should head for **Kasongan**, a village of potters eight kilometers (five miles) south of Yogyakarta. Pottery here is literally a cottage industry since nearly all of the village's 465 families have backyard kilns. While old women mix clay and water with their feet and teenagers sculpt stylistic animals, small children stoke the kilns with rice straw. There are no addresses or telephones in Kasongan, but since every house is a store just

Outside the city are several villages known for their excellent handicrafts. Six-and-a-half kilometers (four miles) east of Yogya is **Kota Gede**, a village whose artisans have produced most of the silver and gold adornments found in the museum of the sultan's kraton. Kota Gede produces two kinds of silver: white and black, the latter being called "burned silver." **Tom's Silver** at Jalan Ngeksigondo Nº 60, ℂ (274) 2818 has an excellent selection of decorative silverware, much of it inlaid with gold. Open daily from

walk around until something catches your eye. Temu and his father Karya Reja, who together have more than 100 years of experience, understand quality control and have the ability to pack and ship overseas. Except for large special orders, Kasongan's potters work on a cash and carry basis.

Perhaps Yogyakarta's oldest handicraft is the manufacture of **paper umbrellas**. They still are used in religious and cultural events and can be seen alongside the heirlooms in the *kraton*. The tiny village of **Juwiring** has been making umbrellas for several centuries. In Yogya they can be purchased on **Jalan Ibu Ruswo** close to the North Square of the Kraton, or from a store called **Tjokrosuharto** on Jalan Panembahan.

ABOVE: Sun-dried earthenware from Kasongan comes in a variety of shapes and colors.
OPPOSITE: Central Java's volcanos have produced some of the richest soil in the world.

HOW TO GET THERE

Because it is a major tourist destination, Yogya is well served by air. Garuda Indonesia has up to six flights a day from Jakarta and three daily flights from Denpasar. Bouraq links Yogya with Bandung and Borneo. Merpati has daily service between Yogya and Surabaya, Denpasar and Ujung Pandang, and Sempati has daily direct flights to Jakarta and Surabaya.

There is frequent train service connecting Yogya with Surabaya (six trains a day), Bandung (three trains each day) and Jakarta (ten trains every day). The quickest way to travel between Jakarta, Yogya and Surabaya is on the *Bima*, a night train that makes only a few stops. The Bima has air-conditioned first class compartments that contain pull-down beds with linen sheets. The night train that links Bandung with Surabaya via Yogya is called the *Mutiara*. The only day-time train between Jakarta and Yogya worth taking is the *Fajar Utama*. All others are uncomfortably crowded and take FOREVER to arrive.

Night buses travel to all the above destinations, but are considered dangerous even by Indonesians because of the likelihood of accidents.

Yogya's in-town transport runs the gamut from horse-drawn *andong* carriages to hotel rental cars. Because Yogya is relatively flat, the most popular way to get about the city is on pedal-powered *becaks*. Rp 500 will take you almost anywhere in Yogya on a *becak*, though you might have to pay Rp 100 more if your route is uphill. Private cars available for hire outside the main hotels charge $4 an hour for travel inside the city. A four-hour round-trip to Borobudur is $18, while a full day excursion to Solo costs $47. The taxi ride from the airport to the center of town costs $4.50.

The most efficient and inexpensive way to get about Central Java is to go to the front of the Ambarrukmo Hotel and talk with the hire car drivers. Find one who speaks English and then bargain for his best price. The more days you require, the lower the price. The Ambarrukmo also is the best place to shop for a package tour. Ida's Tours, Jatayu Mulya, Matahari Tours, Milangkori, Natrabu, Pacto, Paradise Bali Indah, Rama Royal Holiday, Satriavi, Sri Rama, Tunas Indonesia and Vaya Tours all have small offices along the arcade off the lobby. For the comparison, shopper, this place is pure paradise.

Most of the companies offer city tours that center on a visit to the *kraton*. This tour should be avoided. The *kraton* has a staff of official guides who provide free tours on request, though a small tip is appreciated. The "Art and Handicraft" tours offered by Satriavi and Pacto are well worth the time, however, since both include trips to villages outside the city.

CENTRAL JAVA

Beyond the special autonomous region of Yogyakarta and the neighboring ruins of kingdoms past lie the rich paddy lands of Central Java, the spiritual center of "the real Indonesia." It was here the ancient Sailendra and Mataram kingdoms flourished a millennium ago. Here, too, the Majapahit empire spread the Hindu philosophy throughout Java and Bali. And it was here, from the second Mataram empire's capital of Kota Gede near Yogyakarta, that the island's most accomplished warrior, Sultan Agung, extended his rule across the Java Sea to Borneo, Sumatra and the Celebes.

Convinced of his spiritual alliance with Nyi Loro Kidul, the Goddess of the South Seas, the Sultan believed he could carry Islam's banner throughout the archipelago. But his failure to take the Dutch stronghold of Batavia led to his demise and the spread of Dutch colonial rule.

Successors to Sultan Agung remained loyal to the South Seas Goddess, but she remained a fickle mistress. Though the Mataram kingdom endured into the mid-nineteenth century, it was controlled by the Dutch who used it to their own ends, pitting Yogyakarta against Surakarta (Solo) in a series of petty aristocratic wars.

SOLO (SURAKARTA)

In 1745 King Pakubuwono II chose the tiny village of Solo as the location of his new palace, the Surakarta Hadiningrat. The king quickly ended all local rebellions, making Solo the official capital of Javanese culture and classical arts for the next 200 years. Today, the two names, Solo and Surakarta, are interchangeable.

Solo's primacy in Central Java ended following World War II when its sultan displayed ambivalence for independence while Yogyakarta was becoming a center for revolutionary struggle. Today, Yogyakarta's special administrative area has a population nearing 3,200,000, while Solo's population barely exceeds 500,000.

Those who bypass the city miss a great deal, for Solo's history is fully as rich as that of its neighbor. The *kraton*, which recently received $3.8 million in repairs following a disastrous fire in 1985, is much like Yogya's in that a thick outer wall encloses a grid of lanes and alleyways. A soothing marble performance pavilion used for coronations leads to an interior courtyard surrounded by 77 Ming Dynasty porcelain vases. The Royal Meditation Tower on one side, which at 31 m (97 ft) is the tallest building in Solo, resembles a Dutch windmill without the arms.

According to legend, the Goddess of the South Sea, Nyi Loro Kidul, is the spiritual wife of the sultan of Solo, and she demands periodic visits in the tower. The *kraton* is open every day except Friday from 8:30 am to 1:30 pm. Entry fee is Rp 600 plus an additional Rp 1,000 for each camera and Rp 5,000 for a video camera. There is classical Javanese dancing every Sunday from 10 am to 2 pm.

OPPOSITE: Women play traditional game in Solo's Mangkunegaran Palace.

Nearly a kilometer (half a mile) to the northwest of the main *kraton* is **Pura Mangkunegaran**, a smaller, more homey palace built by an offshoot of Surakarta's royal family. Completed in 1866, the outer pavilion is built of solid teak without the use of a single nail. Behind the Pendopo is a ceremonial hall full of antiques that belonged to Prince Mankunegara IV. Be sure to see the ninth century male and female chastity belts. Open Monday through Saturday from 9 am to 2 pm, Sunday from 9 am to 1 pm. Entrance fee is Rp 600 per person.

East of Solo Mt. Lawu rises over 3,000 m (9,940 ft) from the paddy fields into swirling clouds of white mist. Motorists headed for Surabaya skirt the mountain, but you may want to take the Kemuning village road to **Candi Sukuh**, a fifteenth century Majapahit shrine 40 km (25 miles) east of Solo erected by a fertility cult. The temple, which costs Rp 600 to enter, is known for its erotic carvings, but the genitalia depicted seems more anatomical than pornographic. What makes the temple mysterious is its location in a secluded pine forest and the fact it has a flat-topped Mayan appearance.

Before leaving Solo you should consider trying a *jamu*, the traditional herbal medicine Javanese have used for hundreds of years. There are two kinds of *jamu:* dried herbs and leaves that must be boiled in water before being drunk, and powders which are commercially produced and available in packages. Because of its generic nature, *jamu* is cheap and has minimum side-effects. Some physicians believe it has no effect at all, but Javanese swear by the stuff.

The **Jamu Akar Sari** factory at Jalan Slamet Riyadi N° 137 in Solo is famous for its *jamu godogan*, which is said to cure almost every conceivable disease, including cancer. Commercially produced *jamu* powders claim to restore vigor and potency, while curing high blood pressure, diabetes and the 'flu. If you want to lose weight or reverse the aging process, Solo's *jamu* stalls may have just the potion for you.

Depending on the malady, glasses of *jamu* can arrive mixed with raw egg, wine or honey. Several *jamu* stalls are located on the first floor of the **Singosaren Plaza**. **Jamu Jago** is at Jalan Gatot N° 84 Subroto and

Jamu Dua Putri Dewi can be found at Jalan Perintis Kemerdekaan N° 40.

Where to Stay

Solo does not have a large number of hotels from which to choose, but those that do exist are clean, pleasant and moderately priced. Room rates in Solo are quoted both in rupiah and United States dollars. The rates below are subject to an additional 15.5 percent government tax and service charge.

An old Dutch hotel, the **Hotel Cakra** on Jalan Brigjen. Salamat Riyadi was occupied by the Japanese during the second world war. An economy room costs $33 for two; deluxe rooms are $50. Breakfast included. The egg-shaped monument in front is the Victory Over Japan memorial. ((271) 45847, fax (271) 48334.

The **Kusuma Sahid Prince** at Jalan Sugiyopranoto N° 20 originally was built as the royal palace of a Javanese prince. Unlike Solo's other hotels, the Sahid Prince is set back off the main road. A gamelan orchestra plays nightly in the hotel's reception area. Superior rooms are the best value for the money. They cost $70. ((271) 46356, fax (271) 44788.

Single rooms range from $33 to $40 at the **Solo Inn** on Jalan Brigjen. Salamat Riyadi N° 366. Doubles cost $3 extra. ((271) 46075, fax (271) 46076.

Where to Eat

The **Diamond** restaurant at Jalan Brigjen. Salamat Riyadi N° 394, ((271) 33680 and 35027, serves dependable Cantonese food. There is an army of waitresses who will happily play with your kids while you eat in peace. Dinner for two: $17.50. Open daily 10 am to 3 pm and 5 pm to 10 pm.

The **New Holland Bakery** at Jalan Brigjen. Salamat Riyadi N° 135-151, ((271) 32452, offers tasty affordable meals. At $4.50 the New York steak topped with crab meat and red wine sauce is the most expensive item on the menu. The Satay Madura or the omelets, both priced at $2, may be better choices, however. All the fresh baked bread is delicious. Open 9 am to 1 am except Sunday when the hours are 9 am to 4 pm.

Where to Shop

Because the majority is machine made, batik in Solo costs about a fourth of that made in Yogyakarta. **Batik Keris** has several locations around the city that sell clothing for the entire family. Its main store in Block A of the Purwosari Plaza, ((271) 8008, is open daily from 8 am to 8 pm. A second outlet at Jalan Yos Sudarso N° 37, ((271) 3543 sells baskets, pottery and wooden boxes in addition to batik ready-to-wear. Batik Keris also has a factory at Kelurahan Cemani where you can photograph batik being made. Tours are free.

Batik Semar, on Jalan RM Said N° 148, ((271)2937, and Jalan Gatot Subroto ((271) 3224, has natural vegetable-dyed batik in traditional patterns. Both stores open 8 am to 4 pm, except for Sunday when the store is closed.

Handmade batik can be found at **Batik Srimpi**, a small home industry that operates on a cash only basis and is open from 8 am to 5 pm except for Sunday.

It's possible to buy *gamelan* music tapes in Solo, or drive out to **Ngepung** at Route 02, RW.II in the nearby area of Semanggi and purchase an entire *gamelan* orchestra. The proprietor here, Tentrem "Peaceful" Sarwanto, makes classical Javanese instruments in the traditional way. Metal is heated red hot over a fire, then pounded with mallets until the proper shape and tone is achieved.

More prosaic souvenirs can be found at **Pasar Triwindu**, an open-air flea market halfway between Jalan Slamet Riyadi and the Mangkunegaran Palace. Whether the merchandise here is treasure or junk depends on the shopper, but there is no doubt that Triwindu is a good place to find antique belt buckles, charcoal-heated irons, hanging oil lamps and copper batik presses. Prices depend entirely on one's bargaining ability, and can be paid for only with cash.

After visiting a batik factory and checking prices among retailers in Yogya and Solo, the place to go is **Pasar Klewer**, a sprawling, two-story batik market at the eastern end of Jalan Secoyudan. This is a place where professionals in the sarong trade gather to haggle and swap. The pace is frenzied, which means you must know exactly the style and size you want and the price you expect to pay. Colors here are more restrained than those offered by tourist-oriented retailers.

Children play while adults pray. Indonesia is the world's largest Muslim nation.

How to Get There

Solo is exclusively served by Garuda which has three daily nonstops from Jakarta in addition to flights linking Solo with Ujung Pandang. For travelers heading east, there is an overnight bus to Surabaya but it takes 12 hours to reach Bandung even traveling at night. Those going west should fly or take the train.

Solo is on the Jakarta to Yogya to Surabaya train route and is most efficiently served by the Bima train, which departs Solo at 8:10 pm and arrives in Jakarta the following morning. The eastbound Bima also stops at Solo en route to Surabaya, but is less convenient since it leaves in the middle of the night.

The *Siang* train and dozens of buses link Solo with Yogyakarta, but most travelers usually rent a car for the 61 km (38 mile) drive between cities.

SEMARANG

Though it has more than one million people, Semarang is a lazy tropical port that reached its zenith during the colonial period. Besides being the only port, Semarang is the provincial capital of Central Java, but one senses that the people in this overwhelmingly Chinese city would rather sit back and day dream about the days when Chinese and Arab traders brought porcelain in trade for palm sugar and other agricultural products.

General Information

The Provincial Tourist Service of Central Java (*Diparda Jawa Tengah*) is in Semarang at Jalan Pemuda N° 171. ((24) 24146. The regional tourism office is not far away at Jalan K.H.A. Dahlan N° 2, ((24) 311169.

What to See

Nothing underscores the convoluted history of Indonesia better than a trip to the **Sam Po Kong Temple** on the bank of Semarang's Banjir Canal. Dedicated to the memory Cheng Ho, a Chinese admiral who made seven journeys to Java during the fifteenth century, the temple resembles a Buddhist pagoda. Ironically, Cheng Ho was a Moslem explorer-cum-evangelist who helped spread Islam during the twilight of the crumbling Majapahit Kingdom. One of the anchors from Cheng Ho's ships is on display, but the real attraction of the temple is its atmosphere. Swirling with incense, the different shrines are packed with worshippers and fortune tellers who divine the future with bamboo sticks or small birds.

From the Sam Po Kong Temple it is only a short *becak* ride to Semarang's Chinatown which has its own temple, the garishly painted **Tay Kak Sie**. The small lanes leading off Jalan Pekojan have a number of Chinese medicine and spice shops.

Those who have been sufficiently adventurous to try a *jamu* on their journey through Java may wish to visit the two factories where nearly all of them are made. The **Jamu Jago** factory on Jalan Setia Budi will assign a guide to explain how herbs are turned into medicine, but calling (24) 285533 for an appointment is necessary. The other *jamu* factory, **Jamu Nyonya Meneer** (((24) 285732) on Jalan Raya Kaligawe, is further out of town, but it has a herbal medicine museum that helps explain jamus better than most guides could hope to.

Where to Stay

The **Metro Grand Park Hotel** (((24) 27371) has a supermarket and discotheque in addition to deluxe rooms that go for $35 a night plus 21 percent government tax and service. The **Queen Hotel** nearby on Jalan Gajah Mada N° 44-52 (((24) 27063) is not nearly as charming, but the efficiently managed hotel provides breakfast and afternoon tea as part of its $15 room charge.

Where to Eat

There are a number of Chinese restaurants scattered around the city, and many of them serve Cantonese *dim sum* for breakfast and lunch. At night there are dozens of food stalls and small cafes, called *warungs*, at the **Pasar Ya'ik** night market. The only truly distinctive restaurant in town, however, is **Toko Oen**, an enormous old fashioned tea room with a south seas ambiance. Located at Jalan Pemuda N° 52, the Toko Oen's waiters look as if they could have served the Dutch, but they move smartly enough, no matter whether the order is a milk shake or a gin tonic.

How to Get There

Garuda has daily service from Semarang to Jakarta, Surabaya and Denpasar. It also has a connecting flight to Ujung Pandang. Merpati also has numerous nonstops to Jakarta, as well as service to Bandung. Bouraq and Mandala link Semarang with Jakarta. Sempati has direct flights to Jakarta and Surabaya.

Semarang is on the rail line that links Jakarta with Cirebon and Surabaya. For the most comfortable ride to and from Jakarta take the first class *Mutiara Utara*.

There is a PELNI office in Semarang at Jalan Tantular N° 25 (℃ (24) 20488). It sells space on the *KM Kelimutu* which sails to ports in Sulawesi and Nusa Tenggara.

EAST JAVA

Most travelers to Indonesia bypass East Java in their rush to get to Bali. Those who linger for a spell will discover the fertile plains that were home to the powerful Majapahit Hindu kingdom. If the world's most populous island can be said to have a hinterland, then East Java is it. Outside of industrialized Surabaya, the region is exclusively agricultural.

SURABAYA

Surabaya, the provincial capital and Indonesia's second largest city, is an industrial town that lacks Yogya's charm and Jakarta's history. Long a destination of schooners from Macasar, Surabaya finally fell to the Mataram empire in 1625, but its history really began in 1945 when its resistance forces began Indonesia's war of independence by battling the British who had landed to secure Java for the soon-to-return Dutch.

With a population well over 3.6 million, Surabaya has prospered since independence. In addition to being the seat of the provincial government, it is home to Indonesia's navy and much of Java's heavy industry. Most tourist attractions, however, save for the excellent Surabaya zoo, are outside the city.

General Information

In Surabaya the Regional Office of Tourism, Post and Telecommunications is at 242-244

Jalan Jend. A. Yani, ℃ (31) 815312 or 812291. The Provincial Tourist Service at Jalan Darmokali N° 35 can be reached by calling (31) 654-4879.

What to See

Built in 1836, the **Rakhmat** and **Sunan Bungkul** mosques comprise the religious heart of fundamentalist East Java. A more popular attraction for tourists, however, is the **Red Bridge**, or *Jembatan Merah*, which once was the center of Dutch Surabaya. Old office buildings, warehouses and banks with their

high ceilings testify to the lengths the Dutch went to capture a cool breeze. They also serve as evidence of the quality that went into the construction of colonial buildings. Formerly the home of the Dutch governor, the **Grahadi** on Jalan Pemuda today serves as the home of the Indonesian governor of East Java. Also worth visiting is the **Majapahit Hotel**, the Dutch colonial hotel that served as Japanese Officers' Quarters during the war.

The **Surabaya Zoo** on Jalan Diponegoro near the Joyoboyo bus station is Southeast Asia's largest zoological park. Because of

Despite rich soil and intensive cultivation of rice, Java still must import food to feed its growing population.

the heat and humidity, the zoo does not have many mammals. Its space is devoted to exotic tropical birds, nocturnal animals, Komodo dragons and fish. Open from 7 am to 6 pm, the zoo costs Rp 600 to enter.

Across the road from the zoo the **MPU Tantular Museum**, open 8 am to 1 pm. Tuesday through Sunday and closed Monday, has an assortment of Mesolithic farming implements and some stone artifacts from the Majapahit period.

If you happen to be passing through Surabaya in the summer you should not miss the East Java Ballet Festival at **Candra Wilwatika**, an open-air amphitheater 42 km (26 miles) south of Surabaya on the road to Malang. Here Javanese classical dances are performed beneath the Gunung Penanggungan volcano on the first and third Saturday nights between May and October. Unlike the Prambanan Ballet Festival in Yogyakarta that presents a single version of the *Ramayana*, the Candra Wilwatika performances include indigenous East Javan stories in addition to the *Ramayana*. Buses to **Pandaan** take about an hour, and from the bus station it is fairly easy to get a Colt mini-van to Candra Wilwatika.

Where to Stay

The **Hyatt Regency Surabaya** at Jalan Basuki Rahmat N° 124-128 is Surabaya's leading hotel. Built around a swimming pool, its 511 rooms have nice views of the city. Prices start at $159, but substantial discounts are available for those who ask. ((31) 470875, fax (31) 512038.

Located in the center of the city, the **Garden Hotel** on Jalan Pemuda N° 21 has a sauna, swimming pool and a rooftop restaurant. Its 100 rooms range from $42 to $60, but this price includes an enormous breakfast buffet. ((31) 47000, telex 314238 GARDEN HOTEL.

Jalan Panglima Sudirman has two different hotels that both offer exceptional service. The **Elmi Hotel** at Jalan Panglima Sudirman N° 42-44 ((31) 471571, cable ELMIHOTEL) has a modern fitness center and disco. Its 140 rooms cost $60 for singles, $70 for dou-

ble occupancy. The 47-room **Tanjung Hotel** across the street at N° 43-45 has fully equipped rooms that are priced between $25 and $35 with breakfast included. ((31) 44031, fax (31) 512290.

For the ultimate in colonial appeal stay at the **Majapahit** at Jalan Tunjungan N° 65. Built in 1910 around a beautiful flower garden, the hotel today is a bit dowdy, but at $30 the price of its rooms is hard to beat. ((31) 43351, cable MAJATEL, telex 31363 MAJATEL.

Where to Eat

Open from 9 am to 11 pm the **Pasar Kayoon** market has the standard assortment of small, inexpensive *warungs*. **Chez Rose** (Jalan, Panglima Sudirman N° 12, ((31) 45669)

Steaming fissures, bubbling mud, jagged lava and a swirling sea of sand give Mt. Bromo an otherworldly appearance.

has an extensive menu with European, Chinese and Indonesian specialties. But most people go for the luncheon buffet, the largest in Surabaya, which is served from 11:30 am to 2:30 pm.

How to Get There

Surabaya is a major transit hub with daily flights to every corner of the country. In Surabaya, the challenge is not finding a flight, but deciding which flight offered by the four competing airlines is the cheapest.

Garuda is the dominant carrier because of its extensive fleet of jet aircraft, but Merpati, Mandala and Bouraq also have dozens of scheduled flights throughout the day. Garuda is the logical carrier if you need to fly to Biak or Sorong, but on short hops to

places like Denpasar, Ujung Pandang or the coastal cities of Kalimantan the money you save may be worth a slower flight on the Bouraq or Merpati propeller planes.

Located at Jalan Tunjungan N° 29, ((31) 470640, Garuda has 13 daily nonstops to Jakarta, four nonstops to Ujung Pandang and four to six daily flights to Denpasar depending on the day of the week. Bouraq, which has an office at Jalan Panglima Sudirman N° 70 or can be reached by calling ((31) 42383, also has a large profile in Surabaya with many flights to Kalimantan, as well as service to Jakarta and Bandung.

There are three train stations in Surabaya. Westbound trains to Jakarta via Solo and Yogyakarta leave from the Gubeng station. Jakarta-bound trains passing through

Semarang leave from the Pasar Turi railway complex. Commuter trains for Malang depart from the Kota station or Gubeng.

The cheapest way to move about East Java, or across the island for that matter, is by overnight bus. But the margin of cost savings offered by the bus is not worth the danger associated with traveling Java's narrow, traffic-clogged highways. Scarcely a month passes without some bus careening off a highway with substantial loss of life.

As befits the home port of the Indonesian navy, Surabaya is well served by all manner of ocean going vessels. Nearly two dozen cargo ships leave Surabaya each day for various parts of the archipelago and most have limited accommodation for passengers. But given the busy PELNI schedule, traveling on a cargo ship isn't really necessary. The PELNI office at Jalan Pahlawan N° 20 has ships leaving daily to various destinations. Telephone (31) 21041 or 21694 for a schedule, or go by from 9 am to 1:30 pm weekdays.

MADURA

Thirty minutes by ferry from Surabaya is the sparsely populated and often spectacular island of Madura. Largely ignored by tour groups, Madura initially seems a rather imposing place. The north coast is arid, rocky and treeless, a desolate cattle breeding area where goats browse on tufts of weedy scrub. The fertile south coast, however, more than compensates. Covered with tobacco plantations, orchards and edged with golden beaches, the south coast is home to most of the population and the location of the island's most famous attraction: *karapan sapi* bull racing.

Background

Reputed to be the fiercest people in the archipelago, the wiry, hot-tempered Madurese were incorporated into the Mataram empire in 1624 by Sultan Agung. The Madurese were not content to become vassals, however, and eventually, through intermarriage, succeeded in achieving hegemony over the eastern half of Java. But Madura was no match for the Dutch, who exiled the Madurese warrior-prince to South Africa, despite his assistance in helping the Dutch subdue the sultans of Central Java.

What to See

The main attraction here is the *Kerapan Sapi* bull races that are staged from the middle of August until the end of October. The races, which originated long ago when bored farmers began racing their plow animals across the fields, are run on an elimination basis. Small villages hold the first races in August and the winners go on to stiffer competition in larger district towns. The grand finale in Madura's capital of **Pamekasan** takes place in October when as many as 100 flower-bedecked bulls parade through town in preparation for several days of 100-meter races.

Events in Pamekasan makes Pamplona's running of the bulls seem like a walk in the park. In Pamekasan bulls are roused to fever pitch with frenzied *gamelan* music, then given a jolt of arak wine to insure fire-in-the-belly competitiveness. Shorn of ribbons and flowers, they are lashed to heavy wooden sledges atop which drivers, who also have partaken of the arak, drive the bulls toward the finish line with whips and piercing cries. Entry into the stadium outside Pamekasan costs only a few hundred rupiah, but you may wish to sign up for a tour organized by Surabaya's Orient Express, ((31) 43315, at Jalan Basuki Rachmat N° 78 since it will provide seats roped off from the general madness.

Where to Stay

Pamekasan's main hotel is the **Garuda**, ((324) 81589, a rambling center city establishment on Jalan Mesigit N° 1. Double rooms here cost $12 with attached *mandi*, a water-filled cistern from which you can take a slosh bath. A smaller, quieter alternative to the Garuda is the **Hotel Trunojoyo**, ((324) 81181, located in an alley just off Jalan Trunojoyo. Breakfast is included in the price of the rooms, which can range in price from $4.50 to $11 depending on whether they are air-conditioned.

How to Get There

Ferries leave the Surabaya port of Tanjung Perak about every 15 minutes for the brief

30-minute crossing to Kamal on the south-west tip of Madura. At Kamal Colt mini-buses wait to take passengers to villages throughout the island.

MALANG

Malang is a pleasant mountain town with broad streets, well tended parks and an abundance of colonial architecture. A care-fully planned coffee plantation market town on the banks of the Brantas River, Malang was founded a century ago. Dozens of old Dutch villas still line jalans Ijen, Kawi and Semeru and Dutch can still be heard spoken by older Indonesians.

General Information

Local businessmen have chipped in to fund a local tourism office at Jalan Tugu N° 1, but there is not much there in the way of printed information. Still, it's worth a stop to check to see if there are any local festivals coming up.

What to See

At the **Pasar Besar** several blocks south of the main square, you'll find a large clothing market and an antique section full of Dutch and Chinese items. Not too far from the Pasar at N° Jalan Ijen N° 25 you'll find the **Brawijaya Army Museum**, ((341) 2394, an artillery packed arsenal that chronicles the history of the locally based Brawijaya Divi-sion of the Indonesian Army.

East Java has its share of temples, but unlike those in Central Java you'll need some travel time to get to them. **Candi Singosari**, **Candi Jago**, **Candi Kidal** and **Candi Penataran** are all impressive com-plexes of temples dating back to 1200 AD that are difficult to get to, so tours are defi-nitely the best way to go. Apexindo Ex-press has a six-hour Triple Temple Tour that visits Singosari, Jago and Kidal be-fore returning to Surabaya. The price of $92 per person drops to $37 if four to six peo-ple go together in one van. Satriavi Tours offers a similar package that costs slightly more. Contact both companies in Jakarta at ((21) 376524 for Apexindo and ((21) 380-3944 for Satriavi. In Surabaya the Natra-bu travel group at Jalan Dinoyo N° 40 also can arrange a mini-van and guide. ((31) 68513.

Where to Stay

The venerable **Hotel Pelangi** (((341) 27456) in the middle of Malang on Jalan Merdeka Selatan catered to *tuan blanda* (Dutch over-seers) in the heyday of Dutch rule and still exudes an air of fusty colonialism. The large, air-conditioned rooms still have operating ceiling fans and wicker recliners that impe-riously survey the town square Dutch engi-neers laid out a century ago. Double rooms range from $12 to $18 depending on the view.

The **Splendid Inn** on Jalan Mohopahit N° 2-4, ((341) 23860, is a smaller hotel with similar ambiance. The inn actually is an old Dutch mansion that has been divided into bright and airy rooms each with their own bath. Tariffs can start as high as $20, but that price includes breakfast and afternoon tea. Even if you stay elsewhere stop by the Splen-did Inn's informal bar for a sundown liba-tion. If anyone interesting is in town, he'll probably be there drinking Bintang from a frosted mug.

Incredible as it may seem, there is a hostel in Malang where you can sleep for $2 a night. It is called the **Bamboo Denn** and is located at Jalan Semeru N° 35 at the corner of Jalan Arjuno. True, the eight beds are in a one-room dormitory, but the place is friendly enough, mainly because it is a lan-guage school. In return for the discount digs you'll be encouraged to spend a few hours talking English with young Indonesian stu-dents the following day.

Where to Eat

The restaurant at the **Splendid Inn** has a reasonably priced western menu. In the mood for al fresco dining? Then spend the evening at **Pasar Senggol**, a colorful assort-ment of *warungs* near Jalan Majapahit.

How to Get There

There is no airport at Malang, but there are more than a half dozen trains that make the three-hour run from Surabaya every day. The bus from Surabaya takes about the same amount of time as the train, but for $4 it is possible to charter an air-conditioned mini-bus and make the trip much more rapidly.

Bali

A MYSTICAL Island of music and dance, Bali is Indonesia's number one tourist destination. Covered by emerald rice terraces, sparkling rivers and slumbering volcanoes, the island is home to 3,000,000 Balinese who spend their lives never far from the swirl of incense, the hypnotic cadence of the *gamelan* or the brooding shadow of 2,750-m (9,500-ft) Mt. Agung. The great Majapahit Kingdoms of Central and Eastern Java brought the Hindu influence to Bali in the fifteenth century when the Muslims invaded Java. Their culture, music, art and philosophy have developed ever since in tandem with the native Buddhism.

THE BALINESE

Balinese look at their island and see perfection. Indeed, they believe Bali is an earthly paradise guarded by a pantheon of Hindu spirits, which they honor with daily offerings and elaborate temple ceremonies. Women in form-fitting sarongs walking beside the road with bowls filled with fruit, flowers and rice cakes balanced on their heads invariably are heading to the local temple. There they are greeted by the men of their village, some of whom already are playing gamelan instruments, while others are costumed as characters from the *Ramayana* or *Mahabharata*.

Temples in Bali are settings for colorful morality plays between good and evil that pit characters like the mythical animal *Barong* and the witch *Rangda*, a vampire with tusks, fangs and bulging ebony eyes. Whether it ends in frenzy or a trance, the struggle is always epic in dimension, a lesson that never grows old no matter how many times it is told.

Balinese believe in the God *Sanghyang Widi*, who has three manifestations: Brahma the Creator, Vishnu the Preserver and Shiva the deity who dissolves the material universe and returns all things to their basic elements at the end of each cycle of creation. For Balinese, life is a series of spiritual steps, the final being cremation, which frees the soul from its last ties with the material world.

Indian traders who first visited Bali centuries ago called the island *Wali*, the ancient Sanskrit word for religious festival. The intrusion of the twentieth century has not dampened the island's fervor. A day seldom passes without some village performing a *kris* dance or the *Legong Keraton*, a sensuous dance in which two lithe maidens wrapped in hand painted gold brocades move in unison to the chime of a gamelan orchestra. Though Balinese music and dance initially may seem similar to those performed on Java, the tempo here is much faster. After living on Bali for several months, actor Charlie Chaplin perceptively explained the difference: "The Javanese dance the idea, the Balinese dance the action."

BALINESE DANCES

Drawn largely from the stories contained in the great Hindu Epics, the *Mahabharata* and the *Ramayana*, Balinese dancing remains an integral part of the island's culture. Every day in dozens of villages Balinese gather to perform dances. Visitors to Bali should see as many dances and temple purification ceremonies as possible, preferably in villages north of Denpasar. All of the dances explained below are performed on a regular basis. Consult the *Bali Tourist Guide* which is

OPPOSITE: A young performer in the *Barong* Dance. ABOVE: Young dancers are "purified" with lustral water prior to a performance on Kuta Beach.

distributed free throughout the Kuta–Sanur–Nusa Dua area, or ask your hotel concierge for times and locations. If you'd prefer a guide to take you to the dance and explain what you're passing along the way, call Satriavi Tours in Denpasar at (361) 24339, 26458 or 24887.

The **Baris** originally was a temple ceremony performed by colorfully costumed guards carrying long lances. Later, the dance was transformed into an individualized warrior dance. In the dramatic *baris* the dancer freely expresses himself while the *gamelan*

in love. Alas, the Princess refuses to tie the knot with a frog. So, the Frog Prince meditates, and in time is returned to human form by Vishnu. The couple marries and lives happily

Originally a ceremonial temple dance in which a group of young girls bring offerings to the temple shrine, the **Panyembrama** today is a welcoming dance in which young girls dance with bowls full of flowers, eventually throwing the petals to the guests as a gesture of blessing.

Oleg Tambulilingan begins with a female bumble bee darting about a beautiful gar-

orchestra follows his improvisation. The formula creates a tense, yet intimate, relationship between dancer and musisians.

Kebyar Duduk is the most difficult Balinese dance because the dancer must hop about cross-legged while remaining in the seated position. Developed in the 1920's, the dancer's movements are accompanied by sudden bursts of sound and intricate variations of rhythm from the *gamelan* orchestra.

The **Genggong** story dates back to the days when Hindu princes ruled Java. It tells the story of a prince who was fond of chasing dragon flies. One day he disappears while chasing a golden dragon fly and emerges several years later as a frog. The frog then encounters the Princess of Daha and they fall

den. Later a male bee appear and a flirtation commences. The two dancers swerve and whirl about each other, finally ending the dance by departing for the hive.

The **Kecak** (Monkey) tells a portion of the *Ramayana* story in which Rama, the prince of Ayodhya, is exiled to the forest with his wife Sita and brother Laksamana. The lecherous demon king Rahwana kidnaps Sita when Rama's back is turned. Hanoman, the King of Monkeys and a friend of Rama, locates Sita, but before Rama can rescue his wife he is bound by writhing snakes loosed by Rawana's son, Meganada. In desperation, Rama calls the Garuda bird who pecks him free. The dance ends when the large male chorus enters into a frenzied trance during which they stage a battle between Hanoman's monkey army and the demon legions of Rawana.

The **Barong** and **Kris** Dance, the most colorful in Bali, represents the struggle of good versus evil. Good is symbolized by a mythological animal called the Barong. Evil is embodied in the witch Rangda and her servants. An evil spirit unleashed by Rangda enters Dewi Kunti, who then promises to sacrifice her son, Sadewa to the greater glory of Rangda. The God Shiva saves Sadewa from death, but he must fight a series of evil

creatures. Sadewa wins all his battles until he encounters Rangda. He then changes himself into a Barong for the final struggle, which ends in a draw.

HISTORICAL BACKGROUND

Though the history of the island is intertwined with that of Java, Bali always has managed to retain its share of independence. Local leaders, for example, traditionally have taken the title *Dewa Agung*, meaning "Great Deity." The first Europeans to arrive in pursuit of plunder instead fell in love with the island, jumped ship and took Balinese wives. In 1904 the Dutch finally arrived in strength,

determined to incorporate the island into the Dutch East Indies. Unable to resist, the Rajah of Denpasar assembled his court before the Dutch authorities in a grassy open area in front of what is today the Bali Museum and ordered his high priest to plunge a jeweled *kris* into his heart. Then, one by one, the Rajah's family and courtiers calmly committed suicide. Balinese remember the mass suicide as the *puputan,* or "the end."

Today, "old Asia Hands" often decry the commercialism of Bali, insisting that Southeast Asia's most exotic culture has been com-

promised by beer, bars and bikinis. In reality, Balinese culture and arts have never been stronger. Money brought in by tourists has helped preserve many crafts that might otherwise have died. While the golden triangle of Kuta, Sanur and Nusa Dua has an alien appearance, the atmosphere remains Balinese.

From the terraced rice fields surrounding the village of Sayan to the multi-leveled "Mother Temple" at Besakih, Bali is a place that begs to be photographed. Bring plenty of film and a telephoto lens, if possible, in order to capture the facial expressions of dancers.

OPPOSITE: Ritual dances begin with the arrival of a gamelan orchestra. ABOVE: Though hospitable to foreigners, the Balinese were fierce foes of colonialism.

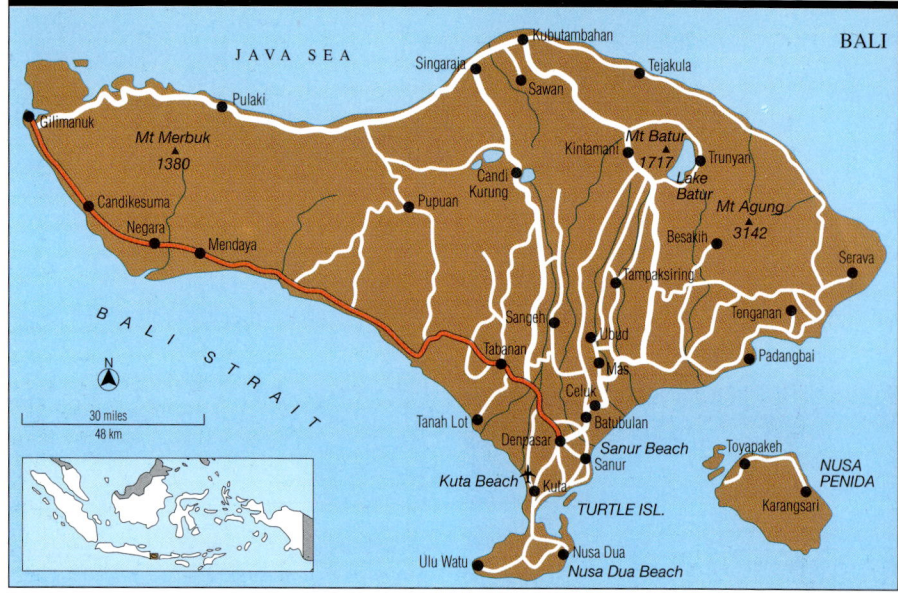

Bali has a wealth of beautiful beach hotels, but no sane person goes there simply to get a tan. Bali is an experience; an encounter with Asia's most exotic and vibrant culture. To really see Bali is to watch the sun setting over the temple at Tanah Lot. Drive to Kintamani and drink hot lemonade while the cold mist swirls above Lake Batur. Contemplate the serenity of the temples at Besakih and Penelokan. Finally, when you see a village that embodies your idea of tropical paradise, stop the car and go for a visit. Balinese villagers are more than happy to show off their little corner of paradise.

DENPASAR

Not even the Balinese have anything nice to say about Denpasar. Before you're even out of the airport the taxi drivers will explain that Singaraja was supposed to be the island's capital. "Denpasar was just a market town," they scowl, searching for an appropriate explanation, "that just grew." Listen to them. Don't buck the conventional wisdom and try to discover gourmet restaurants or exotic lodging in Denpasar. Whip on through town just like every one else toward more colorful locales up north. It is worthwhile, however, to pause briefly and see a couple of sights.

One is the **Bali Museum** across from Puputan Badung Park. The museum consists of several buildings and pavilions that serve as good examples of palace and temple architecture. The large structure with the verandah in the second courtyard is an example of the type of royal building in which rajahs would hold audiences. Open from 9 am to 5 pm except Sunday, the museum costs Rp 450 to enter and contains the island's best collections of woodcarving, textiles and weaponry.

Follow the course of the Badung River several blocks and you'll arrive at **Pasar Badung**, the morning market. Across a narrow bridge is the **Kumba Sari** shopping center. The morning market has three floors that contain, going from top to bottom, clothing, spices and fruit. Floors one and two are great for picture taking. Be sure to save film for **Pura Melanting**, a small temple in front of the Pasar. This is one of the most active temples in Bali, a place swirling with incense, full of women in sarongs offering fruit and flowers to the Gods. If the fervor here seems unusually high it's because the women are Pasar Badung merchants praying for a profitable day.

Along Gajah Mada, Denpasar's main street, there are several curio stores. The best antique store in Denpasar, **Arts of Asia Gallery**, is a few blocks away at Jalan Thamrin

27-37 Block C5, ((361) 23350. All the items on sale here have been personally collected by Verra Darwiko, the store's English-speaking owner, who once each year takes a boat and sails through the Nusa Tenggara and Maluku island chains looking for treasures. Much of the pottery and wood carving here is museum quality.

GENERAL INFORMATION

There are two tourism offices in Denpasar. The regional Office of Tourism, Post and

Telecommunications office is in the Komplex Niti Mandala on Jalan Raya Puputan Renon. ((361) 25649. The Provincial Tourism Agency is on Jalan S. Parman. ((361) 22387.

KUTA BEACH

Once Bali's poorest district, Kuta now is the most westernized (perhaps more accurately, Australianized) part of the Island. A haphazard assortment of bars, beach hotels, curio shops and simple inns called *losmen*, Kuta has given itself over entirely to tourism. Despite the touts and traffic, it still has the best beach in Bali, accommodation that is both excellent and affordable and some of the

best nightlife entertainment in Indonesia. Travelers searching for Bali's magic should remember that Kuta is not a self-contained destination but a base of operations from which you venture forth each day in search of the real Bali.

WHERE TO STAY

Bali experienced a boom in hotel construction in 1992 with an addition of 8,000 new hotel rooms. It's doubtful prices will decline, however, since supply is barely keeping up

with demand. Due to rapid inflation, Bali's better hotels list their room rates in United States dollars. All hotel rates are subject to an additional 15.5 percent service charge and government tax. With the exception of small *losmen* and guest houses, Bali hotels accept most credit cards.

Built right at the ocean's edge, **Bali Intan Cottages** has two swimming pools, a landscaped children's playground and a pool bar that serves popsicles. Its spacious standard rooms, which cost $70 based on double occupancy, look out over thatched bungalows to the sea. Cottages closer to the ocean

Young travelers have made Kuta their favorite beach in Bali.

rent for $75, with an extra $5 added for two people. But they have open air bathrooms that look out on a private fish pond and rock garden. Jalan Melasti N° 1, Legian Beach; ((361) 51770, fax (361) 51891.

The **Kuta Palace Hotel** is located on Jalan Pura Bagus Teruna at Legian beach about three kilometers (two miles) away from the *bemo* corner. To compensate for the relative isolation, this 280 room hotel provides guests with a broad, sandy beach, two pools surrounded by coconut palms and queen size beds in every room. Single rooms cost from $75 to $85. Double rooms with a view are $95. ((361) 51433, fax (361) 52074.

Owned by Indonesia's state oil company, **Pertamina Cottages** was Kuta's only luxury hotel when it opened back in 1975. It remains a favorite of visiting state dignitaries, which can be a mixed blessing depending on your need for security. Executive cottages next to the beach go for $140. Deluxe cottages further back from the ocean yet still in a garden setting cost $115. IDD telephones and CNN via satellite in every room. ((361) 51161, fax (361) 52030.

Ten kilometers (six miles) outside the clutter of Kuta, the **Puri Ratih**, a hideaway with eight Balinese style bungalows, sits in splendid isolation. Surrounded by rice fields, this hotel rents tropical beach homes for people who value privacy. On the ground floor of each bungalow two air-conditioned bedrooms, a bathroom with sunken tub and a kitchen are built around a living room open to the sea. A circular wooden staircase leads to a loft that contains a bamboo bed and a desk. Robert Louis Stevenson would have loved this place. Nurses for the handicapped and private cooks are provided free of charge by the hotel. Ask in advance and the manager will have a computer, fax machine and IDD telephone waiting for you in the loft. During Christmas and summer the bungalows rent for $290 a night. The low season rate is $250. Fifteen percent off for people staying 10 days or longer. P.O. Box 1114, Tuban Kuta; ((361) 51546, fax (361) 51549.

Across the street from the beach and a 20 minute walk from the *bemo* corner, the **Rama Palace Hotel** on Jalan Pantai Kuta has 150 spotlessly clean rooms supplied with solar heated water. The Rama's massive dining hall sits atop two large fish ponds stocked with 2,500 catfish. Children (adults, too, for that matter) are welcome to borrow fishing tackle and catch their own fish. Cooked to order and served with salad and fries, the $7.50 fish dinner is one of Bali's best bargains. Superior rooms are priced at $100 with double occupancy costing $5 extra. Surcharge of $20 per night during the Christmas-New Year's fortnight. ((361) 52063, fax (361) 53078.

The entrance to the **Sahid Bali Seaside** on Jalan Pantai Kuta is a bridge that traverses a series of terraced lily ponds. Its lobby is a replica of a sultan's *kraton*. These and other architectural touches lend human dimension to this sprawling 400-room hotel located across the coast road from Kuta beach. A deluxe room for two costs $80. Standard rooms are $75. There is a $15 surcharge during the July-August "high season" that increases to $20 over the Christmas holidays. ((361) 53855, fax (361) 52019.

Set back 100 yards from one of Kuta's best surfing beaches, **Wina Cottage** on Jalan Pantai Kuta has a variety of complimentary services that include an hourly shuttle to the *bemo* corner, a fresh basket of fruit every afternoon and pots of hot tea on request. Air-conditioned rooms with an ocean view cost $55 for one person; $60 for two. Fan cooled rooms range from $26 to $30. No charge for children 12 and under. An extra bed costs $8. ((361) 51867, 53061, fax (361) 51569.

Kuta Beach has dozens of small bungalows within a few steps of the restaurants and shops along Legian Road. Most cater on a cash only basis to young Australian singles on a limited budget looking for basic accommodation. Those listed below, however, aspire to higher standards, and for the person willing to walk a few minutes to the beach offer both exceptional value and location.

Agung Cottages on Jalan Legian (((361) 51147) is a five minute walk from the ocean. Agung has 45 rooms with thatched roofs and Balinese calendars decorating the walls. A fan cooled bungalow with large sunken bath tub costs $18 for one person, $20 for double occupancy. A similar room with air-conditioning cost one person $24, $30 for two. Breakfast included.

A double with air-conditioning costs $30 at the **Matahari Bungalows** on Jalan Legian.

Two people sleeping under a fan pay $18. Breakfast included. ℂ (361) 51616, fax (361) 51761.

From the outside, **Mutiara Cottage** on Poppies Lane looks like a Balinese temple. Its 50 rooms are arrayed about a courtyard ablaze with tropical flowers. Fan cooled rooms cost $15 for one, $18 for two. ℂ (361) 52091.

The 20 thatched bungalows belonging to **Poppies Cottages** on Poppies Lane I are the best value-for-money-lodging in Kuta. Tucked away in a jungle setting, each cottage has a private verandah, a soaring nipa ceiling and access to an inviting swimming pool. $55 for single occupancy; $60 for a double. Reservations required months in advance. ℂ (361) 51059, fax (361) 52364. **Note**: On Poppies Lane II there are four less expensive cottages also operated by Poppies that should be avoided as they fail to meet the standards of the main hotel.

WHERE TO EAT

There are dozens of good, affordable seafood restaurants in Kuta. Most of them have European and Chinese items on the menu as well. There are only two caveats to dining in Bali. The first is ignore the wine. Indonesia imports cheap, generic "table wine," then taxes it exorbitantly. There is no reason why you should pay French chateau prices for Australian plonk. Secondly, beware the beef. I know it's difficult to resist a $6.50, but remember, Bali is a Hindu island. There are no cattle ranches or feed lots on Bali. The beef set before you today recently was a buffalo — a very old buffalo — used to plow rice paddies. If you must have beef, make sure it's imported. The volume of chilled beef shipped from Australia is so enormous that the price usually is quite reasonable. Most hotel restaurants only serve imported beef. Outside the major hotels, it's best to ask. Kuta restaurants open and close with alarming frequency. Be adventurous and go exploring, or follow the crowds and find something new. If you can't decide, then consider the following restaurants that over a period of years have consistently offered excellent food.

One final note: though many restaurants claim to take credit cards, it's always best to carry cash.

One kilometer (just over half-a-mile) south of the *bemo* corner on Jalan Kartika Plaza is a small bar and restaurant called **Dewi Sri** ℂ (361) 51490. Its owner, Wayan Arthur Tanala, is the Rama Palace hotel food and beverage manager. Open from 8 am to midnight, it serves a variety of fresh fish. For about $2 you can try the frog legs in butter sauce or have a crab meat omelet. There is an imaginative drink menu. Try the Boom Atom (a blend of fruit juices with gin and triple sec) or the Claude Rain (bourbon, rum and Peter Herring). Free transport from any hotel in Kuta.

Fifteen years ago, Jalan Kuta Theater, a narrow lane next to the *bemo* corner was the Haight Ashbury of Bali. Restaurants openly spiced their "Blue Meanie Soup" and "Sgt. Pepper Omelets" with mind-scrambling "magic" mushrooms. Today, the hippies are gone, but the mushrooms remain. **Jimmy's**, whose hours of operation are at the whim of the owner, specializes in soup costing approximately $5, $6 or $7 a bowl depending on the number of mushrooms. A few steps away, **The Garden** (8 am to 10 pm) puts mushrooms in omelets and pineapple frappes for approximately $6.50. Cash only both places.

Two kilometers (one-and-a-half miles) north of the *bemo* corner on Jalan Legian, **Glory** ℂ (361) 51091 is the place to go for Indonesian and Balinese food. Open daily from 8 am to midnight, dinner for two comes to $14. Every Saturday at 7 pm there is a Balinese buffet with a suckling pig for about $6.50 a person.

Poppies (Poppies Lane I, ℂ (361) 51059) is arguably the best restaurant in Kuta. An outdoor garden restaurant with well prepared Indonesian dishes and seafood, Poppies has a great tuna fish steak for $6.00 and tall glasses of Long Island iced tea that can only be described as "soothing." Don't worry about ordering the inexpensive sashimi; the modern kitchen is exceptionally clean. If curry is your main course, be sure to order a fresh fruit *lassi* to drink. For desert try the Black Rice Pudding, a Balinese favorite sweetened with palm sugar and coconut milk. Open daily 8 am to 11 pm.

The **SC Restaurant** ℂ (361) 53769 on Jalan Legian is one of the best places in Kuta for grilled seafood. The day's catch is displayed on a bed of shaved ice. Pick out what you

want, order a beer and in minutes you'll be enjoying tasty shrimp, fish or lobster. Dinner for two: $15. All credit cards.

WHERE TO RELAX

Every night is party time in Kuta. Actually, the beat goes on around the clock, but 9 pm is when the live entertainment begins in most of the bars. There is no one place to be since everything happens at once, but the following bars are perennial favorites. Remember, bars in Kuta open around 1 pm, reach their frenzied peak about 11 pm and operate on a cash only basis.

The **Cock 'N Bull** bar in the Kuta Ria shopping center on Jalan Legian is a fair dinkum place for sheilas, but no place for families. Here it pays to be an Aussie.

If there is a *primus inter pares* among night spots in Kuta it is probably **Casablanca** ((361) 51333 on Jalan Buni Sari south of the *bemo* corner. This two-story bar has extremely cold beer, an upstairs dance floor and great vocalists who usually have patrons dancing on the tables by midnight.

Though Casablanca does have a dance floor, **Peanuts** is the only bona fide disco in Kuta. Located in the back of the Komplex Kuta Ria, Peanuts opens at 9 pm (it closes at 3 am) but doesn't really click until midnight. A $5 cover includes two beers or soft drinks.

A bit farther down Jalan Buni Sari on the other side of the street is **The Pub** ((361) 51905, a smaller, more subdued bar with guitar players fond of mellow Seventies rock. The Pub's chicken satay and black bean soup go well with cold cans of Foster's beer.

The **SC Bar** ((361) 51854 is across the street from the Kuta Ria complex on Jalan Legian. A sprawling outdoor beer garden, this place is Libido Central for cruising Aussies. There is a band and a large video screens, but the main attraction is the enormous crowd itself.

WHERE TO SHOP

Balinese artisans produce wood carvings in the village of Mas, stone carvings in Batubu-

lan and paintings in Ubud. All are reasonable priced and of the highest quality. Kuta, which produces nothing of its own, has a wide variety of Indonesian goods from Bali and elsewhere in the archipelago, but not always at the best price. So why shop in Kuta? Because the merchandise that is for sale here is styled to western tastes and adjusted to foreign sizes.

The best price for batik, for example, can be found in Central Java. But in Kuta the batik is faded, made into contemporary fashions or used to accent denim wear. One

of the many places worth investigating is **Mr. Richard's Sunshine Moonshine** store at Jalan Legian Tengah N° 439. All of the batik here comes from Solo via Surabaya and creatively used as patches on pants and jackets.

Kuta has several antique shops only two of which appear to have much worth buying. Open from 10 am to 6 pm, **Polos** on Jalan Legian ((361) 51316 has the best carvings and antiques in Kuta. It is actually four galleries each linked to the other by small doors, so don't leave after seeing only the items from Irian Jaya in front.

Yanwar north of the Peanuts Disco on Jalan Legian has excellent baskets, *ikat* (tiedied) textiles and primitive carvings from northern Sumatra.

PREVIOUS PAGES: A fishing *prahu* on the beach at Sanur. ABOVE, RIGHT: Hotels like the Tanjung Sari cultivate Bali's mystical allure.

Though Indonesia has copyright laws that protect computer software, rock music tapes seem to have slipped through the net. So stock up on the latest releases for only $6. Two stores with excellent selection and good quality sound open from 9 am until past midnight are **Dynasty** on Jalan Bakung Sari ((361) 53256 and **Mahogany** on Jalan Legian just north of the *bemo* corner.

SANUR BEACH

Developed as an alternative to Kuta, Sanur offers a more orderly environment and a beach conducive to swimming because of a protective offshore reef. Sanur, along with Ubud, was one of the first Balinese villages to be "discovered" by European artists like Belgian Le Mayeur. Mayeur's house next to the Bali Beach hotel has been turned into a museum and is worth a brief visit, if only to capture the feeling of what it must have been like to live in Sanur a half century ago. You can't watch the sunset in Sanur, but on clear days you can see Lombok's Rinjani volcano soaring above the clouds. During the day, the exotic triangular sails of fishing boats the Balinese call *jukungs* skim across the horizon. At low tide it's possible to walk across the sand and coral to the reef and watch crabs skittering in the shallows. The late afternoon belongs to kites, many of them with spans up to one-an-a-half meters (five feet). Kite flying is the favorite sport for young boys in Sanur and on the nearby "Turtle Island" of Serangan, and many of the shops along the main street sell animal-shaped kites painted in pastel colors.

WHERE TO STAY

Following the construction of the ten-story **Bali Beach Hotel** (P.O. Box 275, Denpasar 80001; ((361) 88511, fax (361) 87917) a law was passed that no building in the future could be higher than the surrounding coconut trees. Bali's only western style hotel has three swimming pools, a nine hole golf course plus an adjacent bowling alley. Most international airlines serving Bali have ticket offices in the shopping arcade. Single rooms are priced from $105 to $120. Double occupancy costs $12 more.

Surrounded by 15 hectares (36 acres) of frangipani, bougainvillea and hibiscus, the **Bali Hyatt's** 387 rooms have a tropical feel with grass mats on the floors and balconies large enough for breakfast. A double with a garden view costs $155. Add $10 for a similar room facing the ocean. There is a $20 high season supplement. Located on Jalan Danau Tamblingan, the Hyatt can be reached on ((361) 88271 or by sending a fax to (361) 87693. There is a second Hyatt resort at Nusa Dua

and a shuttle bus operates between the two hotels. Guests can use the facilities at either Hotel. See under NUSA DUA BEACH, page 93 for details.

The pool is no more than a puddle at the **Santrian Beach Bungalows** ((361) 88009) but with 50 thatched bungalows only a few steps from one of the best beaches in Bali none of the guests are complaining. Linked by meandering paths leading through a jungle garden, the bungalows don't have television, but fresh fruit and flowers arrive every day. You don't need a shirt or shoes to be served at the Nirwana Reef restaurant.

No new hotel in Bali can be built higher than the surrounding palm trees.

Set right on the sand, the Nirwana obtains its catch of the day from local fishermen who tie up on the beach. For $4.50 a hour you can charter one of the boats and go snorkeling out on the reef. $75 for a single room, $80 for double occupancy.

The three main wings of the 430-room **Hotel Sanur Beach** (((361) 71793, fax (361) 87566) are built around courtyards dominated by statues of Balinese gods. Recreational facilities include two swimming pools, but most guests prefer the beach where the water is clear and calm because of an off-

shore reef. The Sanur Beach is also home to the romantically informal Warung Seahorse restaurant, whose grilled prawn lunch is one of Sanur's best bargains. Comfortable single rooms with polished parquet floors range from $105 to $135 depending on the location. Add $10 for double occupancy.

In Bali the swastika is the ancient Hindu symbol for safety and peace. And there is no shortage of either at the **Swastika Bungalows** on Jalan Danau Tamblingan, Batujimbar, Sanur. ((361) 88693, telex 35457 SWTIKA. A cluster of two-story cottages built to resemble the cosmic dwellings of the five gods who guard the "corners" of the winds, the Swastika is set back 400 yards from the beach, which means the rate charged for its 60 rooms is well below the Sanur average. Fan cooled rooms are only $35 a night, while those with air-conditioning rent for $45. A complimentary breakfast served from 8 am comes with the room. Air-conditioned rooms 43, 46, 47, 52, 53, 56 and 57 overlook the pool and have balconies large enough for lounging. Fan rooms on the

ground floor have no balconies, but six feature secluded, grotto-like bathrooms conducive to showering under the stars.

WHERE TO EAT

Most of this area's better eating spots are located in the beach hotels. There are a few restaurants, however, on Sanur's main street, Jalan Danau Tamblingan, that serve freshly grilled seafood and tasty Indonesian dishes at prices well below those charged by the hotels. Most offer free transportation to and from hotels in the Sanur area.

Grilled lobster and Balinese dancing are the main items on the menu at the **Legong Restaurant**, ((361) 88066. Located midway between the Hyatt and Sanur Beach hotels, the Legong looks like a Balinese temple, especially on those four nights a week when the Mask and Legong dances are performed at 8 pm. Begin your meal with a steaming bowl of crab and asparagus soup ($2) and end with a plate of chilled pineapple slices. Dinner for two comes to around $19. Reservation advisable at night. Lunch 11 am to 2 pm; dinner 5 pm to 10 pm.

Just outside the entrance to the Bali Hyatt is **Madelo's**, ((361) 88773, an Indo-Chinese cafe that advertises itself as "the house of good food & cold Aussie beer." Both claims are true. Dinner for two: $9.

The **Penjor** restaurant at Sanur's Batu Jimbar ((361) 88226, serves up a traditional Balinese dance every night along with dozens of Indonesian dishes. There are six set menus (Indonesian, Japanese, Korean, etc.) at lunch, the best of which is the seafood. A la carte dinner for two runs to $20. Open 10 am to 11 pm.

he menu at the **Swastika Garden Restaurant** ((361) 88573 next to the Swastika Bungalow is pure Indonesian. A seafood dinner for two costs about $18. Brochures touting the Swastika Garden available at the bungalow office next door are worth a 20 percent discount when presented at the restaurant.

WHERE TO SHOP

Shops in Sanur offer mostly curios, ready-to-wear batik, paper kites and children's toys.

Though you probably won't find too much else to buy, an early morning stroll along the main shopping street is a nice way to begin the day. One place worthy of more detailed investigation is **Sekar Tanjung**, Jalan Pantai Br. Pekandelan, ((361) 88027, an antique junkyard near the Bali Beach intersection. No high pressure selling here. Ornately carved doors, pediments and headboards are simply jumbled together awaiting discovery. Open daily 7 am to 4 pm.

NUSA DUA BEACH

This unabashedly upscale, meticulously planned resort area 10 km (six miles) southeast of the airport is the Brasilia of Bali. Nusa Dua has everything the rest of Indonesia lacks: immaculate sidewalks, tree-lined boulevards, street signs and landscaped traffic circles. Unattached singles, of course, regard Nusa Dua as antiseptic, but Bali's newest tourist area appeals to families and more established travelers. Like Sanur Beach to the north, Nusa Dua benefits from an offshore reef that makes beaches perfect for swimming. The area has no restaurant row or nightclubs outside the hotels, but there is a small shopping center with a modern supermarket that is served by a free shuttle bus that stops at the major hotels. Buy soft drinks here and avoid the hotels' extortionate minibar prices.

WHERE TO STAY

The ceiling of the lobby at the **Melia Bali Sol** is covered by a three-tiered mural depicting the transmigration of souls from the animal kingdom to Nirvana, where frolicking Gods dressed like Balinese are depicted at play. The fun continues outside where honking geese patrol the perimeter of a lagoon that extends down to the pool. The hotel's 500 rooms, all of which have spacious balconies, are divided into four blocks. Unless you like to hike, ask for a room in Block Four right by the pool and the beach. Because it's owned by a Madrid hotel chain, the Bali Sol's management staff speaks Spanish. Standard rooms cost $120 while junior suites go for $180. ((361) 71510, fax (361) 71360, 71362.

Nusa Dua Beach Hotel. Question: What do King Hussein, Lord Litchfield, Senator Robert Dole and President François Mitterand have in common? Answer: They all stayed at the Nusa Dua Beach Hotel.

And why not? The rooms are elegantly furnished with teak molding, parquet floors and French doors that open into spacious balconies. A curtain of coconut palms shades the fringe of a spotless beach. On Mondays the Ramayana ballet is performed outside in an old Balinese temple. The Legong is performed on Fridays. A deluxe single room

costs $110, or $130 for two people. A supplemental fee of $13 is added to the normal rate during peak vacation periods. ((361) 71210, 71220, fax (361) 71229.

Eighty percent of the 384 rooms in the U-shaped **Putri Bali** have ocean views. All the rooms have hardwood floors, IDD phones and twin double beds. Five nights each week there is Balinese dancing out by the beach. There are two happy hours every night at the Paseban Bar where two drinks are served for the price of one. Single rooms range from $90 to $100 with double occupancy costing $10 more. One bedroom suites cost $220. Because of the hotel's architectural design, there are six suites, one at the end of each wing, that come with extra large balconies at no extra cost. Ask if one is available when you check in. ((361) 71020, fax (361) 71139.

The **Grand Bali Hyatt**, (((361) 71102) opened in 1991 with 750 rooms in four low-rise buildings set in 16 hectares (40 acres) of

On Bali handicrafts OPPOSITE are more expensive than elsewhere. ABOVE: Many travelers spend their afternoons on native *prahus*.

gardens and sand banks. Recreational facilities cater for every type of sea sport, also tennis, badminton and beach volleyball. The Grand Hyatt is slightly more expensive than the Bali Hyatt at Sanur, but its facilities are available to guests of either hotel via a 20 minute shuttle bus. A standard single room is $130; double rooms are $20 extra, Children under 18 stay free in the same room as parents; a second room is available at half rate. Suites cost $290. There is a $20 high season supplement through August and from December 20 to January 6.

Another similarly recent addition to the choice is the **Sheraton Lagoon Nusa Dua Beach Resort** (℃ (361) 71328), which has a truly magnificent serpentine lagoon with children's pool and play area. Standard rooms (double or single occupancy) are $165, rooms with lagoon access start at $205 and suites commense at $375. Children under 17 free in the same room as parents.

UBUD

Twenty-nine kilometers (18 miles) north of Sanur Beach, Ubud (population 5,600) looks and feels much like Bali used to 20 years ago. Electricity didn't arrive until 1975, and even today it is viewed as a mixed blessing by those who prefer the more subtle glow of oil lamps. There are only two main streets, neither of which requires traffic signals. In the morning, men squat along the perimeter of the market, gently stroking their fighting cocks while women in *sarong kebayas* haggle for produce. As the day progresses, the pace slows rapidly as people return to nearby villages and paddy fields.

Nearly all of Ubud's hotels have been built within the past seven years, but none are intrusive. It is still possible to stroll from the monkey forest just south of town to nearby rice fields and waterfalls without seeing a single alien structure. **Peliatan** is a village famous for its graceful dancers, **Nyuh-kuning** is famous for its woodcarvers. Both are easily reached on foot, even for families with children. The walk from the Amandari

Ubud's serenity makes the highland town an attractive alternative to Kuta Beach.

Hotel to the Hotel Tjampuhan is one of the most pleasant on Bali, passing as it does through **Penestanan**, a village of young artists whose unaffected surroundings belie their passion for depicting the beauty around them.

For decades Ubud has cast a magic spell over artists from all parts of the world. European painters Walter Spies and Rudolf Bonnet arrived here in the early 1930's, built Balinese homes and founded the *Pitha Maha*, a society dedicated to encouraging young Balinese artists to experiment with perspec-

tive and different textures. Young painters from Ubud accepted the challenge, as did woodcarvers from Mas. Today, the early work of European masters like Spies, Bonnet, Arie Smit, Theo Meier and Han Snel proudly hangs in local galleries beside that of their now famous students.

For persons who have walked endlessly around Kuta and spend several days on the beach in Sanur, Ubud may be the place to finally rent a car and drive along the slopes of Bali's great volcanoes. Certainly rental cars are cheaper here, and the traffic is much less.

ABOVE: The misty Ayung River gorge is a backdrop at Ubud's luxurious Amandari Hotel. OPPOSITE: Tourists size up the Elephant Cave or Goa Gajah, near Ubud.

WHERE TO STAY

Designed to resemble a Balinese village, the 30 pavilion suites of **Amandari** which overlook the terraced rice fields of the Ayung River gorge offer the most luxurious accommodation in Bali. Each of the two-story suites has a private outdoor garden for sunning, an upstairs bedroom with a king-size canopy bed and a private garden just off the dressing area with a sunken marble bath. Moments after being escorted to the suite by your personal assistant manager, a chilled bottle of Möet & Chandon arrives. Sip it while listening to the distant tinkle of the *gamelan* orchestra which performs nightly by the pool from 8 pm to 11 pm. The hotel employs its own trekker who will escort you free of charge on country walks to local caves, temples and waterfalls. There are several secluded grottos along the river where the hotel can arrange a romantic picnic. Indeed, one is never far away from the soothing sound of running water since irrigation water for the surrounding rice paddies has been ingeniously channeled to flow around the suites. There is an excellent library with books and tapes that can be enjoyed in your room. Deluxe suites cost $325. Identical suites with a private pool cost an additional $150. Ask for villa N° 15, a regular suite with a million dollar view. Complimentary transfers to airport. P.O. Box 33, Ubud 80571; ((361) 95333, fax (361) 95335.

Ananda Cottages' 35 non air-conditioned bungalows are planted in the middle of rice paddies. It is literally quite possible to see rice being planted within 10 yards of your balcony terrace. A wooden bridge across an irrigation canal leads to a swimming pool. Upstairs rooms cost $45; those at ground level are $35. All rooms have polished camphor wood floors and king-size beds. P.O. Box 205, Ubud; ((361) 95375, telex 35428 UBUD.

Five minutes from the center of Ubud, **Cahaya Dewata** offers spectacular 180-degree views of the Ayung River. Suite rooms 1, 2, 3 and 6, the best in the house, each have two balconies and secluded, open air showers shaded by coconut palms. The Ayung Restaurant, which seems to hang suspended in mid air, has luncheon buffets, and with a

day's notice will prepare smoked duck for two ($25) or a suckling pig feast for 15. Suite rooms are $70. Double occupancy in a standard room costs $55. ((361) 95039, fax (361) 95115.

Built and managed by Australians, the **Kupu Kupu Barong**, Kedewatan, near Ubud, is designed for lovers. Eleven private bungalows cling to the side of the Ayung River gorge. The rooms are reached on a funicular tram that drops 55 m (180 ft) past bamboo and frangipani. You can put on a sarong and go swim in the river, or take a dip in the pool, which is fed by a natural mineral spring. Two-bedroom bungalows with marble floors, wicker furniture and queen size beds cost $305. Luxury bungalows with a private swimming pool are $365. American breakfast included. ((361) 95478, fax (361) 95079.

Siti Bungalows, Jalan Kajeng N° 3; ((361) 28690. Across the street from the old *kraton* in the middle of Ubud are six non air-conditioned bungalows operated by Dutch painter Han Snel and his Balinese wife. The rooms come with either double or twin beds and range in price from $40 to $45. Breakfast included. Hotel restaurant and bar closed on Sundays.

Located in a tropical ravine right in the middle of Ubud, the **Hotel Tjampuhan** — Bali's first hotel — originally was an artist colony. One of the hotel's 40 rooms is the original house of German artist Walter Spies. There is a tennis court and swimming pool, plus several trails that lead through the gardens and along the river. All of the rooms have a verandah or balcony overlooking the river and a personal room boy who can be summoned by a bamboo bell. None, however, have air-conditioning. Single rooms range from $50 to $72 depending on the view. Add $15 for double occupancy. Breakfast included. ((361) 95368, 95369, fax (361) 95137.

Centered in the heart of Ubud's artist colony, the **Ubud Inn** on Monkey Forest Road may be too rustic for most people. The rooms have nipa covered walls, bamboo furniture and a small light for reading. Singles are $20. Doubles are $27. Breakfast included.

The **Ulun Ubud** in Sanggingan (((361) 26414, cable SUNDT, telex 35190 SUNDT) has 16 rooms overlooking the Campuhan River valley. The rooms have double beds, old Dutch

lamps and large balconies where complimentary breakfast can be served. The hotel also has a restaurant and pool, but no air-conditioning. Standard rooms are between $55 and $65, with suites costing $85.

WHERE TO EAT

Coconuts Cafe at Jalan Suweta N° 7 is a local favorite specializing in pasta and pizza. At slightly less than $4.50 the small pizza makes a meal for one. The Crepe Balinese with banana, coconut and palm sugar is a tasty dessert for $1.50. Open 11 am to midnight, except Monday when closed.

Griya on the main road of Ubud is the place to go for barbecue. A grilled tuna or chicken dinner costs $3.50. Fresh strawberry *lassis* are $1.25. Open 9 am to 10 pm.

A short walk down the main street past the Ubud Museum is **Cafe Lotus**, an outdoor restaurant built next to a large lotus pond and temple. Open daily from 11 am to 11 pm, the Lotus serves a variety of salads, eggs Byzantine (with yogurt and cheese instead of Hollandaise sauce) and pasta with smoked duck for $4.50. Dinner for two is $14.

Murni's Warung on the banks of the Campuhan River serves large two-egg breakfasts for $4.50, brown bread hamburgers for $2.50 and tuna fish steaks with rice, potatoes and salad for $4.80. This is a good place to stop for a milkshake and a slice of cashew or banana cream cheese pie. Open daily from 10 am to 10 pm.

Cafe Wayan on Monkey Forest Road has been a favorite of foreigners for years. Wayan the cook, who began her career stirring up *jamus* for the locals, and her husband Ketut Krinting, a painter when he's not serving as maitre d', make everything from scratch. The smoked duck dinner must be ordered a day in advance, but it's worth the wait. Twelve herbs and spices are mixed with oil and lemon juice until a paste is formed. This is spread over the duck which is wrapped in palm and banana leaves and put in a large clay bowl to cook for 12 hours in a fire made of rice and coconut husks. The duck and its juices are served with rice, *sambel* and *lawar*, a Balinese dish consisting of finely chopped green beans and grated coconut. Open every day from 8 am to midnight.

WHERE TO SHOP

Ubud has a wide variety of shops and galleries, most of them located on the main street. It's possible to find art just about everywhere you might walk outside Ubud, but the best place to begin is the central market (go early in the morning) which is a good place for photography. On both sides of the market are dozens of shops selling carvings and paintings on consignment from artists in the surrounding villages.

First stop of any one seriously interested in buying Balinese art intelligently is **Agung Rai**, a fine-art gallery open daily from 7 am to 7 pm. Fifty artists exhibit their work in Agung Rai's six large galleries. But the best aspect of the gallery is the willingness of its personnel to give tours that explain the evolution of Balinese painting. Painted with modest vegetable dyes, traditional paintings are unidimensional. Younger artists of the modern school use tempura and acrylics, and deal with bolder themes. All credit cards.

A smaller gallery closer to the Campuhan River, **Neka** ((361) 26941 is also worth visiting. Open from 8 am to 5 pm it shows the work of 40 local artists. **Note:** you must bargain in both galleries.

Though stores in Kuta and Sanur offer a wide variety of merchandise, some of the island's best buys can be found in smaller towns north of Denpasar. It is difficult to separate exploring from shopping. For that reason, be prepared to stop when you see interesting shops along the roadside. Many of Bali's best artists sell some of their finest items directly out of their houses. This is especially true of painters around Ubud, so don't pass through towns too quickly.

BATUBULAN

About 45 minutes north of Kuta on the road to Mas and Lake Batur is Batubulan, the village of antiques, stone carving and *barong* dancing. Though there is no hotel or home stay of note here, you will want to spend several hours, if only to catch the *barong* dance, a Kodachrome attraction worth at least three rolls of film that is staged every morning at 9:30 am Be sure to arrive early since the dance is one of the most colorful on the island. Seats near the open air stage are the best in the temple complex, but tend to be occupied last since they're in the direct sun. By the time the performance begins they'll be in the shade, so grab the front row if it's free.

If you have any interest in stone carving it's worth while to spend several hours after the dance looking at the stores along Batubulan's main road. Carving is a living art in Bali because village temples are constantly reordering new statues. Carved from soft sandstone, the statues weather quickly in the tropical climate, and after a decade or so must be replaced.

Across from the *barong* dance is a collection of carvings owned by **Made Kakul**, the cashier at the temple where the dance is performed. Made has a varied assortment of carvings from Temple guards to Chinese mandarins and speaks English, but bargaining is essential in this cash-only establishment.

If you decide to make a purchase, you can get the statue carefully packed and shipped out of the country at **Rote Adhi**, on Jalan Brig. Tegal Tamu ((361) 35622, a packing

---

Dozens of galleries make Ubud the artistic center of Bali.

company a few minutes walk north up the road. Shipping of stone carvings out of Bali is quite reliable and inexpensive, costing at the maximum around $300 for one cubic meter. Since weight is no factor in the shipping price, which falls dramatically as the volume increases, stone carvings are one of the best buys on the island.

On the other side of Brig. Tegal Tamu is the store of **Wayan Parka**, a stone and woodcarver who specializes in griffins and the Hindu God Ganesh, and **Majapahit**, a gallery selling large stone carvings by Abu Naim.

Batubulan has some of Bali's biggest antique stores and one of the best is **Mergepati Palace**, a rambling gallery on the south side of the village. A half dozen antique sewing machines just inside the door make this gallery seem as if it only sells western antiques, but if you walk through the back door into a courtyard you'll find elaborately carved temple doors and Balinese wedding beds displayed in a setting that itself is worthy of a photograph.

Two Batubulan galleries are worthy of note because they specialize in items you're not likely to find elsewhere in the island. The first is **Oka** (℡ (361) 32703) a small art shop that has the village's best collection of old Balinese masks. Though new Balinese masks are not hard to find, the old ones are highly prized because the use of organic-based paint and vegetable dyes gives a subtlety to the colors that no modern mask can match.

Nyoman Suetha's **Puri Antiques** (℡ (361) 35755) focuses more on Sumatran textiles

the narrow road crosses the Ous River and dips briefly south before heading north again. The first town after the river is the district center of Sukawati. Most Balinese tour operators offer shopping oriented day trips to Batubulan and Celuk but none stop in Sukawati, which is unfortunate since it is home to **Nyoman Erawan**, 33, one of Indonesia's most promising young painters. A Balinese "modernist" whose paintings have been selected to tour the United States during the "1991 Visit Indonesia Year," Nyoman is a graduate of Java's most prestigious art academy. His impressionistic, mixed media creations are put together in an open air studio on Melati Lane which runs into the main Denpasar to Ubud road just before the Sukawati Art Center. In Ubud his paintings sell for $5,000, but at his studio the price can fall to $1,000 or below after bargaining.

Between Sukawati and Mas is a stretch of road lined with typical Balinese houses. The houses are much larger than they appear from the road. The typically narrow gate that leads into a Balinese house opens onto a courtyard with four to five buildings, each used for a separate function. The Balinese are very hospitable and invariably welcome visitors who first ask permission to enter.

MAS

A 15 minute drive north from Sukawati brings you to **Mas**, an art center favored by Bali's best woodcarvers. Mas has a population of 3,000, 90 percent of which is involved in woodcarving. Carvers in Bali tend to work in groups, so don't be surprised if you find eight men and women busily at work in the back of a gallery. The **Adhi Art Gallery** (℡ (361) 95228) on the main road of Mas has several large rooms filled with carvings in both Balinese and European styles. Because Bali is a small island with a very large population, only mahogany and light colored hibiscus wood is locally grown. Ebony hardwoods come from the Celebes and Borneo. East Timor supplies sandalwood. There is always

and blue and white porcelain. Don't miss the collection of baby carriages from Borneo.

Before leaving Batubulan you should make one last stop at the **Bali Souvenir Artshop**, ℡ (361) 24063 a small gallery on the north side of the road just east of the turn off for Celuk. Unlike the stores in Batubulan proper which all feature locally produced carvings, Bali Souvenir has wooden masks and temple ornamentation from Sumatra and the lesser Sunda Islands as well. The prices are competitive and credit cards are accepted.

SUKAWATI

North of Batubalan, just past the village of **Celuk**, which is famous for its jewelry

Men pretend to impale themselves on sharp *krises* during the climax of the *Barong* dance performed daily in the village of Batubulan.

a group of Balinese working out back; men carving while women sand the finished pieces. Don't be shocked if you see Kiwi shoe polish being applied to a statue. The Balinese use shoe polish to stain wood. Open daily 9 am to 5 pm.

About 100 yards further along is **Barong**, (✆ (361) 24925, telex 35144 NATRABU), an even larger manufacturer and exporter of carvings, open from 7 am to 8 pm. Don't be put off by the front building, which is the shipping room. Head directly to the back where there is a two-story display area. The large

beautiful **temple** that means "the place to look."

There are three restaurants in Penelokan that offer $9 luncheon buffets to tourists. The **Batur Garden Restaurant**, the **Puri Selera** and the **Kintamani Restaurant** are all similar in that each is open from 11 am to 4 pm and has a spectacular view of Lake Batur.

Warning! Numerous vendors sell crudely carved figurines outside these restaurants. They are the most unpleasant people on Bali and should be avoided. They can become extremely unpleasant if, having shown in-

statues are on the first floor. Smaller items like picture frames, Balinese masks and animals are located upstairs.

While in Mas be sure to stop at the **Puri Rasa Cafe** (8 am to 9 pm) for a Balinese lunch. Owned by a woodcarver, the cafe accepts only cash for meals, but will take credit cards if you want to buy one of the antique Balinese doors on display.

terest in their wares, you do not purchase anything. Have a nice lunch. Enjoy the view. Ignore these vendors.

KINTAMANI AND LAKE BATUR

The high mountain town of Kintamani (elevation 1,400 m or 4,600 ft) is a mile or so beyond Peneloken. Houses here are constructed of wood and earthen tiles to ward off the evening chill. The crisp, spring-like climate does not seem to bother vegetable and fruit growers, whose produce appears in profusion at the morning market every three days. The cool weather also makes Kintamani the best place in Bali for trekking. The island's

PENELOKAN

Just beyond Ubud the road begins to climb up to the crest of Bali's mountainous spine. A steady climb eventually leads to Penelokan, a tiny village with a dramatically

most reliable mountain guide, Gede Merta, can be found at **Gede's Trekking** on the village's main street. Merta's tailor-made walking tours for groups or individuals include ascents of the Batur volcano and Mt. Agung that cost from $30 to $60. It is even possible to take mountain trails all the way back down to Ubud, a pleasant six-hour trek that costs about $44.

The tourists who stop for lunch in Penelokan and Kintamani usually return to their hotels on the coast by mid afternoon, missing the sunset over Lake Batur. Persons who'd

charter an ancient *prahu* for $2 and cross Lake Batur to the village of **Trunyan**, the home of the primitive *Bali Aga* who call themselves "the original Balinese." The village itself is extremely primitive and can be bypassed in favor of the lakeside cemetery. The 300 people of Trunyan do not believe in cremation. They place their dead in rows beneath an enormous tree and allow nature to take its course. A nominal donation is expected when entering the cemetery. Place the money next to the skull at the gate.

like to spend a cool evening sleeping under a blanket, and those wanting to get an early morning start on a trek back to Ubud with Gede Merta, should consider spending the night at **Losmen Gunawan**, a peaceful 14-room lodge overlooking Lake Batur and the surrounding mountains. There's no need for air-conditioning in these simple rooms that cost $11 a night. The Gunawan has a small restaurant in which menu items range from $1.50 to $3 for chicken steak and French fries. Take your meals in the restaurant or have the dishes delivered to a special pavilion built for contemplating the beauty of Bali's highland.

From **Kedisan**, a small boat landing directly below Losmen Gunawan, you can

SINGARAJA AND BALI'S NORTH SHORE

From Kintamani it's possible to follow the road north over the mountain to Bali's north shore, an area of heavy rainfall rarely visited by tourists. The road down to the black sand beach is arduous with dozens of cutbacks and corkscrew turns, but after reaching Kubutambahan, it's a fairly easy drive to Singaraja.

Until 1953 Singaraja, an old town the Dutch had made their administrative center,

ABOVE: Balinese temples, and the friezes that decorate them, reflect contemporary life on the island. OPPOSITE: It takes about four hours to climb Mt. Batur, the highest point on Bali.

was the gateway to Bali. Today it has been eclipsed by Denpasar, but it remains a major historical center with a library that contains thousands of ancient Balinese manuscripts. Pacto Tours in Sanur Beach is one of the few companies to offer trips to the north coast. To sign up for a day-long excursion to Singaraja via Ubud, Kintamani and Lake Bedugul contact Pacto at ((361) 8247 or go by their counters at the Bali Beach, Bali Hyatt and Putri Bali hotels.

HOW TO GET THERE

Bali is a major international destination served by nine major airlines in addition to Indonesia's flag carrier Garuda. Every day more than 150 planes arrive and depart Denpasar's Ngurah Rai airfield, which is in the process of being enlarged to accommodate an even larger number of passengers. Garuda makes it easy to get to its leading tourist destination. From Los Angeles there are five flights each week with intermediate stops in Honolulu and Biak. It also has daily service linking Bali with Singapore, Hong Kong, Tokyo, Taipei, Seoul and Australia. There are four daily nonstops to Singapore and two to Hong Kong.

Inside Indonesia, Denpasar is a major hub that can be reached on a daily basis from every island group. Garuda alone has eight daily nonstops from Jakarta, plus three daily nonstops from Yogyakarta and Surabaya. Merpati, Bouraq and Sempati airlines serve Denpasar from smaller cities.

Most major hotels offer complimentary transportation from the airport for guests who advise their arrival times. No organized taxi service exists on Bali. Persons without reservations will find a small army of drivers waiting to take you to their favorite hotels. A Bali Tourism Promotion desk right outside the baggage claim can provide a list of hotels appropriate to your budget.

Years ago travelers rented motorcycles for a few dollars a day and buzzed about Bali on their own. The volume of traffic on the island's narrow roads makes that inadvisable now. Today, there are three basic ways to get around. One is to rent a car and drive yourself. All the major hotels have transportation desks that can arrange a hire car. It may be cheaper, however, for you to go directly to the dozens of small rental companies in the Kuta-Sanur area that charge from $40 to $65 a day for small Suzuki jeeps. **Don't forget to bargain! And make sure your insurance coverage is confirmed in writing!**

Renting a car may be more trouble than it's worth if you're staying in Kuta where there is little parking and a lot of traffic. Option two is renting a van by the hour or for the day. The *bemo* corners in Kuta and Legian are packed with drivers of Mitsubishi vans who yell "Transport" the moment a foreigner approaches.

First timers to Bali are advised to discover the island with a reputable travel agency like Satriavi, which offers reasonably priced van tours with a driver and guide to upcountry temples and villages known for their handicrafts. For people interested in shopping, the five hour trip to Tampaksiring is a great value at $40 since there are visits to woodcarvers in Mas, gold and silversmiths in Celuk and Ubud's art galleries in addition to stops at the Elephant Cave and the royal tombs at Gunung Kawi. A second excursion, not to be missed by newlyweds, is the drive to Asia's most romantic temple, the rockbound offshore temple of Thanah Lot ($50 for two). It stops at the sacred Monkey Forest of Sangeh and Bali's most beautiful temple, Pura Taman Ayun. The van arrives at Thanah Lot just as the setting sun begins to silhouette the temple. Satriavi has offices in the Sanur Beach and Nusa Dua Beach hotels. Its headquarters is in Denpasar on Jalan Veteran N° 7, ((361) 24339 or 24385.

OPPOSITE: Fishing nets and the black sand shore of lonely North Bali which serves as a major footpath, TOP. Threshing rice in North Bali, BOTTOM.

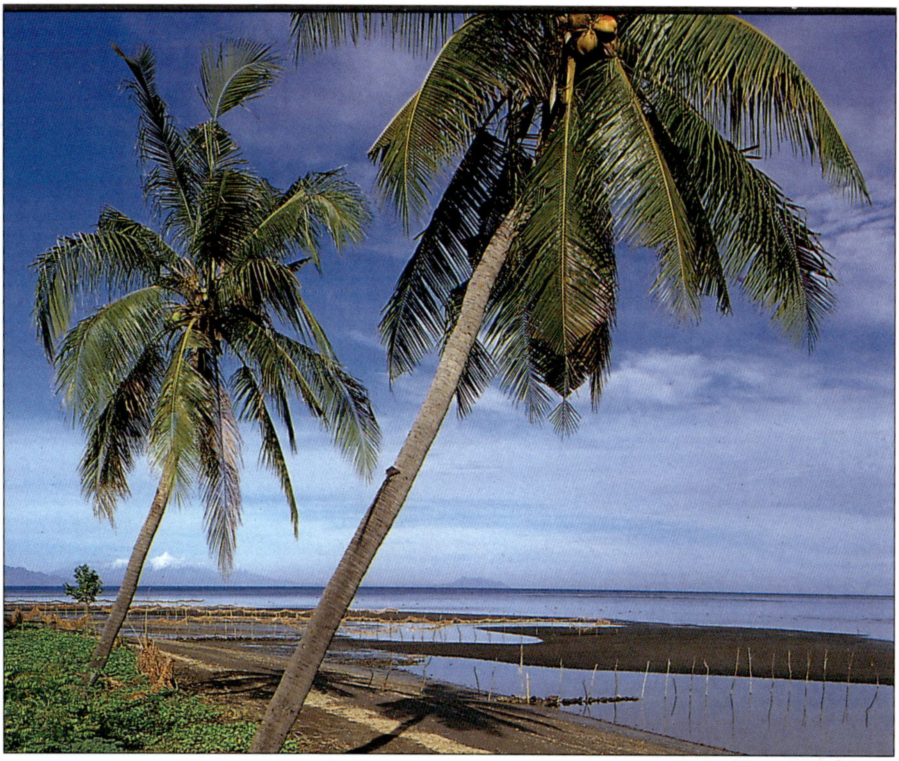

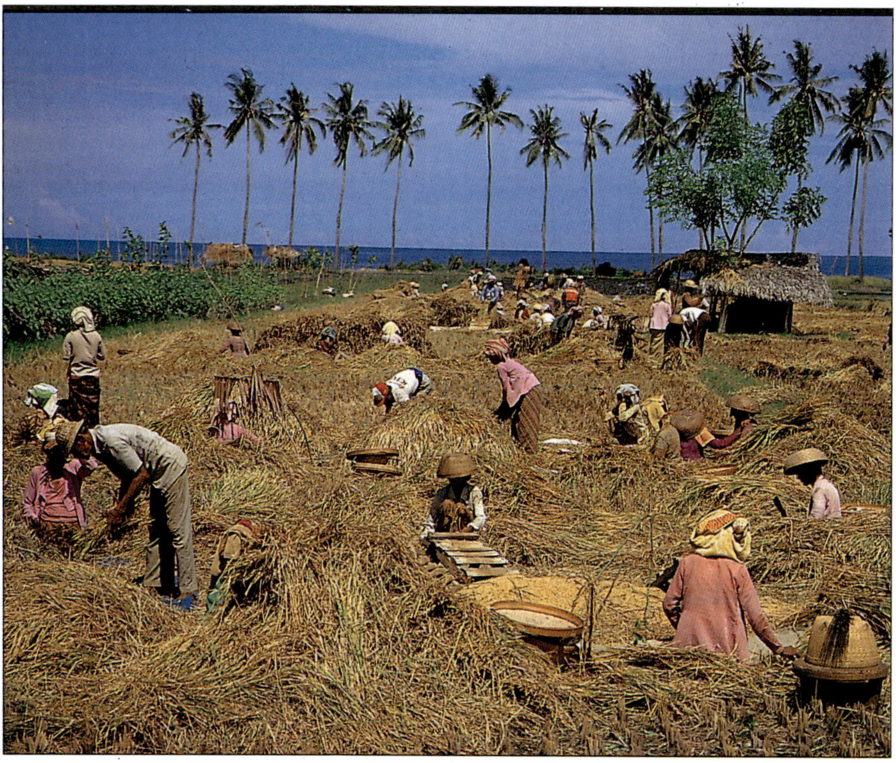

Sumatra

fundamentalist brand of Islam, while Christianity prevails around Medan and Lake Toba. Outside Padang and Bukittinggi on the southwest of Sumatra, the adat system of ancestral worship prevails. On offshore islands like Nias, animism still holds sway.

ACCOUNTING for 25 percent of Indonesia's total land area, Sumatra is the sixth largest island in the world. Lying along the Strait of Malacca, it extends for more than 1,600 km (1,000 miles) and contains some of the most exotic and unusual cultures in Indonesia. Though it has less than a third of Java's population, Sumatra accounts for 50 percent of Indonesia's total export earnings. The island produces three fourths of the country's crude oil. The Minas oil field beneath Sumatra's Riau province has been yielding high quality crude for more than a century. Natural gas tapped at the Arun field in Aceh province fires the industries of Japan. Rubber, palm oil and Robusta coffee beans flow out of plantations covering the foothills of the island's Bukit Barisan Range. Tin is mined and smelted in the Bangka Islands. For the Dutch, Sumatra was an unending source of wealth with the richest area being the *cultuurgebied*, or "plantation area," around the present city of Medan.

Sumatra is home to remarkably diverse groups of people who have evolved in relative isolation because of the island's volcanic mountain ranges and raging rivers. The northern tip of Aceh is noted for its

Sumatra's dramatic architecture, seen at its best in the northern and western portions of the island, has received national imprimatur and can be seen throughout the archipelago. The style is reflected in the typical large rectangular building built atop pilings with a saddle-shaped roof that rises to a point at either end. In the Minangkabau area of western Sumatra highpitched gables often are decorated with buffalo horns. Elsewhere, carvings adorn the pillars and lintels of Sumatran styled auditoriums, airports and convention centers.

LAMPUNG

The southernmost province of Lampung is Sumatra's window on the Sunda Strait and the nearby island of Java. The provincial capital, **Bandar Lampung** is a major entry point to the island.

The brooding volcano of **Krakatau**, which exploded in 1883 killing 36,000 people and blanketing the entire southern portion of the island with volcanic ash, sits 29 km (18 miles) off Lampung's southern shore. The volcano is dormant now. Boats can be chartered in the village of **Canti** for the six hour journey, but the seas can be treacherous so plan your visit for the months of September or October when the weather is best.

Enriched by Krakatau's volcanic ash, Lampung's soil produces abundant crops of cloves, coffee and pepper. Fertility has made the province a favorite destination for Javanese transmigrants, who are sent, at government expense, to create agricultural communities. Today, 12 percent of Lampung's 5,000,000 people are from Java.

GENERAL INFORMATION

The Regional Office of Tourism, Post and Telecommunications is located at Jalan Kotaraja 12 in Bandar Lampung. ((721) 55208. The Lampung Tourist Service, also in Bandar Lampung, is at Jalan Dr. Suprapto 39, ((721) 42565.

WHERE TO STAY

Overlooking the Sunda Strait the 94-room **Sahid Krakatau Seaside** on Jalan Yos Sudarso Nº 294 charges $40 for superior rooms and $44 for cabanas. ((721) 44022; fax 44356. Closer to the center of town the **Marco Polo Hotel** at Jalan Dr. Susilo Nº 4 has air-conditioned rooms starting at $28 a night. Guests also have access to the hotel's swimming pool and health club. ((721) 41511.

HOW TO GET THERE

Ferries from Java arrive and depart from one of Lampung's two ports. Bakauhuni is on the southern tip of Sumatra. Panjang is a bit further up the east coast.

RIAU AND THE RIAU ISLANDS

At the southern end of the Malacca Strait, a thousand tiny Riau Islands stretch between Sumatra's east coast swamps and the Malay peninsula. Rich in oil and tin the islands were used for centuries as stepping stones by fishermen, merchant sailors and pirates. In 1745 the area came under the control of the Dutch East India Company, which immediately set about sweeping pirates from the Matuna Sea. The task remains unfinished to this day.

Riau has two capitals, the provincial administrative center of **Pekanbaru**, which lies in East Sumatra 161 km (100 miles) up the Siak River, and the Bintan Island capital of **Tanjung Pinang**.

Pekanbaru is a blue collar oil town surrounded on all sides by dense, triple canopy jungle. Everything the town has to offer is located on or just off the main street, Jalan Jend. Sudirman. Unless you have relatives working for Caltex, there is really no reason to tarry in Pekanbaru. But if misfortune should strike and you are forced to stay the night, head for the **Sri Indrayani Hotel** (℃ (761) 21878) on Jalan Bangka N° 2 or the **Indrapura** (℃ (761) 25165) at Jalan Dr. Sutomo N° 86. Located in a residential neighborhood, the 110-room Indrapura is an excellent business hotel with a billiard center and discotheque for after hours entertainment. The more luxurious Sri Indrayani is in a shopping district closer to town. Single rooms at both range from $35 to $90 depending on the size and view with double occupancy costing an additional $6.

Remnants of the 300-year old Malay Kingdom of Riau can be found on **Penyengat Island** (adjacent to Bintan), but most travelers head for **Batam**, an island of beach resorts 30 minutes from Singapore by ferry. Batam is a duty free port with clean water and dramatic nighttime views of the Singapore skyline.

Tanjung Pinang on **Bintan Island** is the largest town in the Riau archipelago. Located at the intersection of sea lanes linking Singapore, Sumatra, Sulawesi and Java, it is a colorful port and safe harbor for everything from Chinese junks to Bugis schooners.

GENERAL INFORMATION

The Riau Tourist Service (*DIPARDA RIAU*) is on Jalan Jend. Sudirman in Pekanbaru. ℃ (761) 25301.

WHERE TO STAY AND WHERE TO EAT

In the center of Batam our favorite is the **Holiday Hotel** (℃ (761) 58616, 58626) at Blok B, N° 1 on Jalan Imam Bonjol. Rooms average around $35 to $45. The best hotel at Tanjung Pinang is the **Sampurna Jaya Internasional**. Located at Jalan Yusuf Kahar N° 15, the hotel's 77 rooms are in the $50 a night range, but can be had for 15 percent less if you

present a business card and ask for a discount. ℃ (761) 21555. You either eat in the hotel or try the seafood in the open air restaurants. In Batam there are pizza bakeries, a Kentucky Fried Chicken, excellent *padang* and Chinese food.

HOW TO GET THERE

Garuda has direct service from Pekanbaru to Singapore, Jakarta, Medan and Batam. Merpati has flights to Batam, Medan, Padang and Palembang plus daily service to Banda Aceh, Jakarta and Tanjung Pinang. Sempati has direct flights to Jakarta, Kuala Lumpur and Padang.

PALEMBANG

The provincial capital of South Sumatra is a boom town of 700,000 people, many of whom work in the oil, timber and tin industries. The city is surrounded by rubber, coffee and pineapple plantations, but the main attraction for foreign visitors is the **Musi River** which bisects the city. Along with the Mahakam in East Kalimantan, the Musi is one of the most interesting rivers in Indonesia. Negotiate an hourly fare at the quay near the Ampera Bridge and cruise the river banks before heading to Palembang's other attraction, the **Rumah Bari Museum** on Jalan Rumah Bari. Open daily except Friday, the museum is the best and only repository of objects from the Srivijaya Empire that ruled much of Southeast Asia from the seventh to twelfth centuries.

GENERAL INFORMATION

Directions and printed information on South Sumatra and Jambi can be found at the Regional Office of Tourism, Post and Telecommunications at Jalan Rajawali N° 22 in Palembang. ℃ (711) 28948, 28954.

WHERE TO STAY

Located in the residential section of Palembang, the **Swarna Dwipa** at Jalan Tasik N° 2 is 20 minutes from the airport and five minutes from the city center, this 70 room hotel has singles for $27 and $32, and doubles for $32 and $38. ((711) 28322; fax (711) 28999.

How to Get There

Garuda (((711) 22933) and Merpati (((711) 21604) fly out of Palembang's Talang Betutu airport. Garuda tickets can be purchased at Jalan Kapt. Rivai N° 20. The Merpati office is also on Jalan. Kapt. Rivai at N° 6193.

BENGKULU

Bisected by the Bukit Barisan mountain range, this seldom visited province is divided between dense rain forests and fertile soil enriched by the explosion of Krakatau. Peasants resettled under the *transmigrasi* program do much of the agricultural work. For the moment, at least, the forests still belong to .tapirs, tigers, civet cats and the elusive Sumatran clouded leopard.

Three centuries ago, Bengkulu was the base for Britain's entry into the East Indies pepper trade. The experience was not entirely successful. Malaria so thinned British ranks that it soon was said that "two monsoons were the life of a man" sent to Bengkulu. By the time Stamford Raffles arrived on the scene in 1818 most of the work was being done by the Eurasian progeny of the dearly departed.

Today, Bengkulu is a small town of not much more than 70,000 people. It has no exotic nightlife or fine restaurants. Instead it offers an ambiance, a certain tropical charm, resulting, perhaps, from the fact that its people have made peace with the towering mountain chain at their back, the tempestuous Mentawai Strait at their feet, and the omnipresent ghosts of the past.

General Information

The *DIPARDA* Tourist Service for Bengkulu is at Jalan Soekarno-Hatta, ((736) 31272.

What to See

Fort Marlborough was the most imposing military structure ever built by the East India Company. Today it is occupied by the Indonesian army, whose presence in Bengkulu is

hard to explain. The army has done its best to rob the fort of its former grandeur. Its thick front wall has been plastered over with cement giving it the appearance of an adobe prison. But the back of the fort and its windswept parapets remain much as they were when the British and Dutch were fighting over Sumatra. Before leaving the fort, walk through the graveyard, preferably at dusk, to read the epitaphs on the tombstones.

A few minutes walk from Fort Marlborough is the old **English governor's office**, a hilltop ruin whose beauty is enhanced by

the fact that the crumbling structure is being devoured by jungle.

Bengkulu's most interesting attraction from the Indonesian point of view is **Sukarno's house** where he lived for four years during his exile by the Dutch. Next to the tourist office around the corner from Jalan Soekarno-Hatta, the home can be visited in the morning once permission is received from its present occupants.

WEST SUMATRA

West Sumatra is the most densely populated area on Sumatra. It has a population of 4,000,000, nearly all of whom are Minangkabau, a matrilineal society in which inherited property, land and family surnames are passed on to women. Indeed, the word for family is *saparuik*, which means "from one womb."

Mt. Sibayak's sulfurous fumes don't bother the orangutans which live on the volcano's slopes.

Among the Minangkabau of western Sumatra women are the ones who chose their mates. Men are valued for their strength and semen and have no authority in family or business matters. As a result, thousands of them leave to seek their fortune elsewhere. Sleeping in mosques and eating in restaurants, they become *merantu*, or nomads, who return home only after striking it rich in the "man's world" of Java. Because many men never return home, Jakarta's Minangkabau population is greater than that of Padang.

The buffalo is central to the architecture and dress of western Sumatra. Minang buildings have peaked swooping roofs that resemble the horns of a water buffalo. Large homes of the wealthy can have as many as a dozen gables. The pointed headdresses of Minangkabau women, whose dresses are embroidered with gold and silver thread, also appear as stylized buffalo horns.

PADANG

The center of the Minangkabau society is the provincial capital of Padang, Sumatra's third largest city. A sweltering seaport drenched by tropical rain all year around, Padang is the cleanest, most orderly city in Indonesia. It boasts a number of museums and art centers, the most important of which are the **Museum Adityawarman** and the **Padang Art Center**. Located on Jalan Diponegoro, both are open daily except Monday.

Remember, Padang is close to the equator so it never gets cool. Though rain falls throughout the year, it really pours from November to March.

Padang's port, **Teluk Bayur**, is the departure point for boats to the Mentawai archipelago. Padang also is blessed with scenic **Bungus Bay**, the best spot in the province for swimming.

GENERAL INFORMATION

The understaffed Provincial Tourist Service (*DIPARDA Sumatera Barat*) is in Padang at Jalan Jend. Sudirman 43. A better alternative is the West Sumatra Tourism Office at Jalan Khatib Sulaiman N° 22 in Padang Baru. ℂ (751) 23231, 22118. This fully bilingual staff

also has background about tours and resorts in Riau.

WHERE TO STAY

In the center of Padang the **Natour Hotel Muara** on Jalan Gereja N° 34 (ℂ (751) 25600, 21858) has 63 rooms from $23 and climb to $52 for a suite. The **New Pangeran** on Jalan Dobi N° 3-5 (ℂ (751) 26233, 26632) is recently renovated with 200 rooms. Singles are $26 while double occupancy costs $32.

WHERE TO EAT

Padang is the home of Indonesian "fast food." *Padang* is a spicy assortment of meat, fish and vegetables that are served in a dozen or more dishes. Accompanied by a steaming bowl of rice, the food is cooked in chili, coconut milk or curry. You eat only what you want and pay only for what you eat. **Simpang Raya**, across from the post office, at Jalan Aziz Chan N° 24, is a well managed chain of Padang restaurants that serves excellent food at a reasonable price. Also known for *padang* is **Bopet Buyan** on Jalan Aziz Chan.

HOW TO GET THERE

Padang's Tabing airport is well served by Garuda (ℂ (751) 23823) and Merpati (ℂ (751) 27908), both of which have frequent flights to Jakarta, Medan, Palembang and Pekanbaru. Garuda also has a thrice-weekly nonstop from Padang to Singapore. Garuda is located at Jalan Jend. Sudirman N° 2. The Merpati office is at Jalan Pemuda N° 45A. Sempati (ℂ (751) 55366) flies to Jakarta, Kuala Lumpur and Semarang.

BUKITTINGGI

After visiting Padang most travelers head straight for Bukittinggi, the highland center of the Minangkabau culture which has beautiful jungle trails leading out to villages famed for their arts and crafts. Bukittinggi is reputed to have the friendliest people in Sumatra. Horse-drawn carts called *dokars* ply the well-swept streets which meet in the center of town at the big clock, Jam Gadang, which has been keeping accurate time since 1827. The best place on Sumatra to find Minangkabau antiques and souvenirs, the **central market** expands exponentially on Saturdays when weavers from Kota Gadang come to town to sell elaborately embroidered shawls. A priority stop for all who make it to Bukittinggi is the nearby village of Pariangan, believed to be the original home of the Minangkabau. Built around a mosque and community halls, no new buildings are allowed in Pariangan and no old ones may be demolished.

WHERE TO STAY AND TO EAT

The best choice is **Aerowisata's Pusako Hotel** two kilometers from town which has beautiful mountain views. Rooms are $80. Jalan Sukarno Hatta 7, Bukittinggi, ((752) 22111, fax (752) 21017.

Jalan A. Yani is the place to head to for good budget restaurants. Mountain View Guesthouse, quite often full costs $8 per room and Suwarni's, across from Mountain View, is the same price.

Bukittinggi in Western Sumatra is famous for its horse-drawn carts, ABOVE, LEFT and saddle-roofed homes ABOVE, RIGHT.

MENTAWAI ISLANDS

Four Mentawai Islands — **Siberut**, **Sipora**, **Pagai Utara** and **Pagai Selatan** — are parallel to and about 97 km (60 miles) from the west coast of Sumatra. The Mentawais are actually the peaks of submerged mountains that were separated from Sumatra during the Pleistocene Age and ever since have evolved in splendid isolation, protected by coral reefs, treacherous currents and unpredictable winds.

The Mentawai islanders, who number 35,000 at most, are Indonesia's original flower children. As late as 1980 they still wore banana leaves, bark cloth sarongs and gave birth to children naturally in the rivers. The policy of allowing only anthropologists to visit the islands has been modified slightly, but getting there still requires a surat jalan from the Padang police ((110) on Jalan Prof. M. Yamin.

All of the schools and social services on the islands are run by missionaries, who have succeeded in converting about half the population to Christianity. In theory. In reality, the Mentawai islanders remain animists who believe that everything from a rock to a rainbow to a spirit must be appeased.

SIBERUT

There is a government guest house at **Muarasiberut**, but you will be expected to bring all your own food and drink. Native villages in the interior of all islands are hospitable and will provide shelter plus a dinner of fruit and rice. But you will be expected to offer some food and money to the family that takes you in. Remember, however, that to get to these villages you must first present a *surat jalan* to the police in Muarasiberut.

largest in Indonesia, Medan is Sumatra's main transportation hub, the place that most visitors see first. This is unfortunate since the noise and air pollution almost overwhelm the colonial mansions and government buildings built by the Dutch.

Almost, but not quite. After seeing the **Maimun Palace**, a museum that once housed the sultans of Delhi, the **Crocodile Park** and the **North Sumatra Regional Museum**, there is no better way to end the day than with a pleasant stroll along Jalan Jend. Sudirman in the city's **Polonia** colonial quarter. Stately

HOW TO GET THERE

Merpati flies once a week from Padang to **Rokor Mentawai** on Siberut. Cheaper passage can be had on the government supplies boat that makes the journey from Padang's Teluk Bayur to Muarasiberut every two weeks.

MEDAN

Because its history is shaped by Malays, Javanese, Bataks and a host of Chinese, Arab and Indian traders, Medan is the ethnic melting pot of Sumatra. The largest city (population 2,100,000) on the island, and the fourth

old plantation homes also can be found along Jalan Imam Bonjol and Jalan Balai Kota.

Products from all over Sumatra find their way to Medan, and most end up being sold in shops along Jalan Jen. A. Yani. The chances of finding old batik are pretty slim, but reproductions of Batak calendars, statues and betel nut boxes are well made and worth buying once the price is bargained down to a realistic level.

GENERAL INFORMATION

Both the provincial and regional tourist offices are located in Medan, and they are the best in Sumatra. Both have lists of hotels and guest houses, plus advice on reputable tourist agents. The provincial service can be reached at ℂ (61) 511101 or going by the office at Jalan Ahmad Yani N° 107. The Tourism, Post and Telecommunications center is in Medan's Kampung Baru at Jalan Ifalah N° 22. ℂ (61) 24418, 322836.

WHERE TO STAY

The **Tiara Medan** on Jalan Cut Mutiah has large double rooms from $38 to $75 with suites going for $150. ℂ (61) 516000. Also recommended is the **Polonia Hotel** at Jalan Jend. Sudirman N° 14. Right in the center of Medan, this 174 room hotel has room rates ranging from $35 to $70. ℂ (61) 325300, fax (61) 519553.

Built in 1879, the old Hotel de Boer today lives on as the **Natour's Hotel Dharma Deli**. Even if you don't stay there it is worth a visit since its historical value to Medan is similar to that of Raffles in Singapore or the E&O in Penang, Malaysia. Located at Jalan Balai Kota N° 2, next door to Bank Indonesia and around the corner from the Balai Kota city hall, the hotel has been skillfully renovated in a way that has not diminished its nineteenth century elegance. Rates are $30 to $54 for single or double occupancy. ℂ (61) 327999, fax (61) 327153.

WHERE TO EAT

The **Tip Top Restaurant** on Jalan Jen. A. Yani wins top marks for serving not only western food but also *nasi padang*. The Tip Top has a stylish sidewalk cafe that is a good place to have afternoon tea. For excellent Chinese food cooked without MSG try the **Polonia Restaurant** at the Polonia Hotel.

For quick snacks or excellent American breakfasts, the place to go is the **Holland Bakery** on Jalan Taruma. The Tip Top and the Holland Bakery both are well-known for their ice cream.

HOW TO GET THERE

Medan has one of the most active airports in Indonesia and is well served by both domestic and international carriers. Singapore Airlines (ℂ (61) 51811) and Malaysian Airlines System (ℂ (61) 9333) have regular flights from Singapore, Penang and Kuala Lumpur. Garuda (ℂ (61) 25700) has daily service to Jakarta, Denpasar and Ujung Pandang, in addition to most major cities on Sumatra. Merpati (ℂ (61) 514102), Sempati (ℂ (61) 537800), Mandala (ℂ (61) 513309) and SMAC (ℂ (61) 516617) also have frequent service.

Those who don't fly to Medan usually take the *Gadis Langkasuka* ferry from Penang to Medan's port of Belawan. The Penang ferry makes two round trips each week and takes 15 hours to cross the Malacca Strait. Travel agents in Penang sell a through ticket that allows a traveler to immediately board

a tourist bus from Belawan to Medan after going through immigration.

THE BATAK HIGHLANDS

Sumatra is home to about 2,000,000 Batak tribesmen, the majority of which live in the highlands around Lake Toba, a volcanic crater lake 732 m (2,400 ft) above sea level.

When the Bataks migrated from the Himalayan foothills of Burma's Kachin State more than 1,500 years ago they were animis-

OPPOSITE: Medan is famous for Dutch colonial buildings such as the main Post Office.
ABOVE: Lake Toba is the ancestral home of Sumatra's Batak highlanders.

tic cannibals. The passing of centuries did little to change their culinary habits. When Stamford Raffles saw them in the early nineteenth century the Batak still liked filet of sole, he noted dryly, or the palms of hands if feet were not available. Usually carved from their enemies, both dishes were seasoned with lime, salt and pepper, grilled lightly and served with a side order of rice.

Though many of the northern Batak groups remain animist, a century of Christian missionary work has transformed the population around Lake Toba into Protes-

tants. The Batak are skilled woodcarvers who decorate many of their artifacts with graphically carved fertility symbols.

LAKE TOBA AND SAMOSIR ISLAND

Lake Toba, 161 km (100 miles) south of Medan, is a pristine crater lake surrounding Samosir, an island larger than the nation of Singapore. On Samosir it's possible to rent traditional batak houses right on the lake, though many travelers prefer the more commodious accommodation found in **Parapat** on Lake Toba's eastern shore. Either way Lake Toba is a cool and tranquil alternative to the traffic and humidity of towns along the coast.

Samosir is regarded by many as a place to relax and swim, but travelers who opt to leave their bungalows in Tuk Tuk can take one of several cross-island treks through beautiful alpine forest land.

OPPOSITE: Boats are the only way to get around Lake Toba. ABOVE: Samosir Island produces some of Indonesia's most distinctive architecture.

WHERE TO STAY

The **Atsari Hotel & Bungalow** on Jalan P. Samosir N° 9 in Parapat has tastefully decorated bungalows for $18 to $50. ((622) 41219. Slightly more expensive is the **Natour Parapat** on Jalan Marihat N° 1. This bungalow-style hotel is in the mountains overlooking the lake. It has tennis courts and a golf course. Rooms cost from $45 to $65. ((625) 41012. The **Patra Jasa Parapat** (((622) 41706) is a bungalow hotel in the Parapat suburb of Siuhan near Lake Toba. It has a swimming pool, tennis courts and a golf course. Rooms from $40 to $45 for a single; double $5 extra.

On Samosir the bulk of the accommodation is found at **Tuk Tuk**. Many of the best places to stay are guest houses, but finding them will take some assistance since there are no addresses. Tourist offices in Medan and Parapat have lists of guest houses, some of which have telephones. One place worth calling in advance is the **Carolina**, (((622) 41920). It has nine bungalows on the lake shore that range from $5 to $10 a night. The hotel has an excellent restaurant, an isolated swimming cove and rents motorbikes to guests. Reservations are essential, especially in the summer.

HOW TO GET THERE

To get to Lake Toba and Samosir Island you can either drive south from Medan or north from Sibolga. From Medan it takes five hours to drive to Parapat which has the best ferry connections to Samosir. Depending on how much you want to pay, you can take a public bus or a taxi, but most travelers book a seat in a van operated by one of Medan's numerous travel agencies.

Once on Samosir one gets around by walking, renting a motorcycle or waiting for a *bemo* to come your way.

NIAS

The Indian Ocean island of Nias, just north of the Mentawais, is studded with reminders of a megalithic Stone Age culture that once measured wealth and status in terms

or pigs and human skulls taken in battle. Priapic obelisks and stone monoliths guard villages decorated with intricate stone carvings and paved with flagstones.

The sport of jumping 1.5-m (5-ft) stone columns originally served as training for warriors, who needed to jump stone walls when they attacked enemy villages. In ancient times, bamboo spikes affixed to the top of the pillars provided additional incentive for the jumpers to strive for extra height.

Today, stone jumping is more a gymnastic practice than preparation for battle.

There are regular ferries from Sibolga to Nias. Boats (nin-hour trip) to Gunung Sitoli leave from the new harbor of Pelabuhan Baru. Ferries (12-hour trip) to the more popular destination of Teluk Dalam in southern Nias leave from the old harbor of Pelabuhan Lama.

ACEH

Of all the regions in Indonesia, Aceh, at the northern tip of Sumatra, was the first to come into contact with the outside world.

But villages like **Bawomataluo** and **Hili Simaetano**, where stone homes are covered with bas-relief carvings, evoke images of the villages' combative past.

In recent years Nias has become a destination for surfers, who come from all over the world to **Lagundri Beach**, 13 km (eight miles) from the port of **Teluk Dalam**.

HOW TO GET THERE

The quickest way to get to Nias is to take the SMAC flight from Medan to Gunung Sitoli. SMAC has an office (☏ (61) 515934) at Jalan Imam Bonjol N° 59, and you should go by since SMAC's tiny commuter aircraft sometimes keep an erratic schedule.

Chinese chronicles written in the early sixth century speak of a kingdom on the northern tip of Sumatra called Po-Li. By 1292, when Marco Polo passed through the area, more than six trading posts were active.

Islam is believed to have reached Aceh sometime between the seventh and eighth centuries, and the first Islamic kingdom, Perlak, was established in 804. When the Portuguese captured Malacca in 1511, most of the Arab spice traders moved their facilities to Aceh, further enriching the area. By the start of the nineteenth century Aceh found itself in the middle of the struggle between Britain and Holland for regional hegemony. The 1824 Treaty of London gave the Dutch control of all British possessions in Sumatra, but when the Dutch finally moved north of Medan to impose their authority the Acehnese rebelled. The Aceh War, which continued intermittently from 1873 to 1942, was the longest ever fought by Holland, and cost the Dutch 10,000 lives.

A history of contact with foreigners had not resulted in a tradition of hospitality. In spite of the foreign contact, or perhaps because of it, the Acehnese are the most xenophobic people in the entire archipelago. Fundamentalist does not begin to describe the region's intense Islamic zealotry. Today,

sible from either **Kutacane** or **Takingeun**. The park — Indonesia's largest — has research facilities for the study of birds, insects and small mammals. It also boasts the Orangutan Rehabilitation Center.

Orangutan is a Malay word that translates as "man of the forest," and orangutans do resemble humans in many ways. Unlike chimpanzees or gorillas, orangutans can walk upright, pick up tools and "reason" in a way that suggests the species has humanlike thought processes based on logic. Sumatra and Borneo are the only two places

Aceh's leaders look to Tehran and Tripoli for inspiration, not Jakarta.

Unescorted women would be wise to avoid the province of Aceh. Those accompanied by a man should nevertheless wear long dresses and a veil.

General Information

Call (911) 21365 or go by Jalan Lhok Nga 106 for the Aceh Tourist Service.

Gunung Leuser National Park

The only place a western tourist will feel comfortable, and welcome, in this province is the Gunung Leuser National Park, acces-

where orangutans exist in the wild, and here they are dwindling fast because of unrestricted logging and their susceptibility to human diseases when captured.

The Dutch started the practice of capturing baby orangutans, killing their parents, and raising the babies as household pets. Though the practice was outlawed in 1931, many rich Indonesians still do it regardless. When defenseless orangutans are discovered by police, or, as is more often the case, abandoned once they grow old, they are sent to the rehabilitation center which tries to teach them the skills they need to return to life in the forest.

OPPOSITE: The Grand Mosque in Banda Aceh symbolizes Indonesia's Islamic revival. ABOVE: Acehnese fishing trawlers ply the Malacca Strait.

Sulawesi

AN IRREGULARLY-SHAPED island whose four spindly peninsulas are joined in a mountainous middle, Sulawesi is home to 12 million people, the majority of whom live in the seafaring province of South Sulawesi. Anthropologists believe Sulawesi, like Java, may have been inhabited by prehistoric man. Crude stone implements discovered on the southern portion of the island have been carbon-dated back 500,000 years.

Fresh from their conquest of Melaka in 1511, the Portuguese arrived in the early sixteenth century and called the island Ponto dos Celebres, or "Cape of the Infamous Ones," because of the dangerous shoals off the northern peninsula that had claimed so many of their ships. The Dutch grabbed control of the northern peninsula in the seventeenth century and renamed the entire island the Celebes. Despite periodic attacks from South Sulawesi's Bugis, the Dutch successfully used the Celebes as a re provisioning base midway between Java and the Spice islands of Banda, Ternate and Tidore.

Sulawesi's four leading ethnic groups are the fiercely Islamic Bugis and Makassarese of South Sulawesi, the animist Torajans further up the southern peninsula toward the center of the island and the Christian Minahasans of North Sulawesi. The population largely is concentrated along the southern and northern peninsulas where there is enough flat paddy land to support cities.

Separated from both Australia and Asia since long before the last Ice Age, Sulawesi's plant and animal life has evolved in an isolated biosphere. Nineteenth century English naturalist Alfred Russel Wallace was fascinated by the "anomalies and eccentricities" of the island. In his 1869 book, *The Malay Archipelago*, he noted: "…Celebes must be one of the oldest parts of the Archipelago. It probably dates from a period not only anterior to that when Borneo, Java and Sumatra were separated from the continent, but from that still more remote epoch when the land that now constitutes these islands had not risen above the ocean. Such an antiquity is necessary to account for the number of animal forms it possesses…"

Nearly 40 percent of the birds and 90 percent of the island's mammals Wallace found on the Celebes are endemic. Sulawesi is home to a ferocious pygmy buffalo called *anoa*, the black macaque and the *babirussa*, a pig deer with handlebar tusks.

SOUTH SULAWESI

One of the most exotic locations in the world, Sulawesi's southern peninsula is shared by the Bugis, Makassarese and Torajan cultures. The Bugis and Makassarese, both fervent Muslims who are known as Sea Gypsies live along the coast, are famous for their

handmade *pinisi* schooners that today ply the Maluku, Java and Sulawesi seas much as they did five centuries ago. To the north are the animistic Torajans, whose animal sacrifice and burial rituals remain largely undiluted despite a century of work by Christian missionaries.

Bisected by a longitudinal mountain chain, this Florida-sized peninsula has an economy based on agriculture which is most efficient on and around the Jeneponto plain. Because of the mountains, South Sulawesi has two monsoon seasons: April through September in the East and September through April in the West. The heaviest rains occur in December and January, which makes the summer months of June, July and August the peak tourist season.

The peninsula may depend on its farmers, but it is famed for its pirates, who hunted in packs up until World War II, often ramming their merchant prey with bronze

OPPOSITE: A Toraja general. ABOVE: Bugis schooners make Ujung Pandang one of Indonesia's busiest ports.

bludgeons mounted on the bow. Despite their sails and wooden hulls, Bugis ships are remarkably efficient, often reaching speeds of 29 km (18 miles) per hour in a brisk wind.

UJUNG PANDANG

Once the liveliest port in the East Indies, Makasar was described by Alfred Wallace as a city "prettier and cleaner than any I had yet seen in the East." Novelist Joseph Conrad also fell under the spell of the old Bugis capital. Conrad's first novel, *Almayer's Folly*, begins with a paean to the city's glory days: "At that time Makasar was teeming with life and commerce. It was the point in the islands where tended all those bold spirits who, fitting out schooners on the Australian coast, invaded the Malay Archipelago in search of money and adventure. Bold, reckless, keen in business, not disinclined or a brush with the pirates that were to be found on many a coast as yet, making money fast, they used to have a general rendezvous in the bay for the purposes of trade and dissipation."

Now called Ujung Pandang, the city continues to be the focus of maritime commerce, as well as a major hub for Garuda Airlines. A drive along the coastal road from Taneh Baru to Takalar confirms that the building of shallow-draft, sail-powered schooners with hardwood brought from the interior of Kalimantan remains a major industry. One of Indonesia's greatest spectacles is the sight of a black-sailed schooner beating its way into port as the sun sets over the Makassar Strait.

Ujung Pandang, which means "point of sight," is the fifth largest city in Indonesia. The city's economy revolves around its two harbors; Soekarno, where ocean-going freighters dock and Paotare northwest of town where Bugis *prahu* put to sea.

GENERAL INFORMATION

The Regional Office of Tourism, Post and Telecommunications in Ujung Pandang has a good selection of brochures, maps and background information at its office on Jalan P. Andi Petta Rani. Go by or call (411) 21142. The Provincial Tourist Service (*DIPARDA*)

also has an Ujung Pandang office at Jalan A. Yani N° 2, ((411) 7070. Additional advice and directions can be found at the Department of Information office (((411) 22113, 22503) at Jalan St. Hasanuddin N° 42.

WHAT TO SEE

Perhaps the main attraction is **Fort Rotterdam**, an old Dutch fortress built in the shape of a turtle, that was occupied by the Japanese during the war. Inside the fort is **La Galigo Museum**. Open in the morning six days a week (closed Monday), the museum consists of two buildings full of Chinese porcelain, Dutch weaponry, old colonial seals and musical instruments. In addition to the **Conservatory of Dance and Music** and the **Historical and Archaeological Institute**, Fort Rotterdam also has the cell where the rebel prince Diponegoro was held for 26 years.

Diponegoro, whose name graces the main street in almost every Indonesian town, led an uprising against the Dutch in the 1830's. His grave a few blocks west of the fort is marked with a statue.

Despite its enormous growth over the past 20 years, the best architecture in Ujung Pandang is Dutch colonial. Be sure to take a stroll past the old **Dutch governor's mansion** on Jalan Jend. Sudirman. It is now the residence of the Indonesian provincial governor, but unlike many colonial structures, it is well maintained.

WHERE TO STAY

The 140-room **Victoria Panghegar** at Jalan Sudirman N° 24 (((411) 21429, 21228; fax (411) 21292) consists of two buildings. The larger, an eight-story tower completed in 1990, has swimming pool lanais, a shopping arcade and rooms that cost $90 for a single and $100 for a double. The Hasanuddin Pavilion, the former residence of the Dutch Commissioner to the South Celebes, contains large bedrooms, each with a private dining room and reception area. Pavilion rooms range from $60 to $75. American breakfast is included in the price of a room.

Located in the middle of Ujung Pandang at Jalan Chairil Anwar N° 28, the four-story **Makassar City Hotel** has 79 rooms. Singles

cost $40. Double occupancy is $46. Corner suites are $55 a night. ((411) 317055, fax (411) 311818.

Also in the city center a short walk from the museum and central post office is the **Marannu City Hotel** at Jalan Sultan Hasanuddin N° 3-5. The Marannu's 156 air-conditioned rooms are equipped with color televisions and mini bars. Single rooms cost $50 with double occupancy $5 extra. The Marannu has three restaurants, one of which serves vegetarian and health food dishes. ((411) 21470; fax (411) 21821.

A second Marannu hotel, the **Marannu Paviliun** at Jalan M.H. Thamrin N° 2 has

50 rooms that are equally comfortable but less fancy than its larger sister hotel. Single rooms here start at $32 with double occupancy costing $6 more. ((411) 22234 or fax (411) 21821 for reservations.

WHERE TO EAT

Ujung Pandang has a lively restaurant scene that is dominated by Chinese seafood restaurants that serve the local favorite, *ikan bakar*, or charcoal grilled sea bass. For lunch or a quick dinner try the small restaurants along Jalan Sulawesi, almost all of which serve *ikan bakar* or another delicacy, *cumi*

cumi bakar (grilled octopus). For more elaborate dining head for **Asia Bahru**, a seafood restaurant just off Jalan G. Sala or **Rumah Makan Ujung Pandang**, an Indonesian-Chinese cafe at Jalan Irian N° 42.

Ujung Pandang has several lively bars that are perfect for an after dinner drink. The expat favorite is the bar at the **Losari Beach Restaurant** across from the Makassar Golden Hotel, but **Eva Ria**, a third-floor bar on Jalan Penghibur with large picture windows that look out over the harbor may be a more relaxing experience.

HOW TO GET THERE

Ujung Pandang is readily accessible by air from throughout the archipelago. Garuda (✆ (411) 317704) at Jalan Salamat Riyadi N° 6 has daily nonstops from Jakarta, Surabaya and Denpasar. It also provides daily service from Ujung Pandang to Manado and . Merpati (✆ (411) 4114) at Jalan Gunung Bawakaraeng N° 109 has daily 9 am service to Tanatoraja with a second late morning flight departing on Monday, Thursday and Sunday. Sempati (✆ (411) 327148) at Victoria Penghegar Hotel has daily direct flights to Kendari, Palu and Surabaya. Ujung Pandang also is the first port of call for the National Shipping Lines (PELNI) passenger ships *KM Kambuna* and *KM Kerinci*, which dock at Pelabuhan Hatta every week having come from Surabaya and Jakarta's port of Tanjung Priok. The PELNI office, located at 38 Jalan Martadinata, ✆ (411) 7979, also sells space on the *KM Rinjani* which travels to Maluku and the tip of Irian Jaya.

TANATORAJA

Sulawesi's most exotic locale is Tanatoraja, a scenic highland where the Toraja people place their deceased in caves and limestone niches overlooking their villages. Many of the dead are interred standing up in tree trunk sarcophagi. Others are placed alongside wooden effigies carved to resemble the deceased. In the villages of **Lemo** and **Londa** past generations sit in their limestone balconies, watching over their progeny and paddy fields.

According to the Toraja, death is life's ultimate experience. Though mourning families wear black and symbolically sacrifice a cat to underscore their grief, funerals are actually celebrations replete with feasts and dancing that can last up to a week depending on the importance of the deceased. Tourists are welcome to attend and photograph funerals, which culminate with the blood sacrifice of pigs and water buffalo.

The Toraja live in large saddle-shaped houses whose high pitched roofs are covered with geometric designs and adorned with buffalo horns whose number and size is determined by the family's rank in the community.

The dead watch the living in Tanatoraja.

RANTEPAO

The main town in Torajaland, Rantepao has a number of hotels and restaurants as well as tour operators who can arrange trips to more colorful villages like **Kete** where life-size statues guard coffins. **Londa** offers more of the same with the additional benefit of actually being able to visit the caves and wander around the skeletons. If you arrive in town and have trouble finding the announced ceremony, simply stop the first stranger and ask for the *pesta mati*, the "party for the dead."

Where to Stay

Built around a quiet courtyard, the **Hotel Indra** (℡ (423) 97) at Jalan Pasar N° 63 has com-fortable double rooms for as low as $4. The hotel, which employs traditional Toraja architecture, also has a reasonably priced restaurant that looks out over a tropical garden.

Based on its occupancy rate, Rantepao's most popular hotel is the **Toraja Cottages** on Jalan Abdul Gani. But the best buy for the money is found at the **Marannu City Hotel** (℡ (423) 22028, 22221) in **Makale**. Located at Jalan Pongtiku N° 116-118, the Marannu's 40 rooms cost $42 during the summer tourist season ($6 extra for double occupancy), but can be had for as low as $34 in off peak months. The hotel has a jogging track and tennis court in addition to a swimming pool, and offers free transport to and from the airport.

At the other end of the spectrum are *wisma* guest houses where modestly furnished rooms are provided by a family. Tanatoraja, like Yogyakarta, has excellent guest houses that function like an Indonesian bed & breakfast. If you are traveling with children a *wisma* may be the best place to stay since the children of the host family are available playmates. The owners of **Wisma Maria** at the corner of Jalans Ratulangi and Mangadil across from the Sports Field do not have children, but their tastefully-decorated guest house has beautiful gardens and well lighted rooms that range in price from $4 to $10. Hot homemade bread is served each morning with breakfast.

Where to Eat

The **Restaurant Rachmat** on Jalan Abdul Gani in Rantepao has the best European cuisine in Torajaland. Almost as good, and quite a bit cheaper, is **Kios Mamba**, a modest yet excellently managed restaurant just north of Wisma Monika. The friendliest restaurant in Rantepao is **Chez Dodeng**, a family-run cafe on Jalan Mappanyuki diagonally across from the Hotel Victoria. The cafe provides excellent food and the English-speaking children also can furnish information on upcoming ceremonies and other attractions.

How to Get There

Most people visiting Rantepao for the first time try to drive one way and fly the other. During the dry season from April to September Merpati has ten flight a week to Makale. The alternative is to sign up for a tour or buy a ticket on the bus which takes ten hours to make the journey from Ujung Pandang.

The best times to visit are May and September. Definitely avoid the months of July and August when packs of French and German tourists fill every hotel in the region.

CENTRAL AND SOUTHEAST SULAWESI

Sulawesi is the third most visited island in the Indonesian Archipelago, but few tourists venture into the rugged and under-populated Central and Southeastern peninsulas. The main industry in the southeast is mining. Large nickel mines outside Soroako and smaller silver mines further south provide some employment and lots of crudely-fash-

ioned jewelry for sale in **Kendari**. The bulk of the province, however, is given over to subsistence farmers, many of them Balinese sent into the jungle under the government *transmigrasi* program. The farmers essentially are pioneers, sent from over-crowded to undeveloped areas. Because the land is so poor, the failure rate is high.

Beyond the capital of **Palu**, Central Sulawesi is mostly jungle. In theory, the province has an adequate network of roads, but in reality all movement comes to a halt during the rainy season.

Travel in these two provinces can be an adventure, but a day spent wrenching your jeep out of Central Sulawesi's thigh-deep mud can be tedious indeed, and a night spent camping beside the Wotu to Poso road may have you going *mano a mano* with some of the largest insects in the archipelago.

GENERAL INFORMATION

In Palu the Central Sulawesi Tourism Agency (((451) 21797) is located on Jalan Joyokadi. The Provincial Tourism Agency for Southeast Sulawesi is in Kendari at Jalan Mesjid Raya N° 1, ((401) 21764. The Department of Information also has regional offices in these two provinces. The Southeast Sulawesi office is in Kendari (✆ (401) 21311) at Jalan Imam Bonjol N° 78. In Palui call (451) 21121, 21221 or go by the DOI office on Jalan Dahlia.

NORTH SULAWESI

Northern Sulawesi is a rugged peninsula 777 km (482 miles) long by 103 km (64 miles) wide that is dominated by six extinct volcanoes and enormous coconut and clove plantations. Thanks to the rich volcanic soil

ippines than Indonesia. In contrast to Ujung Pandang, which exudes anarchic cacophony, Manado almost seems European. Here the Imam's call to prayer is replaced by church bells and the large wooden homes are fronted by rose gardens and white picket fences.

MANADO

The center of Minahasan culture is a sophisticated city of 300,000 people. Indonesians consider the fair skinned women of Manado

the Minahasan people are among the most prosperous in Indonesia.

Because of Northern Sulawesi's proximity to established trade routes, it was visited early and often by European sailors. The Minahasans hated the Portuguese and Spanish, however, and were forever grateful to the Dutch for ousting the Iberian Catholics. In return for their liberation the Minahasans by the early nineteenth century had embraced Protestantism, volunteered for the Dutch colonial army and become so loyal that Minahasa soon became known as the "twelfth province of Holland."

The people of Northern Sulawesi still refer to their province as Minahasa and often appear to have more in common with the Phil-

to be the most beautiful in the entire archipelago. Certainly they are the most westernized, preferring to wear tight tee shirts and blue jeans instead of the traditional *sarong kebaya*.

Largely rebuilt after World War II, Manado has few buildings of historical importance. The heart of the city is a commercial center called **Pasar 45**. From Pasar 45 you can walk south along Jalan Sam Ratulangi to the hotel and restaurant area, or north to the **Kuala Jenki** fish market.

Manado is a favorite spot for scuba enthusiasts. **Bunaken, Manado Tua** and **Siladen**

OPPOSITE: The size of the horns decorating a home indicates the family's position in the community.
ABOVE: Toraja villages are neat and orderly.

Sea Gardens are famous coral reefs that ring three small islands just offshore. Boats, snorkeling equipment and certified guides can be hired at the Nusantara Diving Club at Malalayang Beach. Experienced divers claim that the clear water, myriad varieties of fish and spectacular drop-offs make these reefs some of the best diving in the world.

General Information
In Manado the Directorate General of Tourism has a representative at Jalan Diponegoro N° 111, ((431) 51728. *DIPARDA*, the Pro-

vincial Tourist Service, is on Jalan Edi Gagola, ((431) 4299. If DIPARDA can't help you, try the Regional Department of Information office a few doors down Jalan Edi Gagola or call ((431) 53923 or 53052.

Where to Stay
Part of Indonesia's largest privately-owned hotel chain, the **Kawanua City Hotel** at Jalan Sam Ratulangi N° 1 has 100 rooms in the center of Manado. Rooms cost from $34 to $55 with executive suites going for $115. ((431) 52222; fax (431) 52220.

Less fancy but probably better value for your money is the **Hotel New Queen** (((431) 52979) at Jalan Wakeke N° 12-14. The New Queen has large comfortable rooms that start at $14.

Where to Eat
Minahasan food is an acquired taste. Actually, the taste isn't so bad. But you may suddenly develop bulimic tendencies when you discover that the juicy *kawaok* you washed down with Bintang beer was actually a fried forest rat. Stewed bat, goldfish (*ikan mas*) and dog cutlets with chili (*rintek wuuk*) also are local favorites. If you want to eat Minahasan fare, head for **Tinoor Jaya** or **Sehati** near the Minahasa Hotel. For the less adventurous there are a goodly number of Chinese restaurants along Jalan Sam Ratulangi. If you choose to simply skip dinner in favor of desert, try the Italian ice cream at **Turing** on Jalan Sam Ratulangi near the Hotel Japindra.

How to Get There
The most efficient schedule in and out of Manado belongs to Bouraq (((431) 2757) at Jalan Sarapung N° 27. In addition to daily flights to Gorontalo, Palu and Ujung Pandang, Bouraq also has reasonably priced daily service to Jakarta, Yogyakarta and Balikpapan.

Sempati flies six days a week to Jakarta and five to Medan. Contact ((21) 348760.

Heading to Irian Jaya? Then Garuda's thrice-weekly service to Biak and Jayapura is your best bet. If the Bouraq flights to Ujung Pandang and Jakarta are full, Garuda's daily service is a good alternative. Garuda can be reached by calling ((431) 51544 or going by the office at Jalan Diponegoro N° 15.

Merpati (((431) 4027) at Jalan Sam Ratulangi N° 138 flies to Jakarta and Surabaya only three times a week, but it has daily service to Ambon, Ternate and the Sangir-Talaud islands.

Also on Jalan Sam Ratulangi is the PELNI office (((431) 2844) that sells tickets for the *KM Kambuna*, a passenger steamer that makes a fortnightly loop to Java, Sulawesi, Kalimantan and Sumatra. Persons traveling by ship should be aware that, though many ships stop in Manado, Northern Sulawesi's main port is at Bitung on the eastern side of the peninsula.

There are three bus stations in Manado and, in theory, one can drive all the way to Palu. But the journey is extremely uncomfortable and takes several days.

ABOVE: The Minahasan people of Northern Sulawesi are English-speaking Catholics more culturally attuned to Manila than Jakarta.
OPPOSITE: Coral just below the surface of the clear, placid waters of Manado Tua.

Nusa Tenggara

NUSA TENGGARA, Indonesia's "Southeast Islands," stretch for more than 1,300 km (800 miles) from the eastern tip of Bali into the vastness of the Timor Sea. Dominated by the major islands of Lombok, Sumbawa, Sumba, Flores and Timor, Nusa Tenggara has only 4 percent of Indonesia's land and 2 percent of its population. Indeed, the ten million people of Nusa Tenggara often have been bypassed by the swirl of history. But though the area has no exotic spices or tillable plantation land, it is rich with the remnants of ancient Hindu kingdoms, Islamic sultanates and mysterious, megalithic tombs.

Prior to the arrival of the Portuguese, Chinese and Arab merchants frequented the islands of Nusa Tenggara, trading textiles, porcelain and metal implements for sandalwood, teak and tortoise shell. Though the Majapahit Empire claimed the entire region, Hinduism quickly succumbed to the advance of Islam. In 1512 the Portuguese arrived in search of sandalwood, the oil of which was an essential ingredient in sixteenth century perfume.

For the remainder of the sixteenth century the Portuguese clashed constantly with the Dutch over the control of Flores and Timor, the two islands that produced the best sandalwood. Portuguese military prowess began to wane, however, around the middle of the eighteenth century, and in 1859 Lisbon formally ceded all of its former possession, with the exception of East Timor, to the Dutch.

Although ruins of old fortifications are scattered throughout the islands, the absence of colonial exploitation has left Nusa Tenggara largely untouched by commercial development. The dominant feature of the region is the invisible Wallace Line, a 300-m (1,000-ft) deep channel that runs between Bali and Lombok. Named after the nineteenth century naturalist Alfred Russel Wallace, this biological and geological demarcation separates lands once linked to Australia from those attached to Southeast Asia's Sunda Shelf. Islands west of the line are blanketed with dense rain forests and jungles filled with monkeys, elephants and tigers. From Lombok eastward the islands become increasingly arid while wildlife is characterized by lizards, marsupials and exotic plumed birds.

Nusa Tenggara has no modern industry. It is only within the last few years that Merpati Nusantara has scheduled flights serving the major islands. The desert winds blowing north from Australia preclude the cultivation of rice. As a result, the starch-rich diet mostly consists of corn and sago.

Transportation can be unreliable, especially in the November to June rainy season, and tourist amenities are rather primitive. English is not widely spoken, and, apart from Lombok which produces some fine handicrafts, there is little but some interesting silver jewelry to be found.

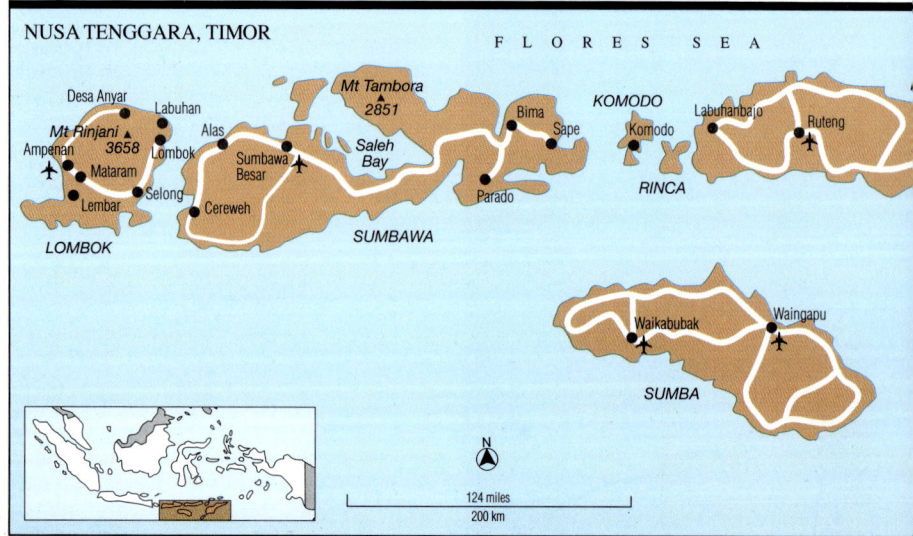

The one product Nusa Tenggara produces that is highly prized throughout the world is woven cotton cloth called *ikat*. In the Malay language *ikat* means "to tie," but in this process threads are tie-dyed before they are woven into intricately patterned shawls, scarves and sarongs.

Though traditionally made from hand spun cotton and dyed with natural tints, *ikat* material today often contains factory-made thread and synthetic dyes. One way to tell the (extremely rare) traditional piece from an artificially-aged copy is to study the colors, which are earthy brown, orange and indigo if made with natural inks.

When a cloth is ready to be dyed it is tied to a frame. Before being dipped into the vat of dye, certain portions of the design are wrapped with palm fiber or coconut leaf. When the thread is dipped, the bound parts reject the dye because of the tightly-bound knots. The batik cloth of central Java also is made using a dye-resistant technique, but its designs are created by using wax instead of knots.

Repeated immersions in different colored dyes can produce varied designs if the bindings are changed before dipping in a new color. Once the designs are in place on the vertical warp threads, the threads can be woven into the weft threads which are stretched on a back strap loom.

Ikat weaving was introduced into the archipelago between the fifth and second centuries B.C. by immigrants from northern Vietnam. These residents of the ancient kingdom of Annam brought with them the Dong Son culture which was based on magical animistic beliefs. Wiped out in regions where Hinduism, Buddhism and Islam took hold, remnants of the Dong Son culture exist today only among Sumatra's Lake Toba Bataks, the Toraja of Sulawesi, Borneo's Dyaks and various people of Nusa Tenggara.

In theory, Merpati Nusantara has scheduled departures to 20 towns in Nusa Tenggara, but flights often are canceled so reconfirmation of tickets is essential. Merpati also has a twice weekly flight from Darwin, Australia to Kupang in Timor that's a great way to sneak into Indonesia through the backdoor. But most people enter Nusa Tenggara from Bali, which has several daily flights from Denpasar to Lombok, Sumbawa and Timor.

LOMBOK

Located just east of Bali, the island of Lombok until recently was a backwater known mostly for the fact that the deep strait separating it from Bali marks the division between lands linked to Australia and those attached to Southeast Asia. Today, developers have discovered its deserted beaches and are hoping to turn it into the next Bali.

Lombok has a population slightly over two million, 80 percent of which are Islamic Sasaks living in the arid eastern part of the island. Officially Muslim since the sixteenth century, the Sasaks live in traditional farming villages that provide most of the island's food in addition to baskets, brightly colored textiles, terra cotta ceramics and rough wood carvings. In general, the mountain-dwelling Sasaks are much poorer than the Balinese (10 percent of the population) who inhabit Lombok's western shore. Here Balinese food, customs and festivals prevail,

and prevailing rains allow rice cultivation in the area of the island's capital, **Mataram**. Around **Selong**, however, Nusa Tenggara's arid nature becomes more pronounced and rice paddies give way to plots of cotton, coffee and tobacco.

Lombok was settled in the fourteenth century by Hindu traders from Java. Several centuries later, Lombok's native Sasaks allowed neighboring Balinese to colonize the western portion of their island in return for help fighting Moslems from nearby Sumbawa. Balinese Hindus then set about enslaving the Sasaks, who immediately converted to Islam and began conspiring with the Dutch. The Sasaks finally gained revenge in 1894 when they took the unusual action of inviting the Dutch to Lombok to help them expel the Raja of Bali.

GENERAL INFORMATION

The Provincial Tourist Service, *DIPARDA* Nusa Tenggara, is located at Jalan Langko N° 70 in Mataram. ((364) 21730, 21866.

WHAT TO SEE

Whether the visitor seeks natural beauty or a fascinating culture, Lombok has much to offer. Indonesia's second highest volcano, the 3,658 m (12,000 ft) **Mt. Rinjani** with its sacred waterfalls and crater lake presides over a landscape dotted with temples, mosques and churches that testify to a rich and complex history. Weavers, woodcarvers and basket makers produce some of the country's finest handicrafts. Best of all, Lombok, at least for the moment, remains a place of quiet seclusion.

Horses still provide much of the transportation on the island. Indeed, a traffic jam in **Mataram**, the capital, or in **Ampenan**, the old port, is a congestion of colorfully decorated horse-drawn carts called *cidomos*.

The main Hindu temple, the **Pura Meru**, stands at the central crossroads of **Cakranegara**, a few kilometers inland from Mataram. Built in 1720 to unify Lombok's various Hindu factions, the inner courtyard has three pagodas symbolizing the Hindu trinity of Brahma, Vishnu and Shiva. The **Royal Palace** opposite the temple has a large water garden called the **Puri Mayura**. A pond filled with pink and white lotus surrounds a pavilion that once served as the court of justice and meeting place for Lombok's nobles.

In the late nineteenth century, the Balinese king built a **summer palace**, an elaborate complex of terraced gardens and ponds, about 10 km (six miles) east of Cakranegara in the volcanic hills. Lombok's Hindus revere the temple at **Suranadi** six-and-a-half kilometers (four miles) further up the mountain because of its holy springs. Nearby, the Suranadi Hotel, formerly a royal pleasure garden looking out over terraced rice fields, has fresh goldfish on the menu.

Hikers can make a strenuous two-day ascent of **Mt. Rinjani,** whose pine-rimmed crater lake, Segara Negara, is believed to be the throne room of the mountain gods. The summit towers 1,200 m (4,000 ft) above the lake, which feeds streams that cascade over cliffs into hot springs below. It is possible to climb Rinjani without a guide, but for the bargained-down price of $90 to $100 an experienced guide will take you through the tangle of criss-crossing trails and show where to rent sleeping bags and an appropriate sized tent.

For the less energetic, Lombok offers **Kute Beach**, a 100-km (62-mile) stretch of deserted sand and surf on the island's south coast that is a bit reminiscent of the way Bali's Kuta Beach looked 30 years ago.

WHERE TO STAY

Though tourist development is just beginning, Lombok has dozens of inexpensive

intimate atmosphere to the resort where poolside rooms cost $95 (double or single). The hotel has 156 rooms. Jalan Raya Senggigi Km N° 8, ((364) 933333 fax (364) 93140.

Much less fancy but equally pleasant is the **Pondok Senggigi**, a garden bungalow motel just down the beach. Individual bungalows start at $7 with smaller attached rooms fronting on a garden going for about half that amount.

The third major resort, **Lombok Intan Laguna**, has 220 rooms arrayed about the island's largest lagoon. The Intan has tennis

hostels and bungalows, and a few excellent hotels. Remember, however, when negotiating the price of your room, that you must add an additional 21 percent government service charge and tax to the basic room rate.

The **Senggigi Beach Hotel**, P.O. Box 2, Mataram ((364) 93210–19, fax (364) 31200, has beautiful grounds, superb service, a range of facilities including tennis courts that compliment 150 rooms, all facing the sea. Standard rooms list for $70, $95 for double occupancy. Deluxe beach bungalows cost $130. Despite the fixed prices, ask for a 30 percent corporate discount, more if you happen to be there during the rainy season.

The extensive palm-fringed lagoon at the **Sheraton Senggigi Beach Resort** lends an

and squash courts plus a fitness center, drug store and shopping arcade. Rooms are $70 for single occupancy; $75 for a double. All credit cards. P.O. Box 50, Senggigi, ((364) 23680.

WHERE TO EAT

The cuisine in central and eastern Lombok falls a few notches below basic. Australian hippies occasionally will open macrobiotic vegetarian restaurants at Kuta Beach on the south coast, but for the most part it's best to

OPPOSITE: Lombok nobility built the Puri Mayura water garden. ABOVE: Fishermen cast their nets off the Lombok coast.

stick with fool-proof dishes like *sate ayam* and *nasi goreng*.

But don't despair. On the western portion of the island you can sample the local favorite, buffalo curry, or try the more palatable *ayam pelicing*, hot curried chicken.

In Ampenan the best food is found at **Cirebon**, a Chinese-Indonesian restaurant on Jalan Yos Sudarso. Cirebon's owners also run the **Pabean** restaurant next door, which features a variety of fresh seafood dishes. Washed down with icy bottles of Bintang beer, dinner for two at either restaurant should

come to no more than $7. Several other good Indonesian cafes are located in the Mataram Shopping Center off Jalan Pejanggik.

At Senggigi Beach, the **Senggigi Beach Hotel** has the most elaborate dining room with meals starting at $6.50. Food equally tasty, but more moderately priced, can be found at the **Pondok Senggigi's** open air restaurant, the area's most popular gathering spot.

In Lombok's major market town, **Cakranegara**, try the garlic fried chicken at **Taliwang** on Jalan Rajawali and the satay at **Rumah Makan Madya 2** on Jalan Hasanuddin.

Balinese temples can be found along Lombok's western coast.

WHAT TO BUY

Antique shops in Ampenan carry three grades of baskets ranging from delicate ones made of horse hair-sized fibers to ones large enough to use as clothes hampers. Jug-shaped, round-bellied baskets sell for $20 on Lombok, about half the price on Bali and a third of what it would cost in Jakarta. There are two or three excellent stores (none of which accept credit cards), the best of which is **Sudirman** at Jalan Pabean N° 16A.

Lombok textiles use a rainbow of colors to create striped panels which are sewn together to make sarongs. Equally distinctive is the terra-cotta ware, especially in the village of Penujak where a cooperative of local artisans turns out bowls, jugs and mammoth water jars. In contrast to sinuous Balinese masks and statues, Lombok wood carvings tend to have strong, primitive lines. Sexual motifs are common, as are dragons which decorate the tops of medicine containers and special boxes that hold spurs for fighting cocks.

HOW TO GET THERE

Mataram's Selaparang Airport is served by Garuda and Merpati, both of which have daily flights to and from the island. Garuda has numerous daily flights between Mataram and Denpasar, and once-a-day service to Surabaya in east Java. Merpati has daily flights to Sumbawa Besar and Bima on Sumbawa.

Two ferries, one at 9 am and the other at 12 noon, leave from Lembar on Lombok's west coast for Padangbai on Bali. Tickets can be bought on the wharf or at ticket offices in Mataram and Ampenan. Three daily ferries leaving at 8 am, 11 am and 12 noon make the shorter voyage from Labuhan on the east coast of Lombok to Poto Tano on Sumbawa.

For people with plenty of time and not too much luggage, a PELNI passenger ship, the *Kelimutu*, makes a two-week long circuit from Semarang in Java to Kupang in Timor with intermediate stops in Ende (Flores), Waingapu (Sumba), Bima (Sumbawa), Ujung Pandang (Sulawesi), Lembar (Lombok), Padangbai (Bali), Surabaya (Java) and Banjarmasin (Kalimantan). The *Kelimutu* is clean and efficient, and gives a real feel for the islands, but passengers wishing to travel first class should reserve space well in advance.

SUMBAWA

A towering, rugged island dominated by irregularly shaped peninsulas and eroded volcanic ridges, Sumbawa is another transition island in which verdant valleys blanketed with Asian rice paddies gradually give way to antipodean savannas. Barren, rocky and unapproachable by sea, the south coast is largely uninhabited. Nearly all of Sumbawa's 900,000 people live in the northern river valleys which are linked to **Sumbawa Besar**, the island capital the by a surprisingly good highway. Traveling across the island is easy even during the November to April rainy season, but real explorers will want to take the dirt roads off the highway to visit the island's Islamic hamlets.

BACKGROUND

For centuries Sumbawa was nothing more than a place marauding Makassarese from south Sulawesi came to for slave labor. Ironically, the Sumbawans embraced the Islamic religion of those who came to pillage, and formed a series of small sultanates along the north shore. Domination by Makassar was ended by the Dutch East India Company, which established a benign hegemony beginning in 1669. Despite excellent harbors and a fertile interior, the Dutch never established a colonial presence and today there is little tangible evidence that they came at all.

The most dramatic event in Sumbawa's history occurred in 1815 when Mt. Tambora exploded, killing 10,000 people outright and forcing two-thirds of the survivors to permanently flee the island. For the past century people have been encouraged to move to Sumbawa from other, more crowded parts of the archipelago. As a result, the present population is a cultural polyglot.

GENERAL INFORMATION

There are no tourism offices on Sumbawa. PHPA, the Indonesian Directorate of Nature Conservation, is a source of information about Komodo and the nature reserve on Moyo Island at the mouth of Saleh Bay. The PHPA office at Jalan GarudaN° 12 in Sumbawa Besar has maps and background information about the western half of the island. The PHPA office (open Monday to Thursday 8 am to 2 pm; Friday until 11 am) on Jalan Pelabuhan in Sape controls access to Komodo and should be visited before catching the ferry.

WHAT TO SEE

The main attraction in Sumbawa Besar is the former sultan's palace, **Dalem Loka**. Built entirely of wood and resting on stilts, the palace was remodeled in 1980 but still retains a seedy tropical elegance.

Persons with three days to spare and plenty of stamina can take a motorboat from Sumbawa Besar across Saleh Bay to the village of Cilacai, hire a guide and climb **Mt. Tambora**. Most travelers, however, take a bus to **Bima**, Sumbawa's most stridently Islamic city, or travel direct to **Sape**, the jumping off point for Komodo and Flores islands, on the eastern end of the island.

WHERE TO STAY

Sumbawa Besar has a number of *losmen* that cost around $3.50 a night. The best hotel in town is the **Tambora** on Jalan Kebayan N° II. Rooms cost from $11 to $25 depending on the amenities, but the Tambora's most valuable services are the knowledge and efficiency with which it assists its guests. The **Hotel Parewa** in Bima has air conditioned rooms for $27.

WHERE TO EAT

In Bima the **Hotel Parewa's** restaurant has an extensive Indonesian menu. The only place to get a cold beer with dinner in Bima is at **Losmen Lila Graha**, which serves tasty, reasonably priced food.

In Sumbawa Besar, eat at the **Hotel Tambora** or take a taxi to **Tirtasari**, a suburban hotel known more for its restaurant than its rooms.

How to Get There

Merpati has a daily 9:30 am flight to Sumbawa Besar from Denpasar with an intermediate stop at Mataram. There also are frequent Merpati flights into Bima from Ende on the island of Flores.

The ferry from Lombok to Alas on Sumbawa's northwestern tip takes 90 minutes. There are three ferries a day, each of which is met by a bus that goes to Sumbawa Besar.

The PELNI office on Sumbawa is in Bima at Jalan Pelabuhan N° 103, ℂ (271) 45203.

KOMODO

Between the islands of Sumbawa and Flores lies an arid and inhospitable jumble of rock called Komodo. It is the land time forgot, the desolate home of the Komodo Dragon.

The large monitor lizards weigh more than 150 kg (334 pounds) and attain a length of three meters (10 ft). Their claws are like talons, their serrated teeth razor sharp. The dragons' saliva is toxic, the better to digest the horn and bone of their favorite meal: the goat. One swipe of their tail can fell a man. They are the earth's land sharks, an animal that lives to eat.

Komodo is not a good place to economize, so don't waste time wandering about alone. Hire a guide to show you around. The dragons feed all year around, but are peppiest during the May to September hot season. For around $30 a congenial group of fellow travelers should be able to buy a goat, which the guide will butcher and string up. At that point you can switch on your motor drive and wait for dinner to begin.

Where to Stay

The **PHPA camp** at **Loh Liang** consists of a number of wooden cabins, each of which has four to five rooms arrayed about a common living area. The rooms each hold two people and cost about $7.50 a night. There is a small restaurant at the camp, but its menu is very limited.

It is possible to walk from Loh Liang into the tiny fishing village of **Kampung Komodo**, but don't expect to find restaurant cuisine. Persons spending more than one night on Komodo definitely should bring their own canned food and bottled drinks.

HOW TO GET THERE

Requests to visit the Komodo Island National Park can be made to the Indonesian Directorate of Nature Conservation on Sumbawa. The agency will direct you toward the ferry to Komodo and provide the opportunity to hire a guide and a sacrificial goat upon arrival. Bring a telephoto lens.

The ferry to Komodo leaves Pelabuhan, Sape, once a week on Saturday. A weekly ferry from Labuhanbajo on Flores to Komodo leaves each Tuesday. Both ferries depart at 8 am An additional nominal charge for transfer from the ferry to the shore is levied once you arrive at Komodo. Persons in a hurry usually can charter a boat from Labuhanbajo for $50. The boat will wait while you spend three hours looking for dragons, then return to Flores in the late afternoon. Charters from Sumbawa cost substantially more and require an overnight stay since the distance is much greater.

FLORES

Second in size to Timor, Flores is so remote that the Dutch exiled Sukarno here during the 1930s. Located atop Indonesia's most active geological fault, Flores is home to 14 active volcanoes, which cause repeated earthquakes throughout the year. Mountains covered with forests and pristine alpine lakes provide a succession of panoramas, but hundreds of narrow gorges bespeak Flores' violent geological past.

Earthquakes and landslides make travel difficult on Flores. The island's roads constantly are being cleaved or crumbled. Movement is further slowed during the November to April rainy season when flash floods join the list of natural disasters. With more than 1,360,000 people, Flores is Nusa Tenggara's most populous island, but the rugged terrain limits development and preserves many cultural idiosyncrasies of the Malay and Papuan ethnic groups.

BACKGROUND

When Java's Majapahit Empire collapsed in the fifteenth century, the Islamic sultans of Powa (Sulawesi) and Ternate (Maluku) immediately began fighting to control the island. Their behavior must have displeased the locals because when the Portuguese arrived in 1512 the population quickly embraced the Catholic faith.

The Portuguese called the island "Cabo das Flores," an especially peculiar description given the fact that the eastern part where they landed is noticeably devoid of flowers. Vivid "coral gardens," however, do blossom in the tropical water offshore.

By 1683 the Dutch East India Company had taken over the island's trade in cinnamon and sandalwood, but Portuguese Dominican missionaries managed to hang on for another 250 years. Today 90 percent of the population is Catholic.

WHAT TO SEE

Though ostensibly Catholic, the people of Flores have many animistic beliefs, most of which stem from the magical, **multicolored lakes** of Mt. Keli Mutu. Set in the craters of extinct volcanoes at an elevation of 1,400 m (4,600 ft), the three lakes are constantly changing color: sometimes appearing green, black and red; at other times purple, blue and black. Many people believe the souls of the dead reside in the lakes. The green lake receives the honest folk, while the enfeebled

OPPOSITE, LEFT: Komodo dragons are prehistoric raptors with serrated teeth. RIGHT: It's wise to hire a guide on the island of Komodo. ABOVE: Volcanoes and earthquakes keep Flores undeveloped.

sink into the red. Thieves and murders sink to the bottom of the black lake.

Skin and scuba divers who arrive in Flores during the dry season are in luck for that is the best time to rent a snorkel and swim around the coral heads off the coast of **Maumere** on the northeast coast. The best place to rent a boat is **Waiara**, about 16 km (10 miles) east of the city. Snorkeling is excellent right off the coast, but more experienced divers may want to head to the offshore islands where the coral formations are said to be more dramatic.

The best place to buy *ikat* cloth is probably **Ruteng**, inland on the western half of the island, which has a colorful market. If vendors down from the surrounding hills don't have the quality you desire, take a taxi to the nearby village of **Cibal where** *ikat* weaving thrives as a cottage industry.

WHERE TO STAY

There are no large tourist hotels in **Ruteng** so most travelers end up at the **Wisma Agung I** at Jalan Wae Cos N° 10, ℂ 80. Rooms with a private *mandi* go for $7 a night. **Wisma Sindha** is slightly cheaper and closer to the center of the city, but unlike Agung I it has no restaurant.

Most *losmen* in the island capital of **Ende** charge around $5 for bed and breakfast. Stop by **Wisma Amica** at Jalan Garuda N° 15 first to see if it has space. Its owner speaks English and can help arrange tours.

Prices in **Maumere** are a bit higher — around $14 to $20 for an air-conditioned room or bungalow — but the quality is better. Air conditioned bungalows at **Losmen Maiwali** look out on a small aviary and tropical garden, and are only a few steps from an outdoor restaurant. Out from the center of Maumere close to the airport, the **Permata Sari Inn** has large rooms close to the Flores Sea.

At an elevation of more than 1,000 m (3,300 ft), the hill town of **Bajawa**, about halfway between Ruteng and Ende, offers a temperate, tranquil break from Nusa Tenggara's usual heat and humidity. Try to arrive on a market day and spend the night at **Losmen Kembang** at 18 Jalan Diponegoro. Continental breakfast and a large room with adjoining *mandi* cost $10.

With only 30,000 people, **Larantuka** the port town on the eastern extremity of the island, is where Flores' Portuguese heritage is most visible. Catholic feast days are celebrated with passion and the chef at **Penginapan Rulies Inn** will make Portuguese African chicken on request. Rooms there range from $3 to $6.

WHERE TO EAT

Most of the *losmen* recommended above have attached restaurants that offer fresh, affordable food. Portuguese cooking can be found in Larantuka and Maumere, but elsewhere the only respite from *gado gado*, the ubiquitous salad, is the occasional Chinese restaurant.

HOW TO GET THERE

Thrice weekly ferries depart Sape on Sumbawa for Labuhanbajo on Flores west coast. Regular ferry service also links Larantuka on the east coast with Timor. The PELNI office in Ende is at Jalan Pabean N° 6, (43. PELNI's *Kelimutu* makes regular stops at Ende, but most travelers end up taking a plane.

From Denpasar, Merpati has daily flights into Ende and Ruteng. There also are several flights out of Bima into Flores' two largest cities. Westbound flights from Kupang on Timor make daily stops Ende, Maumere and Ruteng, and land at Larantuka on Monday and Thursday. Daily flights also link Maumere with Ujung Pandang. During the rainy season when Flores' highways become impassable, Merpati adds flights between Labuhanbajo and Ende.

TIMOR

A large island with a split personality, Timor for centuries was split down the middle: half Dutch, half Portuguese. Due to the extended colonial rule, Protestants in West Timor and Catholics in the East account for nearly 50 percent of the island's two million people, the remainder of whom are animists. Merpati's twice weekly flights from Darwin

The crater lakes of Mt. Keli Mutu change colors depending on atmospheric conditions and the time of day.

to **Kupang**, the island's capital on the western peninsula of the island, have opened the island to travelers, but there has been little development beyond Kupang.

Bisected by a towering volcanic mountain chain that soars to 2,600 m (8,600 ft) at its midpoint, Gunung Tata Mai, Timor alternates between periods of drought and torrential rain (November to March). Originally, the economy was based on beeswax and sandalwood, but all the sandalwood trees have been cut. Today, Timor's broad savanna supports only acacia and lontar palms.

BACKGROUND

Settled by the aboriginal Atoni, Timor was little more than a gaggle of petty kingdoms until the arrival of the Portuguese in the early sixteenth century. When Melaka fell to the Dutch in 1641, the control of Timor, and its valuable sandalwood, came into dispute. Finally, in 1904 the two European countries divided the island. Occupied by the Japanese and heavily bombed by the Allies in World War II, the island's western half became part of Indonesia following the Dutch departure. But East Timor remained a Portuguese colony until 1974 when Lisbon abruptly gave its tiny possession independence.

Fearing that an independent enclave within the archipelago might inspire other islands to rebel, Indonesia invaded East Timor in December 1975 and brutally disbanded the two indigenous political parties. The Revolutionary Front for the Independence of East Timor, known by the acronym Fretilin, doggedly fought back, but eventually was defeated. The Indonesian army's campaign of extermination resulted in the death of one sixth of East Timor's entire population. Open to tourism since 1989, East Timor appears tranquil, but lingering tension and continued police surveillance make it difficult to speak candidly with the citizenry.

GENERAL INFORMATION

The West Timor Regional Office of Tourism is located in Kupang at Jalan Sukarno N° 129. ((391) 21160. The Provincial Tourist Service is at Jalan Jend. Basuki Rachmat N° 1,

((391) 21540. Recently opened in Dili, the East Timor Tourist Office is on Jalan Dr. Carvalito, ((391) 2649.

WHAT TO SEE

The **East Nusa Tenggara Museum** is located in east **Kupang** on Jalan Perintis Kemerdekaan. Exhibits are labeled in English as well as Bahasa Indonesia, and helpful docents are glad to answer questions. The museum has excellent examples of traditional *ikat* weaving, which should be examined before heading to the market.

Kupang's main market, **Pasar Inpres**, is in the southern portion of the city on Jalan Suharto. Remember to bargain for all items you wish to purchase, making sure the seller initiates the process by giving his price. If you don't see what you want in the way of *ikat* cloth, visit **Dharma Bakti** at Jalan Sumba N° 32. In addition to sandalwood oil, this store has well made *ikat* sarongs and blankets from Timor and surrounding islands. The prices are high, but Kupang is cheaper that either Java or Bali.

After a hard day of shopping the best place to cool off is **Teddy's Bar** at Jalan Ikan Tongkol N° 1-3, ((391) 21142. Beloved by Australians, it is the best spot to meet foreigners, and the only bar in the city that has fancooled upstairs rooms for weary revelers.

To the east of Kupang the town of **Soe** also has an excellent market that hums with activity on Wednesdays when people from surrounding villages come into town to sell their crafts. Not much English is spoken here, so practice a few Indonesian phrases before negotiating a price.

Heavily bombed during World War II and selectively ravaged in the campaign against Fretilin, East Timor has few colonial landmarks to evoke its Portuguese past. The town of **Baukau** several hours drive east of **Dili**, the island's second city on the northeast coast, has a certain "forgotten corner of the world" charm that complements miles of deserted beach, but tourist amenities are minimal. Dili itself has several good restaurants and hotels but it lacks the nightlife of Kupang.

Instead of traveling overland from Kupang to East Timor, travelers well may want to hop on a Perum ASPP ferry for the thrice weekly, four-hour trip to **Roti**, the island off the western tip of Timor.

Former allies of the Dutch who prospered in Dutch Missionary Society schools, Rotinese today follow a curious blend of Dutch Reformed Protestantism and animism. Islanders pause frequently for ritual celebrations that mark every phase of life from pregnancy and birth to a child's first step and the advance of puberty.

The island's economy is based on the cultivation of the lontar palm which provides dozens of products including the distinctive palm leaf hats that vaguely resemble the helmets worn by Portuguese conquistadors.

WHERE TO STAY

The fanciest hotel in **Kupang** is the **Sasando International** (((391) 22224) on Jalan Perintis Kemerdekaan. It has air-conditioned rooms that start at $40. Less expensive but equally popular is the **Hotel Flobamor II** at Jalan Sudirman N° 21, ((391) 21346. The **Laguna Inn** (((391) 21559) and **Wisma Kupang Indah** (((391) 21919) are centrally located on Jalan Kelimutu. Both offer moderately priced rooms in the $16 range. The Laguna can be a bit wild at night, so opt for the latter if traveling *en famille*.

Wisma Bahagia in **Soe** has adequate rooms for $13 a night and a good restaurant. It is located at Jalan Diponegoro N° 72, (15.

Dili has several new hotels in the $13 a night range the government hopes will attract foreign tourists. The **Turismo Beach Hotel**, (22029, on Avenida Marechal Carmona has large rooms with balconies and a view of the sea. Similar accommodations can be found at the **New Resende Inn** on Avenida Bispo Medeiros N° 5.

HOW TO GET THERE

Served by Garuda, Merpati, Bouraq and Sempati, Kupang is fast becoming the transportation hub of the entire region. Merpati flies into Kupang from Darwin twice a week. Daily nonstops also link Kupang with Dili. From Kupang you can fly to all of the islands in Nusa Tenggara, if not on a daily basis, at least several times each week.

Kupang also serves as a major marine terminal for PELNI, which has an office at Jalan Pahlawan N° 3 (((391) 21944) near the bus terminal. PELNI's *Elang* loops around the Timor Archipelago, as do the *Baruna Eka* and the *Baruna Fajar*. If no PELNI ship is available on the day you want to travel, check the Perum ASPP ferry office at Jalan Cak Doko N° 20, ((391) 21140. Open from 8 am to 4 pm. Perum ASPP sells tickets in advance for ferries that provide speedy, inexpensive transport to Roti, Sawu and the Flores port of Larantuka.

SAWU

South of the Sulu Sea midway between Roti and Sumba lies the enchanting island of Sawu. Neither strategic nor economically important, Sawu was largely ignored for centuries. The result today is a culture organized around a succession of animistic festivals, animal sacrifice, clan alliances and the phases of the moon. When Capt. James Cook and the crew of the *H.M.S. Endeavor* accidentally stumbled across the island in 1770 they were so entranced that they ended up staying for five weeks.

On Sawu the men consider themselves warriors. Instead of entering into ritual combat, however, they exhibit controlled aggression in dances with sensuous maidens in tight sarongs. The highest ranking priest on the island is called the *deo rai* or "lord of

Ceremonial dress for a Sumba tribesman.

the earth." His assistant, the *apu lodo*, is "the descendant of the sun." Together they worship a variety of spirits, but, in reality, life for the 60,000 people of Sawu springs from the lontar palm.

From the palm comes a juice that is cooling and sweet when fresh, and mildly intoxicating when allowed to ferment into a wine called tuak. Boiled into syrup palm juice becomes the base for a soup. If boiled a bit further it turns into palm sugar that can be molded into blocks and stored for months without refrigeration.

When a baby comes into the world on Sawu he is given a symbolic sip of palm juice before receiving mother's milk. And when that child grows old and eventually dies he will be buried in a coffin hollowed from the omnipotent lontar palm.

Those who venture to Sawu, however, will find some fine Indonesian *ikat* weaving.

HOW TO GET THERE

Merpati flies to Sawu twice a week on Wednesday and Saturday. Ferries from

Sawu horsemen delighted Captain James Cook when he sailed through the archipelago.

Kupang depart with similar frequency. Sawu also is visited fortnightly by PELNI's *Baruna Fajar.*

SUMBA

Known for its intricate ikat fabric, distinctive architecture and sculptured stone tombs, Sumba, like neighboring Sawu, has resisted the advances of the twentieth century. With a population of 400,000, this 11,250 sq km (4,350 sq mile) island midway between Sumbawa and Timor is covered by dusty grasslands and eucalyptus savannah. Sporadic rain from November to March sustains subsistence agriculture on the western half of the island, but on the scrubby plateaus of the east there is little to do save weave ikat and raise horses.

Life on Sumba revolves around fortified villages where ancestors are worshipped by extended families living in enormous clan houses which are built on raised platforms and topped with high-pitched thatch roofs. In the past, women who reached puberty were tattooed and had their teeth filed, but these customs are dying out. Ancestor worship and the custom of preserving sacred textiles remain strong.

WHAT TO SEE

The period from July to October is marked by festival dances, bloody *pajura* boxing matches in which men pummel each other with fists wrapped in thorny leaves. In West Sumba simulated battles called *pasolas* in which clans bash shields and scream are conducted in February and March. Accompanied by a chorus of women trilling the karakul, a high-pitched cry, once used as a greeting for conquering headhunters, the mock wars are fought by mounted horsemen with wooden swords. **Kodi** and **Lamboya** are popular battle sites, as are **Gaura** and **Wanokaka**.

Courtesy demands that the local village chief welcome foreign visitors into his home. In return, travelers should be prepared to reciprocate the generosity with gifts of *tuak wine*, cartons of cigarettes and canned food.

The most elaborate ceremonies, however, accompany the re internment of briefly buried mummies in concrete vaults that are sealed with elaborately carved stone slabs. Performed in traditional coastal villages such as **Mani** and **Rende**, the funerals are accompanied by vigorous dancing, costumed processions and bloody animal sacrifices.

WHERE TO STAY

In **Waikabubak**, in the west of the island, there is only one hotel, the **Rakuta**, which

that bespeak decades of torpor and cold-water washing.

WHERE TO EAT

The only formal restaurants in Waingapu are at the **Sandal Wood** and **Surabaya** hotels. If you are in the mood for fried rice and satay, save some money and snack at the roadside *warungs* near the intersection of Jalan Hatta and Jalan Sudirman. In Waikabubak the best food comes from tiny *warungs* and diners called *rumah makans*.

has large rooms with attached *mandi* for $20 a night. In **Waingapu** near the east coast, and most accessible from Mauhau airport, the best hotel is the **Sandal Wood** (℄ (387) 117) at Jalan Panjaitan N° 23. Air-conditioned rooms complete with breakfast at the Sandal Wood could cost $25, but the rate is very negotiable. The **Hotel Surabaya** (℄ (387) 125) at Jalan Eltari N° 2 has no air-conditioning, but the rooms are large and usually cost a few dollars less than the prevailing rate at the Sandal Wood. People into faded, turn-of-the-century colonialism should consider checking into the **Hotel Elim** (℄ (387) 180) at Jalan Yani N° 55. Illuminated by bulbs of indeterminate wattage, the Elim's fan-cooled rooms are furnished with sway-back beds and mosquito nets

HOW TO GET THERE

Despite being off the beaten track, Sumba has airports outside Waingapu and Waikabubak with Waingapu's Mauhau Airport the more accessible. Flights from Jakarta, Surabaya, Denpasar, Kupang and Bima land at Mauhau several times a week. Merpati also has thrice-weekly nonstops into Waikabubak's Tambolaka Airport from Kupang and Bima. Regularly scheduled ferries from Sawu, Ende and Kupang land at Waingapu.

Ocean-going ferries keep most of far-flung Nusa Tenggara accessible.

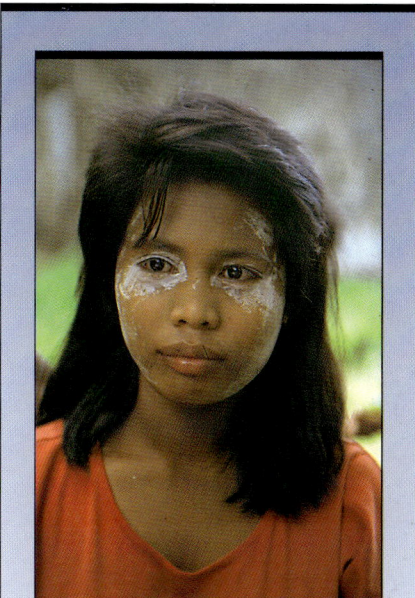

Maluku

NO THREE WORDS in the English language are more evocative of romance, adventure and exotic wanderlust than "The Spice Islands." Just hearing the words makes one imagine swaying palms, tawny native maidens and villages redolent with aroma of coconut, nutmeg and clove. Rarely, however, do we think of spices as basic agricultural commodities. But that is what they are, and 500 years ago they were worth more than their weight in gold.

In the beginning, spices were used as preservatives and breath fresheners. The Han emperors of China chewed cloves, which they called *"fragrant nails,"* prior to royal audiences; Egyptians used them in the embalming process. Later, the Romans used cloves to scent the air in their temples.

It was the Arabs, however, who began the lucrative spice trade. Remembering from the Crusades how bland European food tasted, Arab merchants began selling nutmeg and mace to Venetians at exorbitant prices. Seemingly overnight Europeans were hooked on cinnamon and pepper. They even began adding nutmeg to their alé. The age of exploration that began in the thirteenth century with the voyages of Marco Polo was not a quest for abstract knowledge, but rather an attempt to bypass the Arab-Venetian spice monopoly.

But where were the Spice Islands? The Venetians didn't know and the Arabs wouldn't say. In 1492 Christopher Columbus sailed west looking for the fabled East Indies, but ran into North America instead, much to the dismay of Spain's monarchy who found corn and tobacco poor substitutes for cloves and cinnamon. No European had a clue as to where the Spice islands were until 1511 when Alfonso de Albuquerque conquered Malacca, the key Asian entrepôt of the spice trade, and claimed it for Portugal.

Albuquerque sent three caravels east with Malay pilots. After skirting the Lesser Sundas they finally arrived at the Banda Islands. The three ships immediately filled their holds with cloves, nutmeg and mace. On the way back to Malacca one ship was blown off course and landed at Ternate, which was equally rich with spice. For the next nine years until the remains of Ferdinand Magellan's Spanish flotilla reached Tidore, the Portuguese had the Spice islands all to themselves.

In most respects the Spanish voyage was a failure. Magellan was killed in the Philippines. The Spice islands turned out to lie just inside the Portuguese sphere of influence delineated in the 1494 Treaty of Tordesillas. Only one of Magellan's five ships ever returned to Spain and 212 of the original 230 Spanish seamen perished. But the four tons of cloves that one ship was able to bring back more than paid the Spanish crown's expenses and made the 18 surviving seamen wealthy beyond their wildest dreams.

The 1,000 islands of Maluku constitute one of the most remote provinces of Indonesia. The islands are scattered over an area larger than Borneo with a population of 1.7 million people, but because of infrequent transportation many islands remain unexplored with their deep seas, mangrove swamps and coral reefs. North Maluku includes the original clove islands, Ternate and Tidore plus the Bacon, Obi and Sula archipelagos. Southeast Maluku is rarely visited. Central Maluku includes Banda, the large yet rarely visited islands of Buru and Seram, and the administrative and transportation center of Ambon.

The islands of Maluku are diverse in both culture and geography. Three of the earth's great tectonic plates meet here and, as a result, many islands are volcanic cones that rise abruptly from the sea. The outer arc of islands towards the Arafura Sea, however, are fringed with coral, white sand beaches

ABOVE: Old forts built by the Portuguese and Dutch dot the Spice Islands. OPPOSITE: Islands of the Maluku seen from the air.

MALUKU (NORTH)

Ambon is one of the few places in Maluku that prospered under the Portuguese. So many Ambonese married Portuguese soldiers that when the Dutch arrived many islanders were Catholic. Even under rigid Dutch rule Ambon operated as a free port, welcoming Arab and Chinese traders. When Anna Forbes arrived during the British interregnum caused by the Napoleonic Wars, she described the city as "the most salubrious of towns.

"It is situated on a long, river-like arm of the sea, and commands a fine prospect over the water to the mountains beyond, while it is encircled by verdure-clad slopes, to which shady, arbor-like roads lead from the center of town."

Originally only four square kilometers, Ambon today is constantly being expanded

MALUKU (SOUTH)

and towering palm trees. Those central to the spice trade have sophisticated populations that speak several languages. But large islands like Halmahera, Seram and Buru have natives still influenced by the megalithic stone culture of their ancestors.

Ironically, not much remains of the once fabled spice trade. Grenada produces most of the world's nutmeg. Zanzibar grows more cloves. Today, the most valuable cash crop is copra, followed by cacao and coffee.

The most lasting legacy of colonialism is Christianity. Saint Francis Xavier, the Basque priest who was one of the founders of the Jesuits, established missions in the Moluccas between 1546 and 1547. Today more than half of Ambon's population is Christian.

AMBON

BACKGROUND

Ambon, (population 200,000) lies southwest of Seram. Heavily bombed in 1945, it lacks the charm of Banda Neira, but in the town center of Fort Victoria the residence of the Dutch governor general remains, as do some old fortifications laid down by the Portuguese.

by reclamation of Yos Sudarso harbor. Much of the land created is used for government buildings and retail space. But despite the city's modern appearance and high level of education, society continues to bow to the authority of *adat*, traditional clan relationships that influence where Ambonese can live, buy land and marry.

GENERAL INFORMATION

Both the provincial and regional tourist offices are located in Ambon. If you are heading north to Ternate and Tidore, or out into the vastness of southern Maluku, Ambon is the last stop for information regarding flights and accommodations.

The Provincial Tourist Service, DIPARDA Maluku, is located on Jalan Pattimura at Kantor Gubernur KDH TK.1, ((911) 2471. For information regarding Ambon, Seram and the Banda Islands contact the Kanwil XVI Depparpostel Propinsi Maluku, the Regional Office of Tourism, Post and Tele-communication on Jalan Sultan Hasanuddin Tantui, ((911) 3062.

WHAT TO SEE

Created by volcanic eruptions, the curiously shaped island of Ambon is formed by two loosely connected peninsulas, Hitu and Leitimur, which once were separate islands. Though there have been no recent eruptions, the island continues to shake, spout hot springs and ooze sulfur.

Due to the absence of environmental controls, the Ambonese have taken the sand from many of their beaches to make concrete and allowed lazy fishermen to dynamite the formerly dramatic coral reefs.

Several spots still offer decent scuba diving. One is **Satan's Cove** on the northeast shore. Here one can swim down through clefts in the coral past swirls of tropical fish gliding in unison through the clear water. **Pombo Island** off the northeast coast of Hitu also has preserved its coral reefs. Water here is shallow, however, and snorkels are sufficient to see the remaining coral heads. Serious divers may save time and inconvenience by arranging dives through **Daya Patal Tour and Travel** (((911) 3529) at Jalan Said Perintah SK II N° 27A. Daya Patel can provide a boat, gear and a guide for local dives arrange more extended journeys to outer islands.

WHERE TO STAY

An Ambon institution with 40 rooms, the **Abdulalie Hotel** at Jalan Kapt. Yongker N° 1, ((911) 2057 and 2058 offers clean rooms with an ocean view for around $40.

Ambon's largest hotel, the **Ambonia**, has 42 air-conditioned rooms that cost from $45 to $70 a night. Located at Jalan Kapt. Ulupaha N° 5, the Ambonia offers the advantage of a central location and is the only hotel in town that will accept credit cards. ((911) 3354, cable AMBONIA HOTEL, telex 73111 AHABIA.

Several blocks away from the Ambonia on Jalan Pattimura is the **Mutiara Hotel**, ((911) 3075, cable MUTIARA. The Mutiara's 32 rooms cost from $35 to $50.

A comparably priced yet more modern alternative to the Mutiara is the **Manise**, an efficient Chinese-owned hotel a short walk away at Jalan W.R. Supratman N° 1. A two-story building with guest room balconies, the Manise also has a good Chinese restaurant. ((911) 42905.

WHERE TO EAT

Though menus in Ambon restaurants tend to be typically Chinese or Indonesian, the atmosphere usually makes up for the lack of variety.

The restaurants at the Manise and Mutiara hotels offer standard tourist fare with the accent on large breakfast buffets. The Manise congee, a mix-it-yourself rice porridge, is excellent, but fruitivores will prefer the Mutiara which offers a half dozen freshly squeezed juices with breakfast along with mounds of ripe bananas, papaya and pineapple.

An outdoor eatery on Jalan Sultan Hairun, **Halim** (((911) 2177) is Ambon's best restaurant. Halim's crab soup is an excellent start to any meal. Also an Ambonese favorite is grilled sea bass with *colo-colo*, a sweet and sour sauce made with orange juice and red chilies.

Ambonese moslems pray in filigreed mosques painted in tropical pastels.

The **Tip Top** restaurant next door to Halim has a menu almost identical to Halim's with the addition of several Javanese specialties. With prices about a third less than Halim, the Tip Top is a favorite of Ambonese who, should you be their guest, will no doubt surprise you by ordering local delicacies like kohu-kohu, an undercooked fish salad, and loar, an oleaginous sea worm that when seasoned and stir fried has the consistency of a microwaved cucumber. Fortunately, both Halim and the Tip Top have fiery *sambal* that when applied in sufficient quantity totally masks the flavor of *loar*.

Every sizable Indonesian city has a Chinese cabaret restaurant with willowy vocalists in tight dresses. In Ambon it's the New **Garden** (℃ (911) 41669) on Jalan Pahlawan Revolusi. The New Garden serves surprisingly good Mandarin dishes and can even whip up daiquiris but be forewarned: you may hear a Chinese version of *Feelings*.

WHAT TO BUY

Ambon's most popular curio is a sailing ship made entirely from cloves that you can buy at the airport or any of the tourist stores — **Sulawesi, Jawa**, **Indah** or **Labora** — along

Jalan A.Y. Patty. They are interesting to look at but almost impossible to transport, so don't bother buying one if your next destination is Irian Jaya. Exotic shells, bracelets made from coral or turtle shell and mother of pearl inlaid screens can be found at the city market. Avoid carved sea turtle shells, however, since they will be confiscated in Singapore or Hong Kong because turtles are an endangered species.

HOW TO GET THERE

Ambon is a major hub for Garuda (℃ (911) 2481) whose office is on Jalan Jend. Ahmad Yani. Ambon's airport, more than an hour's drive from the city, is a major stop on Garuda's daily flight from Jakarta to Jayapura. There are numerous nonstops throughout the day to Ujung Pandang with onward service to Balikpapan, Banda Aceh and Bandar Lampung.

Ambon also is well served by Merpati at Jalan Anthony Rebok N° 28, ℃ (911) 3480, which has daily flights to Manado, Sorong, Surabaya and Ternate, as well as Ujung Pandang.

If you're heading for Jakarta, Surabaya or Ujung Pandang and Garuda and Merpati are full, go by Mandala Airlines at Jalan A.Y. Patty SK N° 14-18 or call ℃ (911) 42552 for its less expensive commuter service. Save for its service from Manado to Ternate, Bouraq Airlines does not operate in Maluku.

There is a PELNI office (℡ (911) 3161) in Ambon at Jalan Pelabuhan N°1 that books space on the *Rinjani*, which links Maluku with southeast Sulawesi and the Bird's Head to Irian. For the adventurous, a trip on the *Rinjani* can be a memorable experience, but remember that June to September is the monsoon season during which the Halmahera and Maluku seas are tossed by tropical squalls.

THE BANDA ISLANDS

BACKGROUND

Banda, "the Jewel of the Indies," was Holland's first outpost in what later became the

Dutch East Indies. In 1601 the Bandanese gave the Dutch East Indies Company exclusive rights to purchase nutmeg and mace, the red membrane surrounding the nutmeg seeds. Conflicts over pricing, however, led to several massacres, the last of which established Dutch control over the commodity

they sold in Europe for 320 times its purchase price.

By the end of the eighteenth century, smuggled nutmeg seeds planted in Malaya and on the West Indies' island of Grenada by the British had broken the Dutch monopoly. The advent of refrigeration reduced demand for spices that had been used as preservatives. Public tastes changed. Nutmeg prices plummeted and the Dutch East Indies Company went bankrupt. By 1900, Banda was an impoverished backwater, a remote area where the Dutch exiled dissidents until Indonesia won independence in 1949. Mohammed Hatta, Indonesia's first vice-president, and Sultan Sjahrir, one of the country's first prime ministers, lived on Banda for nearly six years.

The Banda Archipelago consists of nine volcanic peaks surrounded by the azure Banda Sea.

BANDA NEIRA

Banda Neira is the only island large enough to support a town. Restored and developed by Des Alwi, a former Indonesian diplomat turned hotelier, the island is improving its basic amenities, while preserving its rich colonial heritage.

Over 100 distinct ethnic groups speaking 300 different languages form Indonesia's cultural mosaic.

What to See

The seclusion coupled with a rich history and scenic splendor gives the Banda Islands great charm. Virgin coral reefs ring the island. An underwater garden of rainbow-colored tropical fish suddenly disappears into an ocean 2,000 m deep and alive with more marine mammals than any other spot on the globe.

Banda Neira island has many large mansions, some of them more than three centuries old, that once belonged to Dutch *perkeniers*, or estate managers, and Chinese and Arab merchants. A old Dutch church stands at the center of town not far from the ruins of **Fort Nassau**, built in 1609, and **Fort Belgica**, completed two years later. The presence of so many forts in so remote a location attests to Banda's former importance to the Dutch.

Two and a half hours away from Banda Neira by slow boat is the island of **Run**, a barely inhabited hummock of sand and coconut palms that produces the most valuable nutmeg in the world. In the geopolitical history of the world, Run merits a fairly large asterisk. In 1667 the Dutch consolidated their grip on the Spice islands when the British traded Run to the Dutch in return for an undeveloped chunk of real estate in North America called Manhattan.

The Maulana and Laguna inns on Jalan Pelabuhan rent boats, diving equipment and wind surfing boards. Speedboats and launches, large enough to reach **Lontar** island where **Fort Hollandia** is located, cost about $30 an hour from the hotels or $100 for the entire day. Lontar and Karaka islands are perfect for shallow scuba diving since both have colorful reefs. Run Island is better for deeper diving. Be sure to bargain since the price for boats and equipment depends on the volume of tourists and the season of the year.

Where to Stay

Sipping arak laced with honey and lime on the verandah of Banda Neira's **Maulana Inn** at sunset may be as close to paradise as one can get on earth. Elaborately decorated longboats large enough to carry 30 men are beached along the shore. Blue fin tuna dart through luminescent swirls of tropical fish. Across a narrow strait, the Gunung Api volcano emits occasional puffs of fire. The smell of nutmeg and mace mixed with cloves permeates the air, conjuring up visions of colonial powers who three centuries ago vied for hegemony in the Spice Islands. Operated by Des Alwi, an ebullient raconteur and personal friend of Indonesia's first vice-president Mohammad Hatta, the Maulana is reminiscent of a nutmeg planters estate. Alwi provides clean beds, good food, air for scuba divers and a wide verandah with breathtaking views. Located at Jalan Pelabuhan N° 27, rooms start at $40. Three meals a day cost an additional $16.

The **Laguna Inn** is the Maulana's sister hotel next door. Also operated by Des Alwi, it has eight rooms that average about $10 less than the prevailing rate at the Maulana. Meals cost an additional $12. Staying at the Laguna can be just as satisfying as the Maulana if your room looks out on Gunung Api, so economize elsewhere and pay extra for the room with a view.

Where to Eat

Visitors to Banda Neira usually eat at one of Des Alwi's hotels. The only alternative is the **Nusantara** a few blocks down Jalan Pelabuhan. There's nothing fancy about the Nusantara; grilled fish freshly caught a few hours before is served with sliced lime, cold beer and a side dish of *sambal*.

How to Get There

Merpati's subsidiary, Indoavia, flies 14-seat Cessnas from Ambon twice a week. The flight depends on a mostly-full plane, however, and there is a severe weight restriction on the amount of luggage that can be carried. A number of small coastal craft also make the 16-hour overnight trip from Ambon, but none really can be described as comfortable. Two PELNI ships, the *Niaga* and the *Nasuna*, makes swings through southern Maluku about every three weeks, stopping at Banda en route.

The rainy season lasts from June through August and the west monsoon from January to February can cause rough seas. The best time to visit is from October to December and again from March through May when the seas are calm, the breeze is gentle and each day ends with a spectacular sunset.

NORTHERN MALUKU

Just to the west of pinwheel-shaped Halmahera Island the volcanic islands of Ternate and Tidore rise majestically from the floor of the Maluku Sea. Three centuries ago the two islands and their precious crops of cloves and mace were the focus of international intrigue and warfare.

Ternate and **Tidore** are separated by only a one kilometer stretch of ocean. As a result, a small fleet of power boats is constantly

TERNATE

This tiny volcanic island dominated by Mt. Gamalama may no longer be the focus of world attention, but it still remains the second most important commercial center in Maluku after Ambon. First reached by the Portuguese, it was later claimed by Spain, but the Portuguese succeeded in expelling the Spanish and eventually bought the island from the Spanish Crown.

available to shuttle passengers between the two islands or to nearby **Mare**, **Moti** and **Makian**.

Rugged, barely populated and largely undeveloped, Northern Maluku's largest island, **Halmahera** is rarely visited. Scuba enthusiasts, however, may wish to dive the coastal reefs which are rich with lobster. A bit further, but well worth a trip for scuba divers, is a visit to **Morotai** just off Halmahera's northern tip. Occupied by the Allies after a fierce battle with the Japanese, Morotai became the site of a huge air base used in the retaking of the Philippines. Submerged in the shallows off the coast are the coral encrusted remains of destroyers, P51 Mustangs and Japanese Zeros.

In 1547 Francis Xavier passed through Ternate, but his Jesuitical precepts were lost on the island's administrators who enraged Ternate's inhabitants by poisoning the local sultan. After throwing the Portuguese off the island, the new sultan Babullah packed his warriors into longboats called *kora-kora* and for the next 13 years attacked every European he could find.

In 1592 Portugal's nominal rule of Maluku became even more tenuous when a Dutchman working for a Portuguese trading company in Goa published the heretofore secret routes to the East Indies. By 1621

Golden sunsets and local lore are best enjoyed on the verandah of the Maulana Inn on Banda Neira.

the *Vereenigde Oostindische Compagnie*, today better remembered as the Dutch East India Company or V.O.C., had routed the Portuguese and established a spice monopoly by declaring that cloves could only be grown on Ambon. To enforce the monopoly, the V.O.C. exterminated the entire workforce of Banda and uprooted all clove trees on Ternate. The Dutch monopoly gradually eroded as more and more clove seedlings were planted in other parts of the world. But the V.O.C. policy remained in force and every few months until the start of the Napoleonic wars Dutch officials would come to Ternate to crush clove saplings.

Today, Ternate boasts a robust economy and a laid back lifestyle. Its Islamic citizenry is gracious at welcoming foreigners, who should not be overly alarmed by the frequent earth tremors.

General Information
A locally administered tourist office on Jalan Pahlawan Revolusi in Ternate City can provide basic information, but it is short of printed material. The office has no telephone or regular business hours, but some one is usually there in the mornings. For more organized tours contact **Indo Gama**, ((921) 21288, fax (921) 21580, Jalan Jend. A. Yani 131.

What to See
Once the home of the most powerful sultan in the Spice islands, **Ternate City** (population 50,000) is a pleasant tropical port that because it was bypassed by World War II gives a better picture of Maluku's history than does Ambon.

Looking out over the city of Ternate the 758-year old **Sultan's Palace**, or *kraton*, on Jalan Babullah now serves as a public museum where you can see old Dutch cannons, Portuguese swords and Han ceramics brought to the island as trade goods by Bugis merchants. A brief taxi ride down the hill from the *kraton* leads to the **Benteng Oranye** or Fort Orange, a massive Dutch trading post built in the early years of the seventeenth century. Still guarded by Dutch cannons and emblazoned with the V.O.C.

crest, the outpost now serves as a garrison for the Indonesian Army which, in contrast to its behavior elsewhere in Indonesia, is happy to greet camera-toting tourists.

A 30-minute walk north from Fort Orange will take you back a century in time to **Benteng Toloko**, a Portuguese fort built by Alfonso de Albuquerque in 1512. Contrasted to many other colonial ruins, Benteng Toloko was lovingly preserved, ironically, by the Dutch who mistakenly assumed it was one of their own structures.

Benteng Toloko commands a panoramic view of the city that includes **Benteng Kayu Merah**, an old coastal Portuguese fort the Dutch clearly recognized as Portuguese. Allowed to slowly disintegrate, the roundish, wave-splashed ruin still is worth a look. But a much more dramatic trek leads to **Gunung Api Gamalama**, the active volcano to which Ternate City clings. It is possible to climb into the steaming crater with the help of a guide from the mountain village of Marikrobo, but most people are content to just enjoy the view. Am

Where to Stay
The **Chrysant** on Jalan Jend. A. Yani N° 131 has both air-conditioned and fan cooled rooms that cost from $10 to $32 plus a 21 percent government tax and service charge. ((921) 21580. Also in the same price category is the **Nirwana** at 58 Jalan. Pahlawan Revolusi. ((921) 21787.

Where to Eat
Most restaurants in Ternate are found along Jalan Pahlawan Revolusi and offer basic Chinese and Indian food for around $6 per person. The specialty is coconut crab, a beach-dwelling creature that exists entirely on coconuts. The only restaurant to rise above the norm in Ternate is the **Siola**, a short stroll from the center of town on Jalan Stadion. As with other places, crab is the specialty here, but unlike the competition it comes in unusually generous portions. The crab and asparagus soup may be the best in Indonesia, certainly it is the thickest. ((921) 21377.

How to Get There
Merpati has a daily flight linking Ambon and Ternate. There also is daily service to Manado

---

Tropical greenery swathes the gentle waters around Ternate Island.

in northern Sulawesi. Be sure to arrive at the airport early since both flights often are overbooked. Bouraq also flies to Ternate from Ujung Pandang via Manado three times a week. Merpati's Ternate office is on Jalan Bousori N° 81, ((921) 314; Bouraq is located at Jalan Sultan Babullah N° 96, ((921) 21042.

Indoavia, a subsidiary of Merpati, has commuter flights out of Ternate to various locations in Northern Maluku, but service is irregular so check with Merpati before heading to the airport for an Indoavia flight.

PELNI (((921) 21276) has an office in the Komplex Pelabuhan on Jalan Ahmad Yani where you can book space on the *Umsini* which makes a fortnightly trek from Jakarta to Jayapura with a stop at Ternate. PELNI's *Baruna Dwipa* links Ternate with Ambon.

TIDORE

Tidore is a beautiful island that usually is visited on Tuesday and Saturday when the towns of **Run** and **Soa Siu** have their market days. The jungle-covered ruins of an old Spanish fort lie atop a hill at the entrance to Soa Siu. Children also will lead you to the ruins of the old sultan's palace.

Where to Stay

The only accommodation of note is the **Penginnapan Jangi** in the town of Soa Siu whose 12 rooms (breakfast and dinner included) cost $11 a night.

How to Get There

Small outboard boats to Tidore shuttle passengers from Pelabuhan Bastiong on Ternate to Run on Tidore's northwest coast. The boats run from 7 am to 6 pm and cost around 50 cents.

SOUTHEAST MALUKU

On the far edge of the Banda Sea in the most distant corner of the archipelago lie the largely forgotten island groups of **Aru**, **Kai** and **Tanimbar**. Populated by 260,000 natives of Papuan stock, these seldom visited islands have no strategic or economic importance. Historically, the only recorded conflict has been the battle for men's souls

waged between Christian and Moslem missionaries. All three island groups have palm-shaded beaches, traditional handicrafts and coral reefs swarming with tiny tropical fish, but travel to and between islands must be measured in weeks and food and accommodation often are hard to come by.

KAI ISLANDS

Undiscovered until the late nineteenth century, the Kai islands once were covered with forests. The Melanesian natives were renowned boat builders who happily subsisted on a diet of yams, sago and fish. Today, the hills have been largely denuded by Javanese timber companies and disease has prompted many Christians to revert to animism, but the Kai islanders' artistic talents continue undiminished.

Carved stone and wooden statues and finely woven baskets can be purchased in small villages on the two large islands of **Kai Besar** and **Kai Kecil**. On **Palau Tayandu** just west of Kai Kecil villagers produce pottery in the shape of animals and forest spirits. Though villagers will gladly accept rupiah, barter is an accepted practice on all three islands with inexpensive digital wrist watches and calculators being much in demand.

How to get There

Merpati has several weekly flights from Ambon to Langgur via Banda. There also are two flights a week linking Langgur with Saumlaki on Tanimbar.

TANIMBAR ISLANDS

In 1645 the Dutch tried to establish a colony on **Yamdena**, the largest island in the Tanimbar group, but departed with some alacrity after learning that the Tanimbarese were headhunting cannibals. Catholic missionaries later subdued the Melanesian ferocity, but they did not completely dispel the islanders' animism. Today, the missionaries have been joined by botanists who come to observe the islands' unique assortment of orchids.

Of the 66 Tanimbar islands, only seven are inhabited and the total population amounts to less than 70,000. Despite miles of deserted beaches and rainbow colored coral reefs, there is no organized tourism. Those who venture this far south, however, will find some of Indonesia's finest *ikat* weaving and talented silversmiths who make ceremonial headdresses from old coins.

Because the rest of the world is so far away, everything is in short supply. Tee shirts, ball point pens, even leather belts and brandy are valued items that can be traded for textiles, shell jewelry and carvings. One can only imagine what you might receive in return for a Swiss Army knife.

sparsely populated, covered with mangrove swamps and surrounded by abyssal trenches that lead into the shallow Arafura Sea. Wallabies and kangaroo share the land with the Alfuro natives, but the main attraction here are birds of paradise which display their brilliant plumage each summer when it comes time to mate.

Unlike the neighboring Tanimbarese, the dark skinned Alfuro are peace-loving farmers who cultivate melons on their swampy, low lying islands and make tortoise shell jewelry in their spare time. **Dobo** on the

The nearest thing to a hotel on Yamdena is the mission station at **Saumlaki**. Those going beyond this town should carry canned food and drink to share in return for shelter.

How to Get There
Merpati has two flights a week from Langgur to Saumlaki. PELNI's *KM Dukuh* also stops every month on the way to and from the Aru Islands.

ARU ISLANDS

Nearly 700 km (400 miles) southeast of Ambon, the Aru Islands are Maluku's most distant land masses. Located on the edge of a marine plateau, the 21 Aru islands are

island of **Wokam** is the only town of any size. There it is possible to buy painted cassowary eggs and artifacts made from mother-of-pearl.

How to Get There
There is an airstrip outside Dobo, but no scheduled airline uses it. It may be possible to fly in on a missionary flight from Langgur, but getting out could take some time. PELNI provides the only scheduled transportation to Aru, but the journey from Ambon takes three weeks.

A narrow strait separates Banda Neira from the Gunung Api volcano.

Kalimantan

BORNEO. The name evokes images of impenetrable jungles, sluggish rivers, screaming gibbons, leeches and communal longhouses occupied by tattooed Dyak headhunters. In the case of Borneo it's all true, except for the fact that headhunting in recent years has fallen out of fashion.

Kalimantan, which means "Rivers of Precious Stones," occupies the southern two-thirds of Borneo, the world's third largest island. It is a brooding, exotic place that has captivated generations of writers. In *Heart of Darkness*, Joseph Conrad's character Marlow confesses his childhood fascination with maps that depicted Borneo as a sprawling expanse of jungle riven by enormous, undulating rivers. "It fascinated me as a snake would a bird — a silly little bird."

Maps of Borneo still contain many of Asia's most storied locales. Across the border in East Malaysia the state of Sarawak once belonged to the British "White Rajah" James Brooke. Sandakan the pirate prowled the sea off the coast of modern day Brunei. In addition to inspiring *Heart of Darkness*, Kalimantan's rivers often were the focus of Somerset Maugham's *Borneo Stories*.

Kalimantan has a population of only seven million, but because of the oil and timber industries its four provinces are well served by the airlines. Daily nonstops link Banjarmasin in South Kalimantan and the East Kalimantan oil town of Balikpapan with Jakarta and Surabaya. Moving between Kalimantan's major towns also is easy since Garuda, Merpati, Bouraq and Deraya Air Taxi have overlapping service.

Kalimantan is relatively flat with no active volcanoes, but transportation inland from the coast can be difficult. There are no major highways because of the swamps, peat bogs and thick jungle. This means that all commerce must move on rivers like South Kalimantan's Barito, East Kalimantan's Mahakam and the Kapuas River in West Kalimantan. During the rainy season, when the rapids are transformed into foaming torrents, boats reminiscent of *The African Queen* must slowly zigzag up the broad rivers, carefully avoiding the tree trunks sent floating down river by the timber companies. Once the rivers reach the coastal flatland, however, they turn ocherous and meander aimlessly until their final transformation into mangrove swamps.

Some of Kalimantan's towns can be bypassed without fear of missing much. Balikpapan, for example, has little save for an inordinate number of expatriates divided in two categories: "oilies" in the petroleum business and "chippies" who work for logging companies. West Kalimantan's capital of Pontianak which sits atop the equator is mainly a city of Chinese shopkeepers. The beauty of Kalimantan is found on and around its rivers which drain the planet's

last great primary forest. With some 25,000 species of flowering plants (all of Europe has less than 6,000; Africa less than 13,000) Kalimantan is the richest rain forest in the world.

BORNEO'S DYAKS

Dyak is a generic term that identifies any of the 200 tribal groups native to Borneo. Numbering about 1.5 million, Dyaks such as the Iban, Kayan and Punan, are neolithic animists who live along the banks of the island's

OPPOSITE: Dyak settlements line Borneo's many rivers. ABOVE: Dyak women welcome visitors with freshly cut pineapple.

many rivers. Originally, they lived along the coast, but when Arab traders arrived in the fifteenth century the Dyaks moved inland to escape Islam and its prohibition against their favorite food: pork.

Dyaks are skilled boatmen and hunters who transform their bodies into works of art with tattoos. They are also known for their *ikat* cloth and ornaments. The Tanjung Dyaks make a kind of cloth called *Daun Doyo*, which is woven from plant fibers and used for certain rituals in traditional longhouses.

Traditionally, the Dyak's highly-structured society revolves around the longhouse. Wooden structures built on pilings that reach 150 yards in length, longhouses can shelter as many as 100 families. Though each family has a separate apartment, most of the day and evening is spent in the unpartitioned corridor that runs the length of the house.

Frontier hospitality prevails in nearly all of Kalimantan's longhouses. Visitors receive a welcome tour, an explanation of how the human heads hanging from the rafters were taken, dinner and a place to sleep on the split-bamboo floor. In return you are expected to provide cartons of cigarettes and several five-gallon cans of rice wine. The extent and intensity of the festivities that follow will be largely determined by the amount of wine you bring. It's also deemed thoughtful to bring several bags of hard candy for the kids, but only wine and cigarettes are mandatory.

HEADHUNTING

When Sir James Brooke, the nineteenth century British adventurer who became the "White Rajah" of Sarawak, first met the Dyaks he wrote that "they are the most savage of tribes - and delight in headhunting and pillage."

According to Dyak lore, nothing prevents plague, increases fertility or insures a bountiful harvest like a brace of freshly-severed heads. Heads brimming with the spirit of the departed are the perfect wedding gift and are basic to any respectable dowry. For Dyaks, taking heads was essential to the well-being of a community. Indeed, following a death in the family, heads

taken from an enemy tribe served as a spiritual transfusion.

Because a head's power faded as it aged, fresh skulls always were needed. Those taken from rival warriors received VIP treatment. After being drained of its brains and dried over a fire, a head often would be stuffed with rice or betel nuts. On occasion a cigar would be inserted between the desiccated lips.

Tolerated by the Dutch, who viewed it as a primitive form of population control, headhunting fell out of fashion after Indonesia gained independence. The last confirmed case of headhunting occurred in the early 1960's when Iban warriors loyal to the British lopped off the heads of Sukarno soldiers who had ventured too far inside Northern Borneo. Today, it is a serious felony. But new legislation doesn't completely dispel old beliefs, and in most upriver longhouses heads smoked over generations of cook fires continue to occupy a place of honor.

EAST KALIMANTAN

BACKGROUND

Indonesia's petroleum industry got its start in East Kalimantan at the turn-of-the-century when British Petroleum discovered oil outside Balikpapan and on the offshore island of Tarakan. Oil, natural gas and timber have made the province of East Kalimantan vital to the economy of Indonesia. Indeed, more than 25 percent of the country's export earnings come from East-Kal's natural resources.

Logging is concentrated in the forests west of Balikpapan and Samarinda. It was here that 35,000 sq km (13,500 sq miles) of woodlands burned from 1982 through 1983 when fires started by peasants using the slash-and-burn method of cultivation got out of control. The fire devastated an area the size of Holland and cost Indonesia $6 billion worth of timber.

BALIKPAPAN

The large number of American, European and Australian expatriates working in the

oil and timber industries makes Balikpapan one of the friendliest, most welcoming towns in Indonesia. The foreign presence and wealth, however, underscores Indonesia's lack of development. It is incongruous to see two-cylinder becaks parked in front of gleaming office towers. Foreign workers for Pertamina, Total and Union Oil live in a leafy enclave atop the hill where they enjoy the benefits of a country club and other suburban amenities.

Where to Stay
The **Altea Hotel Benakutai** in Balikpapan's city center is the best choice. Single rooms are $95 to $130 and doubles from $130 to $145, plus an additional 21 percent service charge and tax. Jalan Jend. Achmed Yani, ((542) 23522, fax (542) 23893. Borneo's other four-star hotel, the **Benakutai** (((542) 21804) on Jalan Pangeran Antasari in Balikpapan, has single rooms for $78 per night. Doubles cost an extra $10. A shopping center with several restaurants is attached to the hotel.

The **Balikpapan Hotel** at Jalan Garuda N° 2 (((542) 21490/3) is a quiet bungalow hotel that has air-conditioned rooms for $45 a night.

An expat favorite with a lively restaurant and bar is the **Blue Sky Hotel** on Jalan Suprapto N° 1. Rooms with attached shower start at $30. ((542) 35845, fax (542) 24094.

Where to Eat
Because of East Kalimantan's swampy soil, most of the food served in restaurants is imported. This drives up the cost of what turns out to be rather ordinary meals.

Balikpapan's best restaurant is probably the **Seafood Restaurant** at the Benakutai Hotel. Lobster and grilled tiger prawn dinners costing around $7 are presented in an atmosphere that almost seems elegant. Excellent seafood served in a livelier atmosphere can be found at the **Rainbow Coffee Shop and Restaurant** (((542) 22267) at the Blue Sky Hotel.

The **Florida Cafe** at the intersection of Jalan Ahmad Yani and Jalan Pengeran Antasari serves large American-style breakfasts that will ward off hunger until the evening, at which time the cafe prepares an excellent assortment of grilled seafood. For afternoon snacks try the burgers, baked goods and ice cream from the **Holland Bakery** at Jalan Gunungsari N° 3. Persons short of time should try the bakery's fresh fruit milkshakes.

How to Get There

Balikpapan is the main transportation hub for Kalimantan. Garuda, Merpati, Sempati and Bouraq all have daily flights to Jakarta and Surabaya. Garuda's jet aircraft take two hours to reach Jakarta compared to the three hours needed by Bouraq and Merpati's prop planes. But if cost is a factor the latter may be preferable since tickets on the smaller airlines are cheaper. Sempati (℃ (542) 34555) is at the Hotel Benakutai. The Bouraq (℃ (542) 21107), and Garuda (℃ (542) 22300) offices are in and diagonally opposite from the Hotel Benakutai. Merpati reservations can be made by calling (542) 22380 or going by the office at 29 Jalan A. Yani.

From Balikpapan, low cost buses run on a regular basis to Samarinda and Banjarmasin. The trip to Samarinda takes two hours. The 12-hour journey to Banjarmasin is an interminable, gut-wrenching experience that may leave you wishing you had flown.

The PELNI office on Jalan Yos Sudarso (℃ (542) 22187) sells tickets for *KM Kerinci* and *KM Kambuna*, two passenger steamers that sail to Jakarta, Surabaya and Ujung Pandang with intervening stops at Toli Toli, Tarakan and Pantoloan. A first class cabin for the trip to Ujung Pandang costs only $48, while Surabaya is $60.

THE MAHAKAM RIVER

An enormous river that is more than three kilometers (two miles) wide in many locations, the Mahakam functions as the aorta of East Kalimantan. Ocean-going freighters steam upriver as far as Samarinda, which serves as the terminus for thousands of logs floating downstream.

Most of the Mahakam is navigable year-around, but travelers bound for remote destinations such as **Long Pahangai** should plan their journey from September through December when increased rain makes it easier to negotiate upriver rapids.

SAMARINDA

A colorful town on the Mahakam River, Samarinda is the center of East Kalimantan's timber industry. Its bustling riverine harbor is packed with freighters and water taxis,

and lined with businesses and homes from which children dive into the river. Indeed, the city's biggest attraction is its harbor, and tourists are well advised to hire a boat with a wooden roof on which they can sit and observe the passing scene. A variety of canals and tributaries branch off from the river. Some extend through commercial neighborhoods, others meander through residential areas. The journey will offer an insight into the nature of Kalimantan's aquatic culture that no book or land-based tour can provide.

General Information

Maps, general advice and lists of authorized tourist agencies can be found at the regional

Kalimantan timber sent down the Mahakam River often clogs the port of Samarinda.

information office on Jalan Jend. A. Yani in Samarinda. The phone is (541) 21073.

Where to Stay

The **Swarga Indah** on Jalan Jend. Sudirman N° 43 (℃ (541) 22066, 22067) has air conditioned rooms that start at $42 for a single with double occupancy costing an additional $5. Breakfast is included in the room charge, which does not include the 21percent government tax and service charge.

For an additional $10 a night one can stay in a single room at the **Hotel Mesra**

away from the Raya mosque in the centre of the town. Here one can order a variety of dishes from more than a dozen food stalls. For a change of pace foreigners often head for **Pondok Indah**, a steak restaurant on Jalan Panglima Batur. Prices there are a bit higher than elsewhere, but the beer is cold and the person sitting next to you at the bar probably speaks English.

How to Get There

Samarinda is served by Merpati (℃ (541) 24553) and Bouraq (℃(541) 21105), both of which

International, ℃ (541) 21011, fax (541) 21017, a resort on Jalan Pahlawan at the northwest edge of Samarinda. The Mesra has tennis courts, a large swimming pool and several restaurants. If the Mesra is full and you want a similar hotel in the same area try the **Lamin Indah** (℃ (541) 23894) at Jalan Bayangkara N° 57. The Lamin's rooms are fully as nice as those of the Mesra, but it lacks the recreational facilities of the larger hotel.

Where to Eat

The specialty of Samarinda is *udang galah*, huge fresh water prawns that nearly every *warung* can grill to specification. One of the cheapest and most efficient places to eat is the **Citra Niaga** hawker pavilion a few blocks

have several flights each day to Balikpapan and Banjarmasin. There is a PELNI office where you can book passage, but you'll have to go to Balikpapan to catch the ship.

TENGGARONG

Forty kilometers (25 miles) up the Mahakam River from Samarinda is Tenggarong, capital of the Kutai regency and formerly the seat of the Kutai sultanate. The sultan's palace at the riverside is now a **museum** where the royal paraphernalia is kept, as well as an excellent collection of antique Chinese ceramics. Every September 24 the **palace** is taken over by dancers and musicians who celebrate the town's anniversary.

MAHAKAM RIVER CRUISES

Tenggarong is the jumping off point for tours to the interior. The village has a number of small tour companies that can organize everything from extended river cruises to overnight stays at a longhouse.

Before leaving Samarinda, however, you should study the Mahakam's traffic to become acquainted with the different types of river craft. Most of the taxi boats in Samarinda have long wooden hulls, a canvas roof

and a small diesel motor. Sleeker longboats have more powerful engines that allow the boat to skim up the rapids. Smaller *keting-tings* are powered by a swivel-mounted engine attached to a long propeller shaft which allows the boat to pick its way through extremely shallow water.

For travelers with time to spare a trip upriver can be the experience of a lifetime. Surrounded by rippling streams, waterfalls and produce gardens, the villages of **Barong Tongkok** not only provide an opportunity to hike through shimmering rice fields and groves of bamboo, but also view a particularly undiluted form of tribal animism. Around Barong Tongkok jungle trails lead past carved statues and spirit offerings of

rice and flowers to villages where the beat of drums and gongs punctuate rituals carried down through the centuries.

Half way up the Mahakam is **Long Iram**, an equatorial village that offers the last call for cold beer and restaurant food. Long Iram is one of the Mahakam's larger transportation hubs with boats leaving often for towns both up and down the river.

Upriver of Long Iram Dyaks with tattoos and earlobes elongated by dangling brass rings become more visible. Elaborately carved longhouses can be visited at **Long Bagun**, but before settling in for the evening visitors are expected to announce their presence to the local police.

SOUTH KALIMANTAN

Bisected by the Barito River, Kalimantan's smallest province is a relatively trackless expanse of jungle which is rapidly being denuded by timber companies. Turned into plywood and rattan products, the rain forest is disappearing at an alarming rate at the hands of Indonesian "chippies" whose elongated logging trucks roar along the Trans-Kalimantan Highway which starts just outside Banjarmasin.

BANJARMASIN

Forest areas which remain standing, however, shelter a wealth of animal life. But perhaps the greatest attraction is the 460-year old provincial capital of Banjarmasin — a veritable Venice of the East — whose canals ebb and flow with the tides. Located 16 km (10 miles) from the sea at the confluence of the Martapura and Barito rivers, Banjarmasin is a riverine city in where houses, cafes and produce markets ride the tidal swell. "Banjar" is a good place to buy Dyak handicrafts and semi-precious stones, though the latter may be purchased more cheaply in the "diamond city" of Martapura 40 km (25 miles) east of Banjar.

Background

Banjarese kingdoms on the northern edge of the Java Sea fell to Java's Majapahit Kingdom at the end of the fourteenth century.

Many Dayak tribes later retreated into the interior to escape the advance of Islam, but the area was forcibly converted and was controlled by the Sultan of Banjarmasin when the Dutch finally arrived. In 1857 Dutch colonialists who had come in search of diamonds tried to depose the Sultan. Their goal finally was achieved but only after a costly 50 year insurgent war thinned both sides.

General Information

In Banjar Baru the Department of Information's regional office is located on Jalan Basuki Rachmat, ((511) 2053. Next to the Grand Mosque at Jalan Panjaitan N° 3 is the provincial tourist office. Neither office has much printed information, but both can recommend reliable guides who can hire a boat for $2.50 an hour and escort you on a tour of the canals.

What to See

Banjar's canals are worth at least a half day. Try to leave early in the morning so that you'll arrive at one of the city's **floating markets**, or *pasar terapung*, between 9 am to 10 am when they are most active.

After a leisurely lunch and a nap hire another boat for the five-mile trip down river to **Pulau Kaget**, an island inhabited exclusively by long-nosed proboscis monkeys. The animals have long noses, red faces and pot bellies, characteristics that prompt Indonesians to call them *kera belanda*, or Dutch monkeys.

Another proboscis monkey island, **Pulau Kembang**, is much closer to Banjarmasin, but it is more difficult to visit because of the long-tailed macaques that make hit-and-run attacks on tourists.

Where to Stay

Banjarmasin's nicest hotel is the **Hotel Maramin** at 32 Jalan Lambung Mangkurat. The hotel's 32 rooms, which start at $45 and can cost $55 for double occupancy, are favored by corporate travelers. ((511) 8944.

The **Febiola Internasional** on Jalan Jend. A. Yani is a resort hotel where rooms range from $46 to $75. ((511) 3174, 3658.

Where to Eat

One of the top seafood restaurants is **Kaganangan** at Jalan Samudera N° 30. A variety of dishes, both grilled and fried, are accompanied by steaming bowls of rich vegetable soup. **Restoran Blue Ocean** on Jalan Hasanuddin is an air conditioned Cantonese restaurant where dishes cost from $3 to $4.50.

How to Get There

Merpati has direct service linking Banjarmasin with Jakarta, Denpasar, Ambon and Surabaya, but the quickest way to enter or leave the city usually is via a connecting flight out of Balikpapan. Garuda (((511) 4203) has an office at Jalan Hasanuddin N° 31 that is open seven days a week. The Merpati office (((511) 4433) is at Jalan Letjen Haryono MT, N° 4, and that of Sempati is on the ground floor of the Barito Palace Hotel, ((511) 66304. Bouraq tickets can be purchased at Jalan Lambung Mangkurat 40D, ((511) 2445.

CENTRAL KALIMANTAN

The largest and least populated of Kalimantan's four provinces, Central Kalimantan, or *Kalimantan Tengah*, is blanketed by a thick rain forest that rises abruptly from the coastal mangrove swamps to the serrated ridge lines of the Schwaner and Muller mountain chains.

Drained by four enormous rivers — the Arot, Barito, Kahayan and Sampit — Central Kalimantan's 900,000 people are predominately Islamic (65 percent) with the bulk of the remainder clinging to native Dayak animism.

GENERAL INFORMATION

The regional office of the Department of Information is at Jalan Brig. Gen. Katamso N° 4 in Palangkaraya. ((541) 21227, 21176.

WHAT TO SEE

During the early 1960's, Sukarno began to challenge the region's old colonial powers with a policy called *konfrontasi*. He forced the Dutch out of Netherlands New Guinea

OPPOSITE: Equatorial torpor and intrusive police prevent Pontianak from becoming the Venice of Indonesia.

(now Irian Jaya) and tried to wrest control of Sarawak and North Borneo, British protectorates destined to join the new nation of Malaysia. To win support from Kalimantan, Sukarno announced a series of Moscow-financed development projects. His principal target was **Palangkaraya**, a dusty, impoverished village bereft of historical importance or geographical advantage. Despite the town's undistinguished past, Soviet engineers went to work building a road that would link the town with the village of **Tangkiling** 35 km (22 miles) away. The result today is advertised as Kalimantan's "Highway to Nowhere," an all-weather turnpike that stretches between towns where people ride bicycles and bullock carts.

Central Kalimantan's main attraction is the **Tanjung Puting National Park**, a 3,000 sq km (1,180 sq mile) preserve inhabited by orang-utans, pythons, crocodiles and several species of monkeys. The entrance to the park is located an hour's drive east of Pangkalan Bun at **Kumai**. Located on the Kumai River, the small town is home to dozens of longboat captains who provide the sole means of transport into the park. Inside the park there are piers where one can get off and hike through the foliage, but except for a few locations like Camp Leakey, where the Orang-utan Research and Conservation Project is located, the heat, humidity and cacophony of circling insects keep most visitors in their boat.

It is possible to direct your boatman down the river to Tanjung Keluang beach on Kumai Bay, but a more rewarding experience lies up the Sekonyer tributary at **Camp Leakey** where Dr. Birute Galdikas teaches captive orang-utans to reenter the wild. Because of their gentle disposition, baby orang-utans often are captured by Indonesian peasants (in violation of the law) who try to turn them into pets. When they realize that the jungle creature is incompatible with urban life, they try to insert the orang-utan back into the jungle, but by that time it is too late. The best time to visit Leakey is in the late afternoon when orang-utans, proboscis monkeys and other primates come down from their trees to feed. Longboats take about four hours to reach Camp Leakey from Kumai.

But the main thing to remember is that a frustratingly bureaucratic permit from the PHPA is required to enter Tanjung Puting. To enter the park not only do you have to bring Rp 1,800 but you also need your passport and a police report showing you have entered Central Kalimantan legally (a hotel registration form is an acceptable substitute).

WHERE TO STAY

Central Kalimantan is not known for romantic lodging. The few losmen that exist in **Pangkalan Bun** are strung out along jalans Kasumayuda and Antasari. Two that are considered the cleanest, the **Abadi** and **Bahagia**, charge $7 for a nice room with adjoining *mandi*. At $21 the **Wisma Andika** on Jalan Hasanuddin offers larger rooms and the benefit of an attached restaurant.

Prospects for lodging in **Palangkaraya** are equally lean. *Losmens* there can be had for $4 a night; the city's two hotels, the **Virgo** and **Adidas**, range from $18 to $21.

WHERE TO EAT

Don't bother asking for directions to the nearest *restoran* or trying to pay with a credit card. Tiny *warungs* and *rumah makans* are all that exist in this part of the jungle. Several *rumah makans* along Jalan Ahmad Yani next to the airline offices offer Palangkaraya's best fare. In Pangkalan Bun, the **Wisma Andika** has a simple restaurant attached to the hotel, but you may wish to be a bit more daring and try the **Warung Makan Hayati** on Jalan Blimbing Manis, which specialized in local specialties such as a zesty curry soup called *soto banjar*.

HOW TO GET THERE

Though the easiest way to reach the provincial capital of Palangkaraya is by river boat from Banjarmasin, travelers in a hurry may wish to take Merpati, Sempati, DAS or Bouraq. Bouraq has two flights a day into Palangkaraya from Banjarmasin and Sampit, plus daily service to Pangkalan Bun. In addition to daily service from Jakarta, Garuda has nonstop flights from Balikpapan. All of the major airline offices and travel agents in Palangkaraya are located along Jalan A. Yani.

WEST KALIMANTAN

PONTIANAK

The legacy of Sukarno's *konfrontasi* lives on in West Kalimantan, a rugged, sparsely populated area administered by suspicious police and immigration officials. Travelers who land in Pontianak must go through a separate immigration, even if they are coming from another part of Indonesia. Outside Pontianak police demand that travelers justify their presence. "We know that this is not a province that tourists usually visit," an official explained during a visit I made in 1987. "What do you want and how long do you plan to stay?"

Background
Prior to the arrival of the Dutch modern West Kalimantan was divided into the states of Sukadana and Sambas. British adventuring along the coast in the eighteenth century prompted the Dutch to install a puppet sultan in Pontianak. Though West Kalimantan produced some diamonds and precious gems, it was never targeted for large scale development by the Dutch.

During World War II West Kalimantan was the scene of numerous Japanese atrocities. Though figures are imprecise, mass graves uncovered after the war indicate that as many as 15,000 people may have been exterminated.

General Information
The Provincial Tourism Agency in Pontianak can be reached by calling (561) 6712 or going by the office at Jalan Achmad Sood N° 25. For additional directions try the Regional Department of Information at Jalan St. Syahrir N° 5, ℂ (561) 2771 or 2690.

Where To Stay
The **Kapuas Permai** on Jalan Imam Bonjol (ℂ (561) 6122, 6123) is Pontianak's best hotel. Its modern suites and bungalows cost from $36 to $55 for a single; double occupancy is an additional $5. The hotel's most distinctive feature is a swimming pool 100 m long which dominates the interior courtyard around which the hotel is built.

In the same price category the **Mahkota Kapuas** is closer to the center of town. Foreign businessmen tend to stay here because of the discotheque, health club, rooftop restaurant.

Across the river from City Hall right in the middle of Pontianak is the **Kartika Hotel**, a nicely appointed businessman's hotel known for its lively Chinese restaurant and its liberal visitation policy. Air conditioned rooms here average $45 a night.

Where to Eat
West Kalimantan is a coffee growing province, so Pontianak has plenty of coffee bars. For more substantial dining try the night *warungs* near the Kapuas Indah ferry terminal or the Chinese cafes along Jalans Diponegoro and Tanjungpura.

How to Get There
Pontianak's Pelabuhan Udara Supadio airport is well served by Garuda, Merpati, Bouraq, and the Deraya Air Taxi service. Located at Jalan Rahadi Usman N° 8A, Garuda (ℂ (561) 21026) has three flights a day to Jakarta, and daily service to Singapore. It also links Pontianak with Denpasar, Banjarmasin, Bandar Lampung, Jambi, Medan and Palembang. Tickets to Jakarta (one hour behind Pontianak) are a bit cheaper on Merpati, Bouraq and Sempati, but take slightly longer because of Garuda's jet monopoly. With six daily departures Merpati (ℂ (561) 2332) offers the most flexible service to Jakarta. The Merpati office is at Jalan Ir. H. Juanda N° 50 A.

Deraya has the most frequent and affordable service to destinations within Kalimantan. Deraya (ℂ (561) 4840) is located on Jalan Sisingamangaraja. For truly remote destinations, Mission Aviation Fellowship on Jalan Jen. Urip will take passengers on a space-available, cash-only basis to 50 air strips hacked out of the jungle.

Pontianak also is served by the PELNI ship *KM Lawit*, which departs every 10 days on a two-day voyage to Jakarta. PELNI tickets can be purchased at the company headquarters on Jalan Pak Kasih.

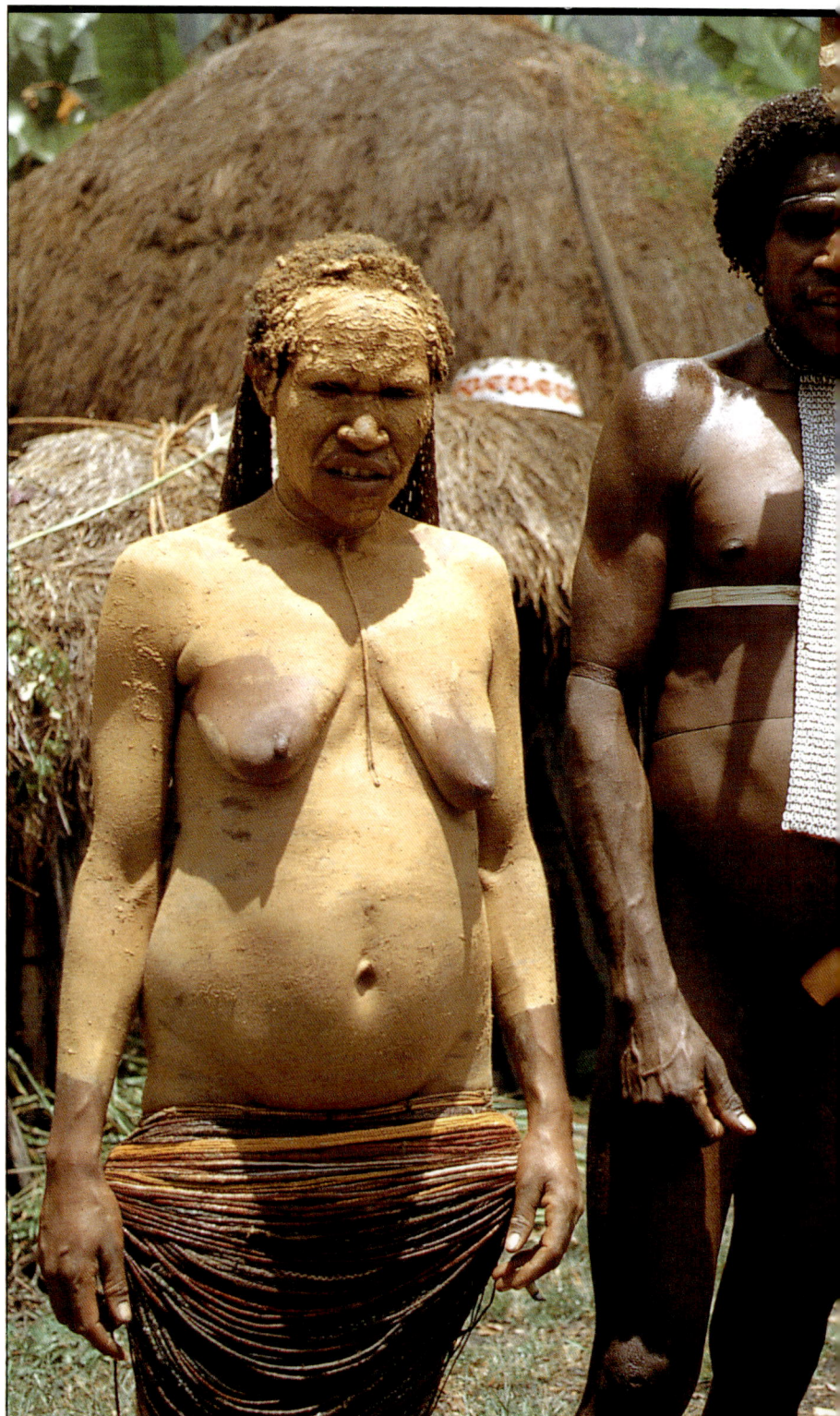

Irian Jaya

COMPRISING the western half of the island of New Guinea, Irian Jaya is Indonesia's largest and least explored province. Roughly equivalent to California in size, it accounts for more than 22 percent of Indonesia's total land area, yet has a population of only 2,000,000, or about one percent of Indonesia's people. Irian's rugged terrain is as beautiful as it is inhospitable. The southern Casuarina Coast consists of pristine white beaches, and malarial mangrove swamps. The Jayawijaya Mountains, Irian's serrated spine, form an impassable jungle wall that, despite being just four degrees below the equator, is permanently covered with snow at higher elevations. More than 200 landing strips cut into the jungle have tamed the region slightly, but transportation remains expensive and often depends on pilots working for Mission Aviation Fellowship (MAF), an organization known locally as the "Missionary Air Force."

BACKGROUND

When Portuguese explorers first arrived at the world's second largest island, they called it *Islas dos Papuas*, the "Island of the Fuzzy-hairs." Dutch colonists changed the name to Netherlands New Guinea since its black-skinned Melanesian people reminded them of natives in the African country of Guinea. The Dutch had little use for the island because of its poor soil. So, they turned its remoteness into a somewhat dubious asset by using it as an internment camp for Indonesian nationalists.

Partitioned toward the end of the nineteenth century, the eastern half of the island, Papua New Guinea, came under Australian control at the start of World War I and continued as a trust territory until 1975 when it gained independence. The lesser developed western half remained in Dutch hands after 1949 when the rest of Indonesia gained independence. But Indonesian president Sukarno maintained military and diplomatic pressure on the Netherlands, which finally agreed to withdraw in 1962 to the consternation of most Papuans.

Sukarno promised the Kennedy administration that citizens of Netherlands New Guinea would be allowed to vote in a 1969 "Act of Free Choice" on whether they wanted to join Indonesia. But when the date for the referendum arrived, Jakarta canceled the election and instead selected 1,025 delegates, who promptly voted (without one dissenting ballot) to join Indonesia. Indonesia's newest province became Irian Jaya, or "Victorious hot land rising from the sea."

Tension between Javanese bureaucrats and Irianese natives continues to this day. Irianese, most of whom continue to live in Stone Age conditions outside the coastal towns, object to the commercial exploitation of their land by Javanese, whose population increases disproportionately because of the government *transmigrasi* program. Jakarta's transmigration program has the laudable goal of moving landless peasants from the densely crowded islands of Java and Bali to relatively uninhabited places like Irian, where they can be given land and the tools to begin a new, and hopefully more productive, life. Unfortunately, the shock of arriving in the middle of a jungle where natives wear nothing but a *koteka* (penis sheath) and cut down trees with stone axes does not bode well for cultural integration. Many transmigrants work only long enough to earn their fare back to Java, leaving scarred plots of land quickly leached by tropical rains.

Despite its thin top soil, Irian Jaya is one of Indonesia's richest provinces. It is blessed with an abundance of gold, uranium and timber, as well as the world's richest deposit of copper.

GENERAL INFORMATION

The Regional Office of Tourism, Post and Telecommunications has free maps, brochures and current information about road and weather conditions. It is located at Jalan Raya Abepura N° 17, Enterup, Jayapura. The telephone number is (967) 21881, 22371. *DIPARDA*, the Provincial Tourist Service is on Jalan Soa Sio Dok II, ((967) 2138 ext. 263.

JAYAPURA AND THE NORTH

Separated from Jakarta by more than 3,000 km (2,000 miles) of ocean and islands, is Irian's capital, **Jayapura**. From Jayapura,

travelers can fly into the beautiful **Baliem Valley**, visit **Vogelkop** (Bird's Head Peninsula) and the nearby **Raja Empat Islands Nature Reserve**, or hop over to Biak, a coral island rich in memories for veterans of World War II's Pacific Theater. Jayapura also is the jumping off point for the **Yotefa Nature Reserve** east of the city along Humboldt Bay.

JAYAPURA

Originally named Hollandia, Jayapura was founded by the Dutch shortly after they annexed the territory in 1828. It is a small, stultifying city largely populated by Javanese bureaucrats who would rather be elsewhere. There is little shopping, and entertainment consists of pool halls, several movie theaters and a bar next to the Dafonsoro Hotel full of aggressive cockatoos and undercover policemen.

One place of possible interest is the **Anthropological Museum** at Cenderawasih University (open daily from 8 am to 2:30 pm except Sunday) in nearby **Abepura**. It has

some excellent Asmat carvings. Beached landing craft and rusting tanks may attract amateur historians to the suburb of **Hamadi** where General Douglas MacArthur landed in 1944. MacArthur's first stop on the road back to the Philippines, Hamadi also has a colorful market specializing in sea food.

If you have an early flight the following day or simply want to escape the torpor of Jayapura, you may wish to spend the night in **Sentani**, the lakeside town 35 km (22 miles) outside Jayapura near the airport where flights leave for Wamena, the Baliem Valley capital of the Dani tribe.

Where to Stay

Hotel Dafonsoro, Jalan Percetakan N° 22-24, (**(** (967) 22285/7) has 27 rooms that range from $40 to $65 for double occupancy. All rooms have attached *mandi*s and air-conditioning, and breakfast is included in the price of the room. The 20-room **Losmen Sederhana** (**(** (967) 21291 or 22357) is right in the middle of Jayapura at 2 Jalan Halmahera. It is convenient to everything in the city, including the night market, but lacks the tranquillity of **Losmen Agung** (☎ (967) 21777) outside Jayapura on the road to Hamadi. Located at Jalan Argapura N° 47, the Agung's nine bright and airy rooms cost only $18 and come with a large breakfast.

Where to Eat

There's always the restaurant at the **Hotel Dafonsoro**, but foreign missionaries prefer the **Jaya Grill** on Jalan Kota next to the outdoor *warungs*. Fronting on the ocean, the Jaya has a mix of European dishes that provides a timely antidote to a steady diet of *nasi goreng*.

THE BALIEM VALLEY

About 110,000 Dani live in the Baliem Valley, which was discovered in 1938 by explorer Richard Archbold. "From the air the gardens and ditches and native built walls appeared like the farming country of Central Europe," he later wrote in the *National Geographic*. After landing his seaplane on a lake, Archbold discovered that the natives were remarkably friendly. They had a diet composed largely of sweet potatoes and gauged wealth by the number of pigs owned by a family. Today, the Baliem Valley has maintained its unique culture. Dani women still wear only grass mini skirts around their pelvis. Men's fashion consists of a penis sheath called a "*koteka*" fashioned from a vegetable gourd. A decade ago, Indonesian bureaucrats tried to introduce clothes, a not unreasonable suggestion since the 73 km (45-mile) long Baliem Valley is more than a mile high. But to this day the Dani on cold nights prefer to smear themselves with pig grease and huddle about a fire in their communal huts.

Outside **Wamena** there is no transportation except for that provided by missionaries. Unless you are staying with a missionary family, you'll have to return by the end of the day since there is no public accommodation except for that provided by the Catholic mission at **Ywika**.

Where to Stay

The **Baliem Cottages** on Jalan Thamrin have eight rooms designed to look like thatched Dani huts from the outside that cost $38 a night. Attached bathrooms separated from each room by a glass partition are open to the sky. In addition to the Baliem Cottages there are several losmen near the airport, the nicest of which is the **Losmen Anggrek**, which has rooms for $22 a night.

Where to Eat

Most of the beef and fruit in Wamena is flown in, which means you should eat the locally grown vegetables when possible. Delicious vegetable soups and curries are served at **Restoran Vemalia** in back of the

central produce market. Next door to the Vemalia the **Rumah Makan Gembira** serves steaming platters of *nasi goreng* chock full of stir fried onions, tomatoes and baby corn.

What to Buy

There is much more to buy in Wamena than Jayapura. Penis sheaths (*koteka*), bark string bags and hand-woven bracelets called *sekan* can be purchased in the market or from shops along Jalan Trikora. Individual Dani with items to sell also cluster outside the hotels. Most of the hand-chiseled stone axes will fit in a suitcase and look surprisingly good when mounted on a wall back home. Asmat carvings also are offered for sale, but the selection is better on Biak.

BIAK

The most comfortable destination in Irian is probably Biak, a coral island 202 km (125 miles) east of Manokwari in **Cenderawasih Bay**. The souvenir shop at the Biak Airport is one of the best places in Irian to buy native handicrafts. While shopping you are entertained by a band of costumed tribesmen whose melodic mumbo jumbo is punctuated by the yelps of small children dressed as apprentice headhunters.

Where to Stay

The best hotel on the island is the Dutch-built **Hotel Irian** on Jalan Prof. Moh. Yamin, ((961) 21139, 21839, 21939. Located across the street from the airport, the 55-room hotel is less than one kilometer from the center of town. Its 24 standard rooms, all with an ocean view, are arrayed motel-fashion around a simple garden and cost $49 for two people. Ten renovated VIP rooms cost $6 more, but are right on the beach. Breakfast, lunch and dinner are included in the price of the room.

The **North Biak Nature Reserve** is full of exotic parrots and cockatoos. After watching the birds, head for **Korem Beach** next to the mouths of two fresh water streams that run through coconut plantations. Nearby **Supiori Island** has an even larger nature reserve that is reachable by boat.

Setia Tours (((961) 21398 or 21956) at Jalan A. Yani N° 36 offers a number of tours for World War II buffs. A five hour tour costing $25 a person visits **Bosnik Beach** where United States marines landed plus the **Japanese Cave** where 5,000 soldiers loyal to Emperor Hirohito chose to die rather than surrender. There also is a $100 trip designed for four people to **Padaido Island** which was the main Allied base during the war.

In the center of town the **Titawaka Hotel**, ((961) 21835, on Jalan Selat Makassar is slightly cheaper than the Irian and provides transport to the airport in addition to three meals a day. Cheaper still are the **Titawaka Home** and **Wisma Titawaka**, two losmen managed by the owners of the Titawaka Hotel.

Where to Eat

There are several small restaurants — **Himalaya, Megaria, Rumah Makan Anda** — along Jalan Jend. Ahmad Yani that offer the

OPPOSITE: Animist artisans use stone axes to carve ceremonial shields. ABOVE: Television programming and stone age technology is a combination that leaves many Irianese bewildered.

usual range of Chinese and Indonesian dishes. If you are looking for an alternative to these places, try the night *warungs* off Jalan Imam Bonjol where fare runs to sate, pickled cucumbers and *gado gado*.

THE BIRD'S HEAD

Sorong and **Manokwari** on the Bird's Head peninsula are oil towns completely devoid of charm, but **Sorong** may be worth a stopover since it's the gateway to the Raja Empat Nature Reserve, a bird watcher's paradise

covering parts of **Waigeo**, **Batanta** and **Gag islands.** Like the island of Komodo, the Raja Empat Reserve is administered by the PHPA, located in Sorong at Jalan Pemuda N° 40.

Where to Stay

In Sorong the **Cenderawasih Hotel** at Jalan Sam Ratulangi N° 54, (℘ (951) 21966, 21740; telex 77127 CHSON) has 22 rooms that cost from $45 to $65 for double occupancy.

THE SOUTH COAST

The Casuarina Coast of southern Irian Jaya is a dark and malarial region. Poisonous adders dangle from areca palms; man-eat-

ing crocodiles rule the mangrove swamps. The Asmat and other cannibal tribes who inhabit the jungle call their home "the land of lapping death." **Agats** on the southwest coast near Flamingo Bay is the departure point for a journey upriver to Asmat villages, but a trip this exotic must be carefully planned far in advance with the assistance of missionaries. The Asmat are prolific wood carvers who adorn their villages with two to three meter (six to 10-ft) -tall totem poles adorned with copulating animistic spirits. More commercial objects such as shields, spears and blow guns are also produced. Dealers in the primitive arts may find a journey into the Asmat jungle rewarding, but less adventurous souls can purchase Asmat carvings in Jayapura or the Biak airport.

Until recently, foreign presence in that area consisted of missionaries and officials of the Freeport Copper Company who ran the world's largest open pit copper mine outside **Tembagapura**, a prosperous little town perched 3,700 m (12,136 ft) up snow-capped Mt. Jaya. Freeport's announced withdrawal (due to pressure from environmentalists) complicates transportation to this area, which has never been easy to reach.

South Irian's greatest mystery concerns the fate of Michael Rockefeller, the 23-year old son of the late American millionaire Nelson Rockefeller, who disappeared suddenly in November 1961.

Drawn to Irian because of his "desire to do something adventurous," Rockefeller worked as a sound man on a documentary film sponsored by Harvard's Peabody Museum. After briefly visiting home, he returned to the Casuarina coast to live with the Asmat, whose art he began to collect for Manhattan's Museum of Primitive Art. Together with Dutch ethnologist Rene Wassing, Rockefeller set out on an expedition to look for elaborately-decorated human skulls, but the small boat they were using quickly was swamped by the rough currents of the Arafura Sea. Rockefeller's two Asmat guides swam for help, but never returned. Wassing told Rockefeller to wait for rescue, but despite the sharks and crocodiles Rockefeller decided to swim for help and was never seen again.

Did Michael Rockefeller drown? Did he arrive safely ashore only to encounter hostile tribesmen? *Argosy* magazine dispatched a correspondent who concluded Rockefeller was killed by an Asmat tribe seeking revenge for earlier indignities suffered from the Dutch. Rockefeller's fate may remain a mystery forever, but recurring stories of his glasses, clothes and skull appearing in the Asmat village of Ocenep persuade some that the heir to one of America's largest fortunes was the victim of cannibals.

HOW TO GET THERE

Three times each week Garuda's international flights from Los Angeles and Honolulu stop at Biak en route to Jakarta. Inside Indonesia, Garuda has daily service out of Jakarta and Denpasar to Jayapura, Biak and Sorong. Unfortunately, traveling from Java to Irian is a tiring, all day affair. Garuda flights from Jakarta leave at 5 am and stop at Ujung Pandang, Ambon, Sorong and Biak before heading to Jayapura. The Merpati flight from Jakarta can take even longer since it makes an additional stop in Surabaya and overnights in Biak before heading to Jayapura the following day.

Inside Irian transportation is provided by Merpati which has service linking Sorong, Biak, Manokwari, Jayapura, Wamena, Merauke and Nabire.

Two PELNI ships, the *Umsini* and the *Rinjani*, make fortnightly trips to Irian and back from the Jakarta port of Tanjung Priok.

Remember when traveling in this part of the archipelago that Irian, like East Timor, is considered a sensitive area. Coastal towns all welcome tourists, but police may demand a surat jalan, or letter of transit, for travel to remote areas near the Papua New

Guinea border. It is occasionally possible to finesse the local police, but if reaching a remote destination is critical to the success of your journey, check in Jakarta first to see if a *surat jalan* is necessary.

Finally, of the more than 200 airfields in Irian less than a dozen are serviced by commercial airlines. The remaining strips are used by MAF or its Catholic counterpart, Associated Mission Aviation, both of which have offices across the road from Sentani airport. It is possible to fly MAF on a space-available, cash-only basis, but MAF is particular about whom they will fly. To insure cooperation at Sentani, call MAF's headquarters in Redlands, California at (1) 714 794-1151 before departing for Indonesia, or write to the organization at P.O. Box 202 in Redlands.

OPPOSITE: Though occasionally the main course at a feast, pigs are more often used as currency.
ABOVE: Since grass skirts have no pockets, Dani women carry valuables in knitted bags slung across their heads.

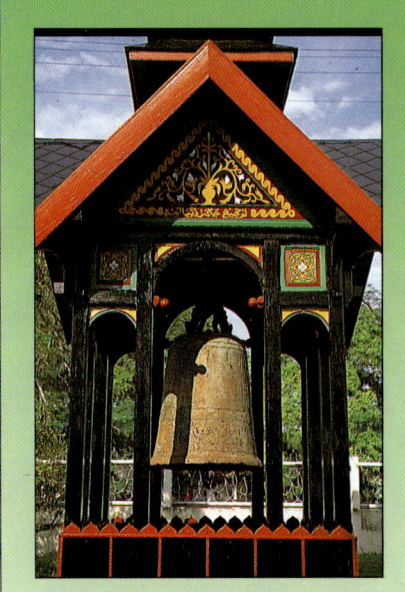

Travelers'
Tips

GETTING THERE

By Air

A quick look at any map will confirm that Indonesia is slightly off the beaten track. It is not a country one "stops over" to visit en route to another destination. That being the case, it is important to plan your trip carefully and shop around for the best travel buys.

The quickest, most economical way to get to Indonesia is by air. From Europe, KLM, Swiss Air, Lufthansa and Air France all have direct service. From the United States, Indonesia's national flag-carrier, Garuda Airlines, offers the most efficient, economical service. Four times a week flights leave Los Angeles for Jakarta, with stops in Honolulu, Biak and Bali's capital of Denpasar. The only United States airline to fly direct is Continental, which has thrice weekly service to Denpasar via Honolulu and Guam.

If a direct flight to Bali or Jakarta is not a priority, you may want to fly through Singapore, the Southeast Asian "hub" city with the most connecting flights to Indonesia. Northwest and United both fly direct to Singapore from the West Coast. Singapore Airlines has daily service from San Francisco and Los Angeles, but the flights make several stops and require changing planes in Singapore.

Once you're in Singapore, getting to Indonesia is easy. Singapore Airlines has ten daily nonstops to Jakarta and once-a-day service to Medan in Northern Sumatra. It also flies to Bali five days a week. Because the number of Singapore Airlines flights between Jakarta, Bali and Singapore is matched by Garuda, the level of service linking the two countries essentially is that of a competitively-priced shuttle.

Executives flying on a full-fare first or business class ticket to Jakarta can get a free one-night stop over in Hong Kong if they fly Cathay Pacific from Los Angeles. The flight from Los Angeles arrives in Hong Kong at 8 pm. The connecting flight to Jakarta leaves at 4:20 pm the following day, leaving the morning free for shopping.

A similar arrangement can be worked out with Malaysian Airline System (MAS) for full-fare travelers who want to see a bit of Kuala Lumpur. Flights from the West Coast to Malayia via Tokyo arrive in Kuala Lumpur in the evening. MAS will provide a hotel for the evening and take passengers to Jakarta or Medan on connecting flights the following day.

From New York, KLM has direct connections via Amsterdam to Medan in Sumatra and on to Bali. Travelers in Bangkok can take Thai International's daily nonstop to Jakarta. Qantas has two weekly flights to Jakarta and three to Bali from Sydney.

From throughout the United States and Canada Garuda reservations can be made toll-free on (800) 247-8380 or sending a fax to (213) 389-1568.

Chicago, Illinois 20 N. Michigan Avenue, Suite 270. ((312) 443-0063.
Los Angeles, California 3457 Wilshire Boulevard. ((213) 386-3323.
San Francisco, California 360 Post Street, Suite 804. ((415) 788-2626.
Honolulu, Hawaii 1600 Kaiolani Boulevard, Suite 632. ((808) 947-5500, 945-3971.
New York, NY 51 East 42nd Street, Suite 616. ((212) 370-0707.
Vancouver, BC 1040 West Georgia Street. ((604) 681-3699.

By Sea

The great irony of this enormous equatorial archipelago is that it is very difficult to reach by ship. The only two established ports of entry are the Medan seaport of Belawan in northern Sumatra and Sekupang on Batam Island in the Riau Archipelago. Both are served by hydrofoils and ferries that connect them with Penang in Malaysia and Singapore.

The ferry linking Penang and Belawan runs twice a week and takes 15 hours. In Medan tickets can be purchased from PT Eka Sukma Wisata Tour and Travel Service at Jalan Brig. Jend. Katamso N° 62 near the Maimoon Palace. In Penang, tickets are sold by Sanren Delta Marine on Jalan Tun Syed Shah Barakbah.

Hydrofoils leave Singapore's Finger Pier on Prince Edward Road five times a day for the 30-minute trip to Sekupang on Batam.

A friendly Savu face. Indonesia's ethnic mozaic is a microcosm of Asia.

After clearing customs there, it's possible to board another ferry for a two-hour journey to Tanjung Pinang.

Adventurous travelers with a yen to experience something akin to the trip upriver in Conrad's *Heart of Darkness* may wish to take a boat from Tanjung Pinang to Pekanbaru in East Sumatra. The ferry goes three times a week and takes 36 hours. The crowded conditions aboard the ferry will not appeal to most travelers (who should take their own canned food and bottled water), but the stops at villages along the rivers provide excellent photographic opportunities and a chance to experience the riverine jungles of Sumatra.

USEFUL ADDRESSES

CONSULAR INFORMATION

In addition to visas, Indonesia's embassies and consulates have valuable information on annual events you may wish to see during your visit.

United States of America
INDONESIAN EMBASSY
2020 Massachusetts Avenue NW, Washington, DC 20036. ((202) 775-5200.
INDONESIAN CONSULATES
Chicago 2 Illinois Center, 233 North Michigan Avenue, Suite 1422. ((312) 938-0101, fax 938-3148.
Honolulu Pri Tower, 733 Bishop Street. ((808) 524-4300.
Houston 5633 Richmond Avenue. ((713) 785-1691.
Los Angeles 3457 Wilshire Boulevard. ((213) 383-5126, fax 487-3971.
New York 5 East 68th Street. ((212) 879-0600, fax 570-6206.
San Francisco 1111 Columbus Avenue. ((415) 474-9571.

Canada
INDONESIAN EMBASSY
287 Maclaren Street, Ottawa, Ontario K29 OL9. ((613) 236-7403, fax 563-2858.

INDONESIAN CONSULATES
Toronto 425 University Avenue, 9/F. ((416) 591-6481, fax 591-6613.
Vancouver 1455 West Georgia Street, 2/F. ((604) 682-8855, fax 662-8396.

Netherlands
INDONESIAN EMBASSY
Tobias Asserlaan N° 8, 5517, KCS Gravenhage. ((70) 469796, fax 643331.

Germany
INDONESIAN EMBASSY
Bernkasteler Strasse 2, 53175 Bonn. ((0228) 328990.
INDONESIAN CONSULATES
Berlin Rudeloffweg. ((030) 831-5076.
Bremen Damhof 26. ((0421) 332-2224.
Duesseldorf Berliner Alle 2. ((0211) 353081.
Hamburg Bebelallee 15. ((040) 512071.
Hannover Georg Platz 1. ((0511) 103-2150.
Munich Widermayer Strasse 24. ((089) 294609.
Stuttgart Lenzheide 65. ((0711) 223729.

Great Britain
INDONESIAN EMBASSY
157 Edgware Road, London W2 2HR. ((01) 499-7661.

Australia
INDONESIAN EMBASSY,
8 Darwin Avenue, Yarralumia, Canberra. ((062) 733222, fax 733748.
INDONESIAN CONSULATES
Adelaide 3/F Walsh Building., 44 Gawler Place. ((08) 223-6535.
Darwin 22 Coronation Drive, Stuart Park. ((089) 819352.
Melbourne 3/F, 52 Albert Road. ((03) 690-7811.
Perth 133 St. George's Terrace. (219821.
Sydney 236-238 Marcubra Road, Marcubra. ((02) 344-9933.

Indonesian Tourism Offices
For additional information and maps contact the Indonesia Tourist Promotion Office:
Australia 4 Bligh Street Sydney 2000. ((02) 232-6044, fax 233-2828.
Germany Wiesenhuettenplatz 17, 60329 Frankfurt am Main. ((069) 233-6778, fax (069) 230840.

Europe's demand for cloves and nutmeg found only on the islands of TOP Ternate and BOTTOM Banda prompted explorers like Christopher Columbus to set out in search of the East Indies.

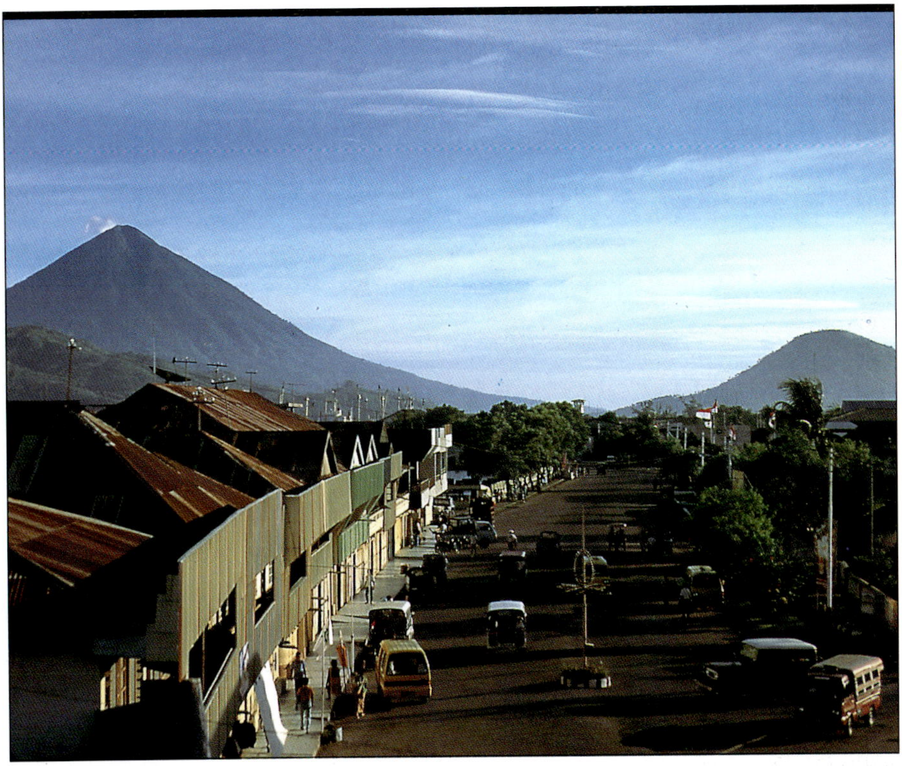

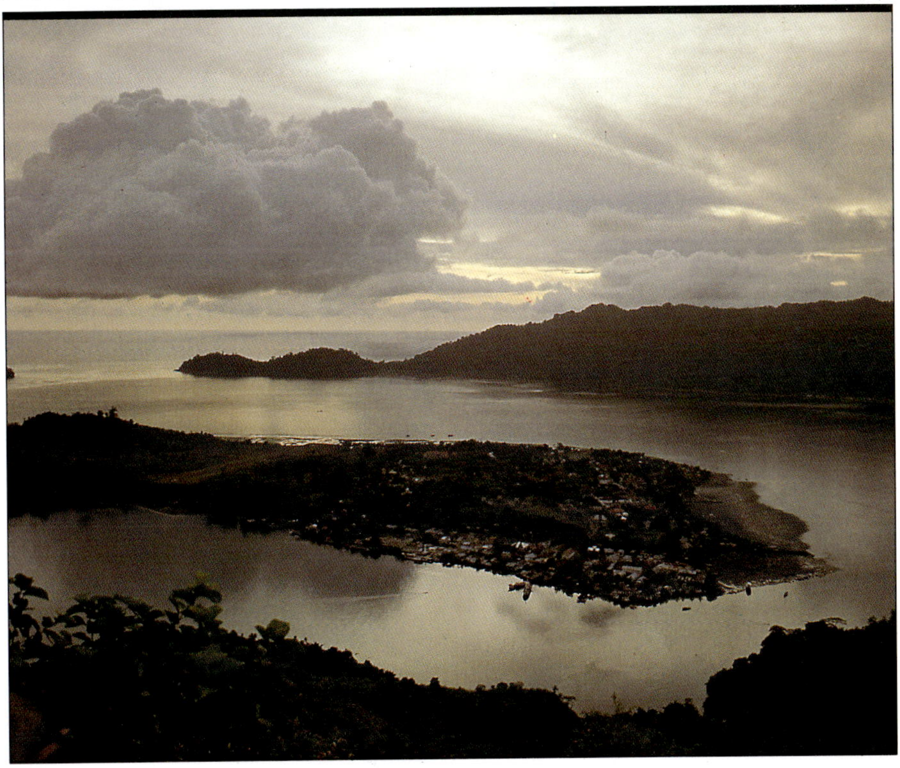

Singapore 10 Collyer Quay, 15-07 Ocean Building, Singapore 0104. (534-2837, fax 533-4287.

U.S.A. 3457 Wilshire Boulevard, Los Angeles, California 90010. ((213) 387-2078, fax 380-4876.

Indonesian diplomats and ITPO officials have several interesting books and pamphlets. One is the *Official Indonesia Handbook*, a statistic-packed 240 page book that provides detailed information on the history, geography and politics of Indonesia. The *Jakarta Visitor's Guide* and the *Jakarta Tour & Convention Planner* are helpful when shaping an itinerary for the capital.

CHARTER FLIGHTS AND TOUR OPERATORS

Garuda Airlines offers a number of Garuda Orient Holiday packages for persons traveling from North America. Brochures containing detailed price information can be obtained toll-free from ((800) 247-8380.

A number of established tour operators in the United States specialize in Indonesia. **Vayatours** at 6420 Wilshire Boulevard in Los Angeles, ((213) 655-3851 offers a variety of packages, as does **Sobek Expeditions** in Angel's Camp, California, ((209) 736-4524.

Sobek Expeditions specializes in adventure travel. Its packages often touch down only briefly in Jakarta before heading to Irian Jaya's Baliem Valley or Sumatra's riverine jungles. Another established adventure travel company headquartered in Jakarta is **PT Tomaco** in the Jakarta Theater Building at Jalan Thamrin N° 9, ((21) 320087. Tomaco puts together jungle river trips that head into the heart of the Borneo rain forest.

Diving coral reefs, climbing volcanoes and sailing the Celebes Sea in Bugis schooners all can be arranged through agencies that specialize in each activity. The Department of Tourism or the ITPO can direct you to the appropriate company.

Persons interested in exploring the seldom visited islands of Nusa Tenggara should contact **Spice Islands Cruises**, Jalan Jend S. Parman N°78, Jakarta Barat, ((21) 593401-2, fax (21) 593403. Spice Islands' 40-m *Island Explorer* will take passengers on a 12-day trip around the Sawu Sea to Flores, Timor, Sawu, Sumba and Komodo.

Jakarta has numerous travel agencies, many of them located on the third floor of the Borobudur Hotel. All of them offer three standard city tours: a morning tour that goes to Old Batavia, the National Museum, the National Monument (MONAS) and the Art Market (Pasar Seni) at Ancol Park; an afternoon tour that visits Jalan Surabaya, MONAS, Ancol Park and the Oceanarium; and the evening excursion to Ancol with dinner included. Frankly, the best investment, both in time and money, is to shop about in front of the major hotels for a taxi driver with a bit of English and hire your own car.

Satriavi Tours at Jalan Prapatan N° 32, ((21) 380-3944 can arrange a variety of guided tours throughout the archipelago. Though it has a thick brochure full of standardized tours, it gladly will personalize individual vacations. A much smaller but equally professional company is **Apexindo Tours** on the third floor of the Borobudur, ((21) 370108.

BIRD-WATCHING SAFARIS

Indonesia is a heaven-on-earth for bird watching. One-sixth of the world's birds, some 1,500 species, live on the country's 13,000 islands. Roughly half of these birds are found nowhere else on earth.

More than a century ago British naturalist Alfred Russel Wallace described Indonesia's king bird of paradise as a "gem of cinnabar red plumage with a gloss like spun silk." Where ever Wallace traveled in the islands he found golden orioles, numerous species of hornbills and "the gorgeous little minivet fly-catcher which looks like a flame of fire as it flutters among the bushes."

Today, although less than 10 percent of the original habitat on Java and Bali remains, bird watchers can visit several impressive national parks and reserves. Some, like the bird sanctuary on Rambut Island in Jakarta Bay, offer easy access. Others, like Ujung Kulon National Park on the southwestern tip of Java, require a more daring spirit.

The islands of Sulawesi, Makulu and Nusa Tenggara have 246 endemic species. Sulawesi alone has 70 birds that are found nowhere else. This group includes two hornbills, five mynas, six kingfishers and an unusual maleo which buries its eggs in hot black sand and then abandons them to hatch on their own.

Persons interested in bird watching vacations should write to Derrick Holmes, editor of *Kukila*, the Bulletin of the Indonesian Ornithological Society, at P.O. Box 287/KBY, Jakarta 12001.

ARRIVING

TRAVEL DOCUMENTS

All travelers to Indonesia must possess passports valid for at least six months after arrival and proof of onward passage.

Neither visas nor immigration fees are required for nationals of Australia, Austria, Belgium, Brunei, Canada, Denmark, Finland, France, Greece, Iceland, Ireland, Italy, Japan, Liechtenstein, Luxembourg, Malaysia, Malta, the Netherlands, New Zealand, Norway, the Philippines, Singapore, South Korea, Spain, Sweden, Switzerland, Thailand, the United Kingdom, the United States and West Germany. Citizens of countries not listed above can obtain one-month, non-extendible visas from any Indonesian embassy or consulate.

Entry and exit from Indonesia must be made either from air or seaports in Jakarta, Denpasar, Medan, Manado, Biak, Ambon, Batam, Surabaya and Pekanbaru. For all other ports of arrival or departure visas are required.

Persons wanting to stay longer than the normally permitted two months must apply for an extension. It is easier to leave the country and reapply.

No matter what sort of visa you have immigration officials can deny you entry if they feel you are not properly groomed. This rarely happens, Indonesia's sartorial standards not being as strict as those of Singapore, but persons judged to be a threat to "the public health and morals" of the country can be sent packing on the next plane out.

CUSTOMS

A maximum of two liters of alcohol, 200 cigarettes or 50 cigars can be brought in duty free. Importing of television sets is prohibited. All video cassettes are subject to seizure and editing by the Film Censor Board.

WHEN TO GO

Indonesia has an equatorial tropical climate tempered by trade winds. Temperatures hover around 28°C (82°F) in the coastal areas, but drop rapidly at higher elevations. The average humidity is 81 percent. The wet season is from October to April and the dry season is from May to September. It can rain any time, however, with the heaviest rains coming in December and January. Kalimantan receives 130 inches of rain a year, while East Nusa Tenggara gets less than 40 inches. Bogor is the wettest spot on the island of Java.

WHAT TO TAKE

Casual and light clothing is best suited to the climate, but for travel in the mountain areas of West Java and Irian Jaya one should have a sweater or jacket. A coat and tie is always appropriate for diplomatic functions, but long-sleeved batik shirts are acceptable almost everywhere else.

GETTING AROUND

BY AIR

Garuda flies to all of Indonesia's large cities and many of its smaller ones. Domestically, it serves 33 cities, including all of the provincial capitals. Garuda has four ticket offices in Jakarta in addition to its headquarters at Jalan Merdeka Selatan N° 13, ((21) 380-1901, 380-6276.

Merpati Nusantara Airlines is the second national carrier and flies to about 110 destinations. It also has a few cross-border flights to Darwin, Australia, Brunei Darussalam and the East Malaysian state of Sarawak. Merpati is particularly active in the smaller islands of eastern Indonesia and the interiors of Kalimantan, Sulawesi and Irian Jaya. Though Merpati and Garuda have made connections more convenient by coordinating their route structures, you still have to buy a Merpati ticket from Merpati airlines. In Jakarta that means going to Jalan Angkasa N° 2, ☎ (21) 413608.

Three privately-owned airlines, Bouraq Mandala and Sempati, try their best to compete with the state-subsidized carriers. Of the three, Bouraq (named after the horse on which the Prophet Mohammed rode to Heaven) has the larger route structure and is particularly useful in getting to coastal cities of Kalimantan and Sulawesi. In Jakarta Bouraq is located at Jalan Angkasa N° 1-3, ☎ (21) 629-5364, and that of Sempati is at Jalan Medon Merdeka Timur N° 7, ☎ (21) 809-4407.

An airport tax of Rp 15,000 ($7.50) is levied on all departing passengers on international flights except Singapore (S$12) and Kuala Lumpur (M$14). For those flying within Indonesia, airport taxes vary from Rp 3,000 to Rp 5,000 depending on the airport.

BY TRAIN

Train service is only available on Java and Sumatra. The most heavily traveled route is between Jakarta and Surabaya. The most comfortable trains by far are the air-conditioned *Bima* sleeper train and the *Mutiara*, which also runs at night. The *Bima* passes through Yogyakarta and Solo, while the Mutiara takes the northern route through Semarang. Another train, the *Senja Utama*, offers express service to Yogyakarta and Solo, but it has no air-conditioning. Bandung is well serviced by the *Parahyangan Express*, which makes four three-hour round trips a day between Jakarta and the mountain city the Dutch built to escape the heat.

BY TAXI

Metered taxis operate in Jakarta, Surabaya, Semarang and Bandung with fares of Rp 600 at flag fall (for the first kilometer) and Rp 300 for each additional kilometer. For air-conditioned taxis flag fall is Rp 700 and Rp 400 for each additional kilometer.

Jakarta has a number of taxi companies. Blue Bird, President and Steady Safe are the best. Blue Bird cabs are clean and the drivers are courteous, but often their English is not

the best so it's always advisable to have a written address for your destination.

Taxis also serve as an efficient and economical way to move about West Java. A number of companies shuttle between Jakarta and Bandung, and one even offers service to Bandar Lampung on the southern tip of Sumatra.

Companies serving Bandung use standard Japanese sedans that accommodate a driver and up to five passengers. Reservations are not necessary. Taxis leave the moment they are full and drop passengers off at whatever address they desire in Bandung. Among the companies serving Bandung are Media Taxi, Jalan Johor N° 15, ☎ (21) 320343; Taxi 333, Jalan Jembatan Tiga N° 36GGI, ☎ (21) 669-6572, fax (21) 602-1133; Metro Taxi, Jalan Kopi 2C, ☎ (21) 674000, fax (21) 675498. In addition to Bandung, Taxi 333 serves the western tip of Java. Passengers bound for Bandar Lampung will be put on a ferry to Sumatra and picked up by another cab following the crossing.

BY SHIP

PELNI, the state-owned shipping company, traverses the archipelago with six modern ships that carry up to 1,800 passengers in five classes of service. PELNI's main office is at Jalan Gajah Mada N° 14, ☎ (21) 343307 or 361635, fax (21) 381-0341 or 345605. Not luxurious but comfortable, the ships are air-conditioned and have attached bathrooms and television sets in the first class cabins.

Society Expeditions also has a ship called the *World Discoverer* cruising Indonesia's waters. For details contact Society Expedition Cruises, 3131 Elliott Avenue, Suite 700, Seattle, Washington 98121; ☎ (800) 426-7794.

BY BUS

Buses are cheap, fast and crowded. Inner city buses are labeled *bis kota* on the side. Long haul buses that travel overnight between large towns are called *bis malam*. Because Indonesian roads are poorly lit and crowded with trucks at night, a trans-Java excursion can have a share of close calls. Indonesians who can afford to fly, do so, and you should too.

If your budget dictates land travel, there are a variety of ways to move between cities. In addition to a *bis malam* you can take a Colt minivan between towns. Cheaper still are *bemos*, small pickup trucks with a bench along each side.

BY CAR

Avis, Hertz and National have self-drive and chauffeured rentals in Jakarta. Avis has offices at the Borobudur and Sari Pacific hotels, and headquarters at Jalan Diponegoro N° 25,

As a rule, driving is not worth the hassle. The exception is Bali where traffic is less intense and jeeps can be rented at normal prices from shops along Legian Road in Kuta Beach. If you decide the drive anyway, remember that Indonesians drive on the left side of the road and call gasoline bensin. If you get lost on Java, ask for the *kepala kampung* (village chief) or the *bupati* (district chief). Avoid police unless you speak Indonesian, and never surrender your driver's license unless forced to do so at a central police station.

〔(21) 331974. Hertz is on the seventh floor of the Chase Plaza just off Jalan Jend. Sudirman, Kav N° 21, 〔(21) 578-2240, it also has an office in the Mandarin Oriental and Aryaduta hotels. National Car Rental is located across the street from the Mandarin on the ground floor of the Hotel Kartika Plaza. 〔(21) 333423.

Import duties make cars expensive in Indonesia, much more costly than in the United States, so expect to pay a premium for the convenience of operating an automobile.

You may regret renting a car once you try to navigate around Jakarta. The main roads are poorly marked, if marked at all. Indonesian streets are rather narrow and are not banked with shoulders that allow a driver to pull off and study a map.

BY THUMB

Beyond the island of Java rides are hard to come by since not many Indonesian families have a car. Those who do seldom use them to travel between cities. The roads on Java, Bali are good there are also some good roads on Sumatra, but beyond these islands the roads are abysmal. Jeeps and pickup trucks can be shaken apart over time; passenger sedans stand no chance at all.

On Java, there is a good road linking Jakarta with Bogor, so hitchhiking is possible

Lake Toba passenger ferries provide the only transportation to Samosir Island.

there. But beyond Bogor it's really not worth the bother. Cheap gasoline makes for cheap transportation. Hitchhiking is a false economy that's not really worth the effort.

GENERAL INFORMATION

Each of the 27 provinces of Indonesia has its own tourist office which can be identified by the abbreviation *DIPARDA* (Provincial Tourist Service) or *BAPPARDA* (Provincial Tourism Agency). All of the offices offer

brochures, maps and other general assistance about their area.

In Jakarta the Department of Tourism, Post and Telecommunications is located at 36 Jalan Kebon Sirih, ℂ (21) 372646, fax (21) 375409. Additional information and advice can be obtained from the Directorate General of Tourism at 81 Jalan Kramat Raya, ℂ (21) 310-3117, fax (21) 310-1146.

EMBASSIES AND CONSULATES

AMERICAN EMBASSY   Jalan Merdeka Selatan Nº 5, Jakarta ℂ (21) 360360.
AMERICAN CONSULATES   **Medan**, Jalan Imam Bonjol Nº 13, ℂ (61) 322200; **Surabaya**, Jalan Raya Dr. Sutomo Nº 33, ℂ (31) 69287; **Denpasar**, Jalan Segara Ayu Sanur Nº 5, ℂ (361) 88478.
BRITISH EMBASSY   Jalan M.H. Thamrin Nº 75, Jakarta ℂ (21) 330904.
BRITISH CONSULATES   **Surabaya**, Jalan Jemur Sari Nº 150; **Medan**, Jalan Jend. A. Yani Nº 2, ℂ (61) 518699.

CANADIAN EMBASSY   5/f, Wisma Metropolitan I, Jalan Jend. Sudirman Kav Nº 29, Jakarta ℂ (21) 510709.
AUSTRALIAN EMBASSY   Jalan M.H. Thamrin Nº 15, Jakarta ℂ (21) 323109.
AUSTRALIAN CONSULATE   **Denpasar**, Jalan Raya Sanur Nº 146, ℂ (361) 35092.
GERMAN EMBASSY   Jalan M.H. Thamrin Nº 1, Jakarta ℂ (21) 323908.
GERMAN CONSULATES   **Medan**, Jalan S. Parman Nº 271, ℂ (61) 324073; **Denpasar**, Jalan Pantai Karang Nº 17, Batujumbar Sanur, ℂ (361) 8535.
FRENCH EMBASSY   Jalan M.H. Thamrin Nº 20, Jakarta ℂ (21) 332807, 333-2375.
FRENCH CONSULATES   **Bandung**, Jalan Purnawarman Nº 32, ℂ (22) 52864; **Yogyakarta**, Jalan Sagan I Nº 1, ℂ 4109; **Surabaya**, Jalan Darmokali Nº 10, ℂ (274) 68639.
NETHERLANDS EMBASSY   Jalan H.R. Rasuna Said Kav Nº S-3, Jakarta ℂ (21) 511515.
DUTCH CONSULATES   **Bandung**, Panin Bank Building, 3/f, Jalan Asia Afrika Nº 166-170, ℂ (22) 439482; **Medan**, Jalan A. Rivai Nº 22, ℂ (61) 519025; **Surabaya**, Jalan Sumatera Nº 79, ℂ 45202; **Bali**, Jalan Raya Imam Bonjol Nº 599, Kuta, ℂ 51094.
JAPANESE EMBASSY   Jalan M.H. Thamrin Nº 24 Jakarta ℂ (21) 324308, 324396.
JAPANESE CONSULATES   **Ujung Pandang**, Jalan Jend. Sudirman Nº 31, ℂ (411) 82323; **Surabaya**, Jalan Sumatera Nº 93, ℂ 44677; **Denpasar**, Jalan Mohammad Yamin Renon Nº 9, ℂ 24203; **Medan**, Jalan A. Yani Nº 12, ℂ (61) 510533.

HEALTH

Western doctors advise getting a battery of vaccinations before arriving in Indonesia, but absolutely none are required unless you happen to be coming from a cholera-infested African country.

Vaccinations may not be essential, but precautions should be taken prior to arrival. Komodo Island is a bad place to have a toothache, so have a dental check up before leaving home. Also, bring any prescription medication you may require. Fungal infections can be a problem because of the heat, so you may want to travel with talcum powder or an anti-fungal spray.

If a medical problem does arise, there are a variety of western-educated doctors practicing in Jakarta. The most centrally located office is the Metropolitan Medical Center in the Hotel Wisata on Jalan Thamrin, ℂ (21) 320408. If you prefer a clinic where all the doctors speak English or Dutch, call the Medical Scheme (ℂ (21) 515597) in the Setiabundi Building on Jalan H. Rasuna Said.

MONEY

At the time of going to press Rp 2,060 was worth US$1.00. In recent years Indonesia's national currency, the rupiah, has been inflating at an annual rate in excess of 10 percent Because it loses value with every passing day, many fixed prices are expressed in United States dollars. Because credit cards are widely accepted in Jakarta hotels and restaurants, some travelers charge every expense believing the interval between the time of their purchase and the time the credit company bills their bank will result in a more favorable rate of exchange. Though deficient in other areas, Indonesian businesses, because of the rupiah's declining value, are remarkably efficient at processing card charges. After returning home don't be surprised if all your expenses appear on the first credit summary you receive in the mail.

Outside Jakarta, Yogyakarta and Bali you must pay cash for goods and services. Carry rupiah in small denominations; large bills are often difficult to change. Personal checks are useless and travelers' checks, if accepted at all, can take hours to negotiate. Only the most tourist-wise businessmen accept credit cards, so their usefulness is extremely limited. Though you may opt for greater security, the best way to finance a trip through Indonesia is to carry $100 bills, which can be exchanged for rupiah when needed at a rate slightly above what is offered for travelers' checks. Don't exchange money until you need it since those unspent rupiah in your pocket lose a bit if their value every day. Neither, however, should you wait until you get to an out of the way place like West Kalimantan, Irian Jaya or Nusa Tenggara since the rate money changers offer there is not competitive with that available in places like Java and Bali.

Banks are generally open from 8 am to 2 pm or 3 pm. Branch banks in hotel stay open longer and money changers may be open until midnight.

TIPPING

Hotels add a service charge of 10 percent to the bill. Restaurants have their own policies, so you must check the bill and add five to

10 percent if service has not been included. Tipping is really not mandatory anywhere. Taxi drivers and hotel porters do not expect a tip, though one will be happily received. Baggage handlers at airports do expect to be tipped Rp 500 for every bag they carry, plus a bit more if the suitcases are large and heavy.

ACCOMMODATION

Unlike other OPEC countries, Indonesia has prospered despite the decline in oil prices

OPPOSITE: Sumatran women take bananas to market. ABOVE: Sumatra's Grand Mosque is the pride of Banda Aceh.

because of expanding revenues from tourism. In 1994 over three millions tourists are expected to visit Indonesia. Two new luxury hotels — the Grand Hyatt, the Meridien — opened in 1992. Together they provided the Indonesian capital with 900 new rooms. The additional lodging will relieve a shortage, not create a glut, so don't expect prices to fall. Still, Jakarta offers some of the most reasonably priced accommodations in Southeast Asia. Because of the rupiah's inflation, Indonesian hotels give their rates in United States dollars. Small *losmen* or guest houses that require payment in cash list their rates in rupiah. All major hotels in the larger cities accept credit cards.

EATING OUT

Indonesian food often is described as an exotic and subtle blend of rich spices. Unfortunately, much of the verbiage is pure hype. The primary flavor in most Indonesian dishes comes from coconut, peanuts or chili, none of which is especially subtle. Indonesian food is not one of Asia's great cuisines. It simply does not compare to Thai or Chinese in taste or diversity. This does not mean you can't have a good meal with great service in Jakarta. Indeed, the city has some very fine restaurants. Just don't expect gourmet dining every night.

Indonesian food is a regional, rather than national, cuisine. When Jakartans consider their dining possibilities they think in terms of Sundanese food from West Java, Central Java's *gudeg* or West Sumatra's *Padang*. Sundanese specialize in grilled fresh water fish, accompanied by an assortment of raw vegetables and sambal, the chili relish found throughout the country. *Gudeg* food is much sweeter and *Padang*, somewhat like the Dutch rijstafel, is served in a series of side dishes from which you can choose and be charged on the basis of only what you eat.

Originally, Indonesian food was eaten with your right hand off a banana leaf. Today, *warungs* (sidewalk food stalls), *rumah makans* (small cafes) and *restorans* (restaurants) serve it on a plate with a spoon and fork. Anything with the word in front of it means it's served with rice. *nasi goreng* (fried

rice) and *mie goreng* (fried noodles) are popular dishes that can be served at any hour of the day. *Gado gado*, the ubiquitous side dish served alongside satay, basically is a vegetable salad with peanut sauce.

Indonesian food goes best with tea, soft drinks or beer. It never was intended to be accompanied by wine, assuming you can find an Indonesian restaurant that has wine. In truth, wine probably should be avoided entirely while in Indonesia since what little there is available largely consists (for reasons stemming from import monopolies) of

inferior Australian jug wine, and even that is heavily taxed as though it were chateau bottled in France.

Finally, a word about credit cards. The informal United States rule that anything above $10 can be charged does not apply in Indonesia. Though many restaurants say they accept credit cards, you may find them reluctant to take yours unless the tab covers four or five people. It's wise to always carry cash, especially outside Jakarta.

RIJSTTAFEL

The term "Rijsttafel" dates back centuries and translates literally as "rice table." No one is certain how the term actually originated, but everybody agrees the dinner itself was a creation of Dutch planters.

Indonesian people traditionally eat rice with fish or meat, perhaps a vegetable dish, and a spicy samba made from fresh red chilies. This rather simple meal was not enough for Dutch planters, however, who labored from dawn till dusk in an unforgiving climate alien to their upbringing. They added more and more dishes—curried beef, fried chicken, turmeric pickles — until the various courses, arrayed around a steaming serving bowl of white rice, covered the entire table.

In the beginning, this type of meal was served only on plantations and at home parties where domestic labor was cheap. But before long fancy hotels like the Hotel Des Indes in Batavia were going the planters one better by having each of the rijstafel's 12 courses served by a different beautiful maiden.

The second world war ended this elaborate method of presentation. Flushed with revolutionary ardor, formerly obsequious Indonesian maidens no longer wanted to serve plates of fish steamed in coconut milk to *tuan blanda* (colonial Dutch). Today those passions have cooled and the rijstafel is making a comeback.

A rijstafel banquet can contain an infinite variety of courses, but it usually begins with chicken soup followed by spicy hard boiled eggs, pan-fried red snapper and a beef stew. After those dishes are empty, chicken in coconut milk, lamb satay, fried grated coconut with peanuts and braised mixed vegetables arrive. Still hungry? That's good since you'll need room for shrimp crackers, pickles and fried bananas before the coffee arrives.

BARGAINING

Finally, finding a bargain depends on your skill at negotiation. With the exception of airfares, package tours and restaurant food the price of every commodity or service in Indonesia is subject to negotiation. Even the toniest luxury hotel will offer a discount during slow periods. The reduced rate, however, depends on the guest's willingness to ask for it.

In bargaining, several common sense rules apply. First, never lose your temper or become abusive. The object, after all, is for both you and the merchant to come away from the transaction feeling satisfied. Secondly, always set a price before the service is performed. If you ride in an un-metered taxi without first agreeing on the tariff, prepare to pay whatever the driver demands.

Good bargainers are coy, devious and deceitful. Mask your lust for every newfound treasure and always strive to project an aura of blasé ambivalence. If a merchant refuses to bargain, or will come down only 10 percent, simply walk away.

Still, at some point in the negotiation, one must put the disputed sum in perspective. If you've spent several thousand dollars to come to Indonesia, it's hardly worth worrying about an additional $20. Yes, you'll wind up paying more than a local, but the price probably will be a bargain compared to what you would have had to spend for a similar item back home.

ETIQUETTE

Handshaking is customary for men and women alike when being introduced or greeting another person. Be sure to shake hands with everyone when entering and leaving a room with a small group of people. To give or receive anything with the left hand is unacceptable, as is touching an adult on the head. It is considered impolite to call people by crooking the finger or point to an

OPPOSITE: You only pay for what you eat in a *padang*-style lunch. ABOVE: Antique *ikat* textiles are worth hundreds of dollars.

individual or objects on the ground with your foot. Neither should you stand with your hands on your hips since the posture evokes unpleasant memories of plantation overseers. Though the majority of Indonesians are Muslims, it is permissible to eat pork and drink alcohol in their presence, except around Banda Aceh in Northern Sumatra where a more fundamental Islam prevails. Beyond the beach communities on Bali women should never wear shorts. If you visit an Indonesian home or office and food and drink is placed before you, do not eat or drink until you are asked. Often steaming coffee or tea will be allowed to cool as the conversation continues and will be verbally offered late in the meeting, after which it should be drunk rather quickly as the meeting is considered at an end.

Naughty children are pinched instead of spanked in Indonesia. A child also is sometimes pinched as a sign of pleasure. If traveling with children be sure to warn them of this custom.

TELEPHONE

Indonesian telephone numbers vary in the number of digits depending on the location. Offices with several telephone lines in some cities often list a six digit number and a seven digit number. The system is not as confusing as it initially appears; Indonesia simply adds new numbers as they are needed. That's why small towns like Jayapura have five digit numbers while Jakarta has six and seven digit numbers. Add "0" before city code when calling city to city within Indonesia

Outside of the major hotels, you won't find many public telephones. Those you happen to find take a Rp 100 coin for a local call. In smaller towns the best place to make a call is the Telephone and Telegraph Office. The offices are remarkably efficient at putting through normal (*biasa*) calls. For even faster service, pay a modest premium for immediate (*segara*) service.

COUNTRY CODES

Australia 61
Denmark 45
Egypt 20
France 33
Germany 49
Hong Kong 852
India 91
Japan 81
Mexico 52
New Zealand 64
Pakistan 92
Singapore 65
Spain 34
Thailand 66
United Kingdom 44
USA 1
USSR 7

INDONESIAN CITY CODES

Ambon 911
Balikpapan 542
Banda Aceh 651
Bandung 22
Banjarbaru 5119
Banjarmasin 511
Banyuwangi 333
Bekasi 99
Belawan 619
Bengkulu 736
Biak 961
Binjai 619
Blitar 342
Bogor 251
Bojonegoro 353
Bondowoso 332
Bukittinggi 752
Cianjur 263
Cibinong 99
Cilacap 282
Cimahi 229
Cipanas 255
Cirebon 231
Denpasar 361
Gadog/Cisarua 251
Garut 262
Gresik 319
Jakarta 21
Jambi 741
Jayapura 967
Jember 311
Jombang 321
Kabanjahe 628
Karawang 267
Kebumen 287
Kediri 354

NEWSPAPERS AND MAGAZINES

One thing Indonesia is short of is news from the outside world. There are several English-language newspapers published in Indonesia and all are dreadful. Imported newspapers are available, but they are heavily taxed. A *Bangkok Post* or *South China Morning Post* from Hong Kong can cost $4. *Time* magazine is widely available. If you crave news of the world, bring along a small short wave radio.

Even English-language books printed in Indonesia are expensive. If you transit at Changi Airport in Singapore, make the most of your transit time and buy books there.

BASICS

TIME

Indonesia has three time zones. Jakarta, in the West Indonesia time zone is Greenwich Mean Time plus seven hours. This means that when it's midnight in London, it is 7 am in Jakarta, 8 am in Lombok and 9 am in Irian Jaya. Because Indonesia is so close to the Equator, the days are the same length all year around.

ELECTRICITY

Outlets in Indonesia supply 220-240 volts, 50 cycles current and require two-prong plugs. Transformers normally are available in hotels for travelers carrying laptop computers or hair dryers. Power surges are not common, but brown-outs are, so be sure to save information periodically when using a computer.

WATER

Don't drink it, at least not unless it comes from a bottle. Most hotels, and many small losmen, provide bottled water at no charge. Mineral water or purified water in plastic containers can also be purchased in small grocery stores. Every restaurant offers Air Minum or boiled water. If you dying of thirst, drink beer.

BATHING AND THE TOILET

In Bahasa Indonesia the term for to wash is *mandi*. *Mandi* also is the name for the large square water tank in most Indonesian bathrooms. Instead of taking a shower, Indonesians use a plastic bucket or dipper to splash themselves with water from the *mandi*. After soaping thoroughly, they rinse off by sloshing more water. It is a thoroughly refreshing way to bath, especially at the end of the day. The *mandi* is refilled periodically and used by everyone. Nothing should be washed or rinsed in the *mandi* itself.

Beyond the tourist centers of Java and Bali toilets tend to be nothing more than a hole in the floor with footrests on either side. The toilet is flushed with water dipped from the *mandi*. Indonesian toilets in restaurants and gasoline stations normally don't provide toilet paper, so it may be wise to carry your own.

CRIME

Compared with the United States and Australia, Indonesia is a very peaceful country. There is very little violent crime of the sort encountered in cities like New York and Chicago. Robbery can be a problem, however, for people who are careless or imprudent. When traveling in remote areas where traveler's checks are not readily accepted, it is advisable to wear a money belt.

In Jakarta and Bali, employees at the better hotels are carefully selected. In general, it is quite safe to leave cameras or travel documents in a locked hotel room. Money and jewelry, however, probably should be put in a safety deposit box or closet safe.

PUBLIC HOLIDAYS AND FESTIVALS

Almost all Indonesian holidays and festivals follow a lunar calendar and therefore the dates vary each year. The dates given are therefore approximate. Check actual dates with the Provincial Tourist Service (*DIPARDA*), or *BAPPARDA* the Provincial Tourist Agency.

HOLIDAYS

JANUARY 1 New Year's Day.
FEBRUARY 12 Prophet Mohammad's Ascension.
MARCH 17 *Nyepi*, Balinese New Year (Day of Silence)
MARCH *Wafat Isa Al-Masih*, Good Friday
MID-APRIL End of Ramadan, the Moslem fasting month
EARLY MAY *Kenaikan Isa Al-Masih*, Ascension of Christ
END MAY *Waisak*, Anniversary of the birth of Buddha
LATE JUNE Moslem Day of Sacrifice
MID JULY Moslem New Year
AUGUST 17 Indonesian Independence Day
MID SEPTEMBER Anniversary of the birth of Mohammad
DECEMBER 25 Christmas

FESTIVALS

January
1ST **Pontianak, West Kalimantan**: Anniversary of West Kalimantan is celebrated with folk performances and art exhibitions
SECOND TO FOURTH WEEKS **East Java village of Bondowoso**: *Sapp-Sapp* and *Tarik Tambang Perahu* are performed. *Sapp-Sapp* is a traditional chicken race in which chickens are released from a boat on the ocean and directed toward shore. The winner is the one that flies the longest distance. *Tarik Tambang*

OPPOSITE: In West Java magic and illusion are popular entertainments.

Perahu is a tug-of-war between two boats afloat in the middle of the sea.

THIRD WEEK **Pager Wesi, Bali**: Balinese flock to temples for , a festival honoring the deity who created the universe.

LAST WEEK **Hila Village, Ambon, Maluku**: Closing New Year celebration. According to Maluku custom, the entire month of January is devoted to celebrating the New Year. This last feast of sago, sweet potatoes and wild game is held in the forest or on the beach, and is accompanied by an all-night sing along.

February

FIRST WEEK **Sidoarjo village, East Java**: Celebration of its shrimp chip and batik industries with various attractions.

Selawu, West Java (30 km or 19 miles from Tasikmalaya): The annual cleansing of heirlooms revives the history of the Suku Naga people.

SECOND WEEK **Siantar, North Sumatra** (137 km or 85 miles from Medan): *Rondang Bintang* means "full moon." This festival is highlighted by a variety of traditional dances and sporting events. The festival is in the a historical city of the Purba Kingdom where old Simalungun houses still stand.

Central Sulawesi: Celebration of *Vunja* harvest festival.

Parang Kusumo beach south of Yogyakarta: Coinciding with the birthday of the Sultan of Yogyakarta, offerings are made to appease Nyai Loro Kidul, the goddess of the South Sea. Similar offerings are given at the peaks of the Merapi and Lawu volcanoes.

THIRD WEEK **East Java**: The *Karo* Ceremony is staged in the Tosari Pasuruan and Ngadisari Probolinggo areas to commemorate the creation of man by the God Sang Hyang Widi. Lasting two days, the ceremony opens with a Tenggerese dance, the *Tari Sodor*, performed by adult male dancers.

March

FIRST WEEK **Southern Lombok in West Nusatenggara:** *Bagedo*k harvest festival.

SECOND WEEK **Bali**: Saraswati Day. Balinese temples bless the island's books in honor

of the goddess of learning and knowledge, Batari Dewi Saraswati.

THIRD WEEK **Bali**: Religious cleaning ceremony prior to Nyepi in which Balinese take temple utensils to the sea for washing. The *Nyepi Day* falls on the Spring equinox and is observed as a day of complete silence. No fires may be lit, no transport taken, no work done. On the night before Nyepi, purification sacrifices and other offerings are made at crossroads and in the centers of villages and towns. Priests chant mantras to exorcise the demons of the old year. People across the island bang gongs and cymbals in their family compounds to make sure all the malingering spirits are rousted. In Denpasar, thousands of boys gather at Puputan Square for a parade through the city. The following

Colorful celebrations occur throughout the year.

day, Nyepi, everyone keeps silent in hopes the demons and spirits roused the night before will think Bali devoid of life and leave for another island.

Kudas, Central Java: Five-day festival marks the beginning of Ramadan.

Semarang, Central Java: The *Dugderan* festival starts one month before the Moslem feasting month of Ramadan and is held in front of the Mesjid Besar. Stalls sell different kinds of food and drink especially for children.

FOURTH WEEK **Pontianak, West Kalimantan** Decorated boat races and cultural performances celebrate the day the sun is exactly above the equator.

Sarangan, East Java (14.5 km or nine miles from Magetan): The ceremony of *Bersih Desa* begins with the burial of a goat's head fol-

lowed by a week of traditional dances and games around the Telaga Sarangan resort.

Bandung, West Java A marathon commemorates the independence struggle against the Dutch.

Besakih, Bali: the largest temple in Bali celebrates its founding with a day of prayer, feasting and entertainment.

April

FIRST WEEK **Majalengka, West Java**: Sugar cane festival.

Muara, Northern Sumatra: boat races.

Siborong-borong, Northern Sumatra: *Batak Horas* festival features horse racing.

Pelabuhan Ratu, West Java: The Sea festival is celebrated by throwing flower petals and a buffalo head into the sea from a colorfully decorated boat. A *wayang golek* puppet show, a *pencak silat* performance and a *ketuk tilu* communal dance are held the night before.

SECOND WEEK **Bitang, North Sulawesi**: Celebrates the city's founding with cultural performances and art exhibitions by different ethnic groups.

THIRD WEEK **Mataram, West Nusa Tenggara:** Celebrates its heritage with parades and exhibitions.

Palu, Central Sulawesi: Anniversary festival.

FOURTH WEEK **Pontianak, West Kalimantan:** *Naik Dago* harvest festival.

May

FIRST WEEK **Subang** (70 km or 43 miles north of Bandung): *Gotong Sisingaan.* Traditional art festival and parade with decorated wooden effigies of lions.

THIRD WEEK: **Gunung Kunci, Sumedang area of West Java**: Ram fighting.

THIRD TO FOURTH WEEK **Prambanan** (outside Yogyakarta): *Ramayana* ballet performed on the open air stage over four nights of the full moon. The four performances are: *The Abduction of Sita, Hanoman's Mission,*

The Death of Kumbokarno and Sita's Trial of Purity.

LAST WEEK **Maumere, Flores, East Nusa Tenggara**: Flores underwater festival.

Surabaya, East Java: *Taman Surya,* Anniversary of Surabaya celebrated with *wayang kulit* shadow plays and popular folk comedies.

June

FIRST WEEK **Cibubur, Jakarta**: Floriculture exposition and festival at the Wiladatika Botanical Garden.

SECOND WEEK **Jakarta**: Dragon Boat races at Ancol marina.

Bali: Art Festival features a month of special dances celebrating traditional Balinese culture.

THIRD WEEK **Pandaan** (45 km or 28 miles south of Surabaya): Javanese ballet. The East Java classical ballet festival held at the Chandra Wilwatikita. Staged against a backdrop of distant volcanoes, the performances are based on the East Javanese Majapahit and Kahuripan eras, as well as the traditional Hindu epics, the Mahabarata and the *Ramayana.*

Prambanan (outside Yogyakarta): *Ramayana* Ballet during the full moon.

Yogyakarta: *Tumplak Wajik* ceremony takes place in the main pavilion of the city's *kraton* when huge mounds of rice are decorated with vegetables, eggs and cakes so they can be blessed and distributed to the poor. The making of the mounds is accompanied by rhythmic chanting and playing of instruments to ward off evil spirits.

FOURTH WEEK **Jakarta**: The anniversary of the city is celebrated with an all night party at Ancol Dreamland Park.

July

JULY THROUGH OCTOBER **Tana Toraja, South Sulawesi**: The *Rambu Solo* religious ceremony is held to insure that the dead will be accepted by God. A buffalo is killed, then bodies are carried to their ultimate resting places in niches on the hanging rock cliffs.

SECOND WEEK **South central coast, Java**: *Asyura* Javanese New Year. A ceremony held to appease Nyi Loro Kidul, the goddess of the South Sea. Pilgrims swim in the Sedudo waterfall 24 km (15 miles) from Nganjuk in the belief the water will keep them young.

Javanese orchestras can be seen every afternoon in Yogyakarta's leading hotels. OPPOSITE: The hypnotic sound of the gamelan can induce a trance-like state in some dancers.

Ceremonial meals are held in the village of Menang.

12TH **Surakarta Central Java**: *Kirab Pusaka Kraton* is the ceremony observed by the two ruling courts of Surakarta, the Kasunanan and the Mangkunegaran, to celebrate the Javanese New Year. Heirlooms are displayed in a procession of court attendants dressed in traditional costume.

14TH **Pager Rejo village, Kretek, Yogyakarta**: *Suran* is an ancient event at Pager Rego on the first day of the Javanese New Year. A black goat and two cocks are paraded

about the village and then slaughtered at noon. The four legs of the goat are planted at the corners of the village with its head in the center to prevent future disasters.

FOURTH WEEK **Prambanan** (outside Yogyakarta): *Ramayana* ballet at Prambanan during full moon.

END OF JULY **Ambon**: Yacht Race from Ambon to Darwin begins.

Padang province, West Sumatra: *Tabot*: A festival held in the West Sumatran province of Padang to commemorate the death of Mohammed's grandchildren Hassan and

Husein. Effigies of Bouraq, the winged horse with a woman's head who saved the souls of the two boys, are carried in a procession before being thrown into the sea.

August

FIRST WEEK **Baruppu Tana Toraja village, South Sulawesi**: *Ma'nene* festival to change the shroud on the corpse of Tau-tau. Taken down from its hillside nook for one night, the newly shrouded statue serves as a center piece for dancing. The following day it is returned to its normal perch.

Rancakalong, Sumedang, West Java: *Ngalaksa*. Rice festival accompanied by night of *jentreng* dancing.

SECOND WEEK **Bandung**: *Pawai Pembangunan*. Independence parade followed by outdoor cultural performances.

Muncar, East Java: *Petik Laut Muncar*. Fishermen fill a boat with a goat's head and other offerings which they then throw into the sea. After the ceremony, there are canoe and sailboat races plus fishing competitions and Gan*drung* dancers.

Yogyakarta: Turtledove Contest. Song birds compete in southern square of the Sultan's palace for trophy.

THIRD WEEK **Pandaan** (45 km or 28 miles south of Surabaya): East Java ballet festival at the Candra Wilwatika open-air theater.

Situbondo, East Java: *Sapp-Sapp* and *Tarik Tambang Perahu* festivities on Pasir Putih Beach.

Palembang, South Sumatra: Canoe races celebrate Independence Day. Canoes used on the Musi river are shaped like animals.

Cianjur, West Java: *Arak-Arakan Kuda Kosong* horse procession has decorated horses escorted by incense-bearing guards.

Prambanan (outside Yogyakarta): *Ramayana* ballet.

FOURTH WEEK **Yogyakarta**: *Saparan Gamping* ceremony. Five kilometers (three miles) west of Yogyakarta there is a limestone hill outside Ambarketawang Gamping village thought to be 50 million years old that has been quarried for centuries. To protect the limestone workers once a year a life-size statues of a bride and bridegroom are made out of glutinous rice and filled with brown sugar syrup representing human blood. The statues are then sacrificed to so that villagers can remain safe for another year.

OPPOSITE: Balinese dancing requires the limber torso of a teenager. ABOVE: *Ramayana* ballerinas personalize the Hindu epic with their own interpretations.

LAST WEEK **Jatinom, Central Java**: *Yaqowiyu* festival honors former Muslim sage. *Apem* pancakes made of rice and corn flour are eaten for good luck.

September

FIRST WEEK **Ambon**: The anniversary of the city is celebrated with Maluku dances and feasting.

Madura island: *Karapan Sapi* bull race championship.

THIRD WEEK **Prambanan** (outside Yogyakarta): *Ramayana* ballet during the full moon.

November

FIRST WEEK **North Sulawesi**: Anniversary of the founding of the Minahasa regency is celebrated with traditional cultural ceremonies.

THIRD WEEK **Pontianak**: Trans Equator Marathon.

LAST WEEK **Malang, East Java**: Anniversary of Malang.

December

FIRST WEEK **Mataram, West Nusa Tenggara:** *Ketupat War*. Farmers from the town throw

Manado, North Sulawesi: Anniversary of North Sulawesi is celebrated with cultural performances, bull races and fashion shows.

LAST WEEK **Tenggarong, East Kalimantan**: *Erau* festival culminates when a mock dragon is thrown into the Mahakam river.

October

FIRST WEEK **Cirebon, Kasepuhan and Kanoman**: *Muludan Panjang Jimat*. Cleaning and blessing of the heirlooms of these princely courts.

SECOND WEEK **Pamekasan, Madura, East Java**: Bull racing championship.

THIRD WEEK **Pandaan** (45 km or 28 miles south of Surabaya): East Java classical ballet festival.

ketupat (steamed rice wrapped in palm leaves) at each other in hopes that they will be prosperous.

Tasikmalaya, West Java: Sea festival. West Javan thanksgiving festival in which a buffalo is sacrificed prior to singing and canoe races.

Kesodo, Nusa Tenggara: At dawn on the fourteenth day of the twelfth month of the Tenggerese year priests of the Tenggerese Buddha Dharma offer fruit, flowers and rice to the God of Bromo who lives in the Mt. Bromo volcano crater.

THIRD WEEK **Bali**: *Galungan Day* commemorates the world's creation with temple offerings and sacrifices.

Bondowoso, East Java: Bull fighting.

BAHASA INDONESIA FOR TRAVELERS

More than 250 distinct languages and dialects are spoken throughout the Indonesian archipelago, but the unifying tongue is Bahasa Indonesia. A refinement of classical Malay spoken on the Malay Peninsula, it is a relatively new language that has been recognized only since Indonesian independence.

Indonesians in large cities tend to speak several languages. In Yogyakarta, for example, Javanese is spoken in the home, while Bahasa Indonesia is the language of the workplace. English is taught in public schools and widely spoken by those in commercial trade service industries. Dutch is also an elective course that some students again are beginning to study. Indonesian professionals age 60 and older usually were educated in the Dutch language. But the general preference for a second language today is English.

GRAMMAR AND PRONUNCIATION

Although study is required to speak Bahasa Indonesia fluently, it is relatively easy to learn because sentence structure is simple, it is written in Roman script and, unlike other Asian languages, it is phonetic, not tonal. There are no articles; *peta* means "a map." To make a noun plural, just double it, so that *peta-peta* (or *peta2* as it might be written in a newspaper) becomes "maps." Neither are there verb tenses. Past and future are denoted by the use of adverbs such as *sudah* (already) and *belum* (not yet).

In speaking the language remember that adjectives always follow the noun, and the order of sentences is subject — verb — object, as in *Saya* (I) *angkat* (carry) *peta* (the map). The possessive is accomplished by putting the personal pronoun after the noun. *Peta saya* means "my map."

In 1972 the country simplified the spelling, making it conform to Malay. Some Indonesians prefer the old spelling, especially when it comes to their names, so that's why

you'll see newspapers spell their president's name Soeharto instead of Suharto.

a is pronounced with a short sound, as in "father."

c has a "ch" sound as in "church."

k is hard at the start of a word, as in "kite," and silent when it comes at the end.

kh is slightly aspirated

j is like the word "James." Under the old spelling dj substituted for j. That's why on old maps Jakarta is sometimes spelled Djarkata.

r is rolled.

u is full as in "ukulele," never like it sounds in the word "but."

y is pronounced as in "you."

VOCABULARY

Numbers

0 *noi*
1 *satu*
2 *dua*
3 *tiga*
4 *empat*
5 *lima*
6 *enam*
7 *tujuh*
8 *delapan*
9 *sembilan*
10 *sepuluh*
11 *sebelas*
12 *duabelas*
13 *tigabelas*
14 *empatbelas*
15 *limabelas*
20 *duapuluh*
21 *duapuluh satu*
30 *tigapuluh*
40 *empatpuluh*
100 *seratus*
200 *duaratus*
243 *duaratus empatpuluh tiga*
500 *limaratus*
1,000 *seribu*
2,000 *duaribu*
10,000 *sepuluh ribu*
100,000 *seratus ribu*
first *pertama*
second *kedua*
third *ketiga*
fourth *keempat*
fifth *kelima*

OPPOSITE: Despite elaborate costuming the monster in the Balinese *barong* doesn't seem that intimidating.

sixth *keenam*
seventh *ketujuh*
eighth *kedalapan*
ninth *kesembilan*
tenth *kesepuluh*
twelfth *keduabelas*
½ *setengah*
¼ *seperempat*
⅔ *duapertiga*

Calendar

Sunday *Hari Minggu*
Monday *Hari Senen*
Tuesday *Hari Selasa*
Wednesday *Hari Rabu*
Thursday *Hari Kamis*
Friday *Hari Jum'at*
Saturday *Hari Sabtu*
day *hari*
today *hari ini*
tomorrow *besok*
yesterday *kemarin*
week *minggu*
month *bulan*
year *tahun*
season *musim*
hot season *musim panas*
dry season *musim kemarau*
wet season *musim hujan*
January *Januari*
February *Februari*
March *Maret*
April *April*
May *Mei*
June *Juni*
July *Juli*
August *Agustus*
September *September*
October *Oktober*
November *Nopember*
December *Desember*

Time

morning (dawn to 11 am) *pagi*
good morning *salamat pagi*
noon (midday, 11 am to 2 pm) *siang*
good day *salamat siang*
evening (3 pm to 8 pm) *sore*
good evening *salamat sore*
good night *salamat malam*
always *selalu*
before *dahulu*
soon *nanti*

now *sekarang*
right now *baru saja*
quick *cepat*
very flexible ("rubber time") *jam karet*
about (approximately) *kira-kira*
then *kemudian*
What time is it? *Jam berapa sekarang?*
Eight o'clock *Jam delapan*
Half-past eight *Setengah sembilan*

Key Words and Phrases

yes *ya*
no *tidak*
I'm sorry *Ma'af*
I beg your pardon *Saya mohon ma'af*
Thank you *Terima kasih*
What is your name? *Siapa nama saudara?*
my name is... *nama saya...*
I come from... *saya datang dari...*
Mr. *Tuan, Pak, Bung*
Mrs. *Nyonya, Ibu*
Miss. *Nona*
and *dan*
but *tetapi*
this/that *ini/itu*
here/there *disini/disana*
more/less *lebih/kurang*
much/very much *banyak/banyak sekali*
very nice *bagus*
big/small *besar/kecil*
young/old *muda/tua*
clean/dirty *bersih/kotor*
hot/cold *panas/dingin*
good/no good *baik/tidak baik*
You're right/you're wrong *Anda benar/anda salah*
open/closed *buka/tutup*
entrance/exit *masuk/keluar*
push/pull *tolak/tarik*
no smoking *dilarang merokok*
I don't speak Indonesian. *Saya tidak bicara Bahasa Indonesia.*
I speak only a little Indonesian. *Saya bisa bicara sedikit saja Bahasa Indonesia.*
please *silahkan*
Please speak slowly. *Tolong bicara pelan-pelan.*
Do you speak English? *Apa saudara dapat bicara Bahasa Inggeris?*
I understand *Saya mengerti*
I don't understand *Saya kurang mengerti*
Goodbye (to person going) *salamat jalan*
Goodbye (to person staying) *salamat tinggal*

In the Post Office
post office *kantor pos*
stamp *prangko*
letter *surat*
package/parcel *paket/bungkusan*
aerogram *warkatpos udara*
airmail *pos udara*
postcard *kartu pos*
tape *isolatip*
overweight *terlalu berat*
I'm looking for the post office *Saya sedang mencari kantor pos*
I want to send this letter via regular mail *Saya mau mengirim surat ini biasa*
This is a special delivery letter *Ini adalah surat kilat*

In Restaurants
restaurant *restoran, rumah makan*
Where is a good restaurant? *Restoran mana yang baik?*
I'm hungry *Saya lapar*
dining room *kamar makan*
breakfast *makan pagi*
lunch *makan siang*
dinner *makan malam*
food/drink *makanan/minuman*
water/boiled water *air/air putih*
Is this water drinkable? *Apa air ini bisa diminum?*
I would like to drink boiled water *Saya minta air matang untuk minum air*
drinking water *air minum.*
ice/iced water *es/air es*
tea/coffee *teh/kopi*
beer *bir*
milk *susu*
bread/butter *roti/mentega*
rice/noodles *nasi/mie*
soup *soto*
chicken *ayam*
beef *daging gapi*
pork *babi*
lamb *domba*
goat *kambing*
fish *ikan*
shrimp *udang*
vegetables *sayur*
fruit *buah*
banana *pisang*
coconut *kelapa*
mango *mangga*
pineapple *nanas*

egg *telur*
fried egg/omelet *telur mata sapi/telur dadar*
boiled/fried *rebus/goreng*
sugar *gula*
salt/pepper *garam/merica*
sweet/sour/spicy *manis/asam/pedas*
hot/cold *panas/dingin*
soya sauce *kecap*
cup/glass *cangkir/gelas*
plate *piring*
knife/fork/spoon *pisau/garpu/sendok*
Where is the toilet? *Dimana kamar kecil?*
May I see the menu? *Boleh saya lihat daftar makanan?*
Waiter, please bring the bill *Bung, saya minta bonnya*

In the Hotel
hotel *hotel*
small hotel, guest house *losmen*
Where is the hotel? *Dimana ada hotel?*
Do you have a room with a private bath? *Apa anda kamar yang pakai kamar mandi tersendiri?*
How much for one night? *Berapa harganya satu malam?*
Does the price include breakfast? *Apakah sewanya termasuk sarapan pagi?*
room/bedroom *kamar/kamar tidur*
bathroom *kamar mandi*
toilet *kamar kecil*
toilet paper *kertas toilet*
towel *handuk*
soap *sabun*
to wash *cuci*
clothes *pakaian*
Please wash these clothes. *Tolong cuci pakaian-pakaian*
to iron *gosok*
I want to check out. *Saya mau keluar sekarang.*
Please get me a taxi *Tolong panggilkan saya taksi*

On the Road
left/right *kiri/kanan*
turn right *belok kekanan*
turn left at the corner. *belok ke kiri di prapatan.*
stop here *berhenti disini*
How far is it from here? *Berapa jauh dari sini?*
to walk *jalan*
to drive *stir*
car *mobil*

bus *bis*
bicycle *sepeda*
train/train station *kereta-api/stasiun kereta-api*
airplane/airport *kapal terbang/lapangan terbang*
I want a ticket to... *Saya mau beli karcis ke...*
What's the fare? *Berapa ongkosnya?*
How long does it take to get from here to...
Berapa lama perjalanan dari sini ke...
ship **kapal laut**
first class/economy class *kelas satu/kelas ekonomi*
I want to reserve two seats to... *Saya mau pesan dua kursi untuk ke...*
gasoline station *pompa bensin*
city *kota*
central *pusat*
I am lost *Saya tersesat.*
What's the name of this street? *Apa nama jalan ini?*
market *pasar*
office building *wisma*
hospital *rumah sakit*
pharmacy *apotik*
taxi *taksi*
How much is this taxi per hour? *Berapa sewa taksi ini per jam?*
Drive faster. I'm in a hurry. *Cepat sedikit. Saya buru-buru.*

Shopping
antique *antik*
How much *berapa*
cheap/expensive *murah/mahal*
like this/like that *begini/begitu*
Just looking around *Saya hanya melihat-nrelihat*
What is this? *Apakah ini?*
I want to buy... *Saya mau beli...*
It's too expensive *Itu terlalu mahal*
I'll come back later *Saya akan kembali lagi*

In Emergencies
I've lost my passport *Paspor saya hilang.*
Please help me. *Tolonglah saya sebentar.*
Is there anybody here who speaks English?
Ada yang bisa berbahasa inggeris disini?
Please go away! *Pergilah!*
Please call a doctor *Tolong panggilkan dokter.*

Picture credits

All pictures by **Nik Wheeler** except those credited below:

Robert Harding Picture Library: 10, 11, 12 *top*, 14, 17,23, 31 *bottom*, 42, 43, 46-47, 66, 69, 111, 113R, 120, 122, 128, 129, 137, 141, 142, 162, 164, 170, 178, 179, 204.
Adrian Bradshaw: 21, 31 *top*, 33, 74, 113 *left*, 116, 117, 121, 123, 126, 138, 168, 194
David DeVoss: 165, 181.
Jill Gotcher: 12 *bottom*, 16,22, 38, 39, 41, 50, 52, 62,73, 107, 115, 130, 131, 133, 145, 146, 174, 175,180, 182, 191, 199.
Chris Stowers: 63.
Joseph R Yogerst: 34, 51, 58, 59. 67,91,92, 96, 99, 133, 136, 140 *left*, 140 *right*, 147, 195.

Recommended Reading

History and Politics

BOXER, C.R. *Jan Compagnie in War and Peace (1602–1799)*. Heinemann, Hong Kong 1979.

CROUCH, HAROLD. *The Army and Politics in Indonesia*. Cornell University Press 1978.

GRISWOLD, DEIRDRE. *Indonesia*. World View Publishers, Chicago 1979.

JONES, HOWARD PALFREY. *Indonesia: The Possible Dream*. Harcourt Brace Jovanovich, New York 1971.

MAY, BRIAN *The Indonesian Tragedy*. Graham Brash Ltd, Singapore 1978.

MONEY, J.W.B. *Java or How to Manage a Colony*. Oxford University Press, Singapore 1985.

MOSSMAN, JAMES. *Rebels in Paradise*. Jonathon Cape, London 1961.

NOTOSUSANTO, Brig. Gen. NUGROHO. *The National Struggle and the Armed Forces in Indonesia*. Center for Armed Forces History, Jakarta 1983. Also *The Japanese Occupation and Indonesian Independence*.

PIGEAUD, T.G. and H.J. DE GRAAF, *Islamic States in Java 1500-1700*. Martinus Nijhoff, The Hague 1976.

SCIDMORE, E.R. *Java The Garden of the East*. Oxford University Press 1984.

STEINBERG, DAVID JOEL. *In Search of Southeast Asia: A Modern History*. University of Hawaii Press 1986.

WALLACE, ALFRED RUSSEL. *The Malay Archipelago*. Graham Brash Ltd, Singapore.

Culture and Religion

AVE, JAN B. *Borneo: The People of the Weeping Forest*. Netherlands National Museum of Ethnology, Leiden 1986.

GEERTZ, CLIFFORD. *The Religion of Java*. University of Chicago Press 1976.

LEE KHOON CHOY. *Indonesia Between Myth and Reality*. Nile & Mackenzie, London 1976.

NEILL, WILFRED T. *Twentieth-Century Indonesia*. Columbia University Press 1973.

RICHARDSON, DON *Peace Child*. GL Publications, Ventura, California. Also *Lords of the Earth*.

VAN NESS, EDWARD and SHITA PRAWIRO-HARDJO, *Javanese Wayang Kulit*. Oxford University Press 1985.

Novels and Essays

ALLEN, CHARLES. *Tales from the South China Seas*. Futura Publications, London.

BANGS, RICHARD and CHRISTIAN KALLEN *Islands of Fire, Islands of Spice*. Sierra Club Books, San Francisco.

CONRAD, JOSEPH. *Almayer's Folly, An Outcast of the Islands, Victory*.

FORBES, ANNA. *Unbeaten Tracks in Islands of the Far East, Experiences of a Naturalist's Wife in the 1880s*. Oxford University Press, Singapore 1987.

LUBIS, MOCHTAR. *Twilight in Djartaka*. Oxford University Press, Singapore 1987. Also *The Indonesian Dilemma, A Road With No End and The Outlaw and Other Stories*.

LULOFS, MADELON. *Coolie*. Oxford University Press, Kuala Lumpur 1982. Also *Rubber*.

MAUGHAM, WILLIAM SOMERSET. *Maugham's Borneo Stories*. Heinemann, Hong Kong 1976.

MULTATULI (Eduard Douwes Dekker). *Max DALTON, BILL. Indonesia Handbook*. Moon Publications, Chico, California 1989.

HUTTON, PETER. *Java*. Apa Productions, Singapore.

Indonesia, Lonely Planet. Hawthorn, Victoria, Australia 1990.

OEY, ERIC. *Indonesia*. Apa Productions, Singapore.

MULLER, KAL. *Spice Islands; The Moluccas*. Periplus Editions 1990.

STEVES, RICK and JOHN GOTTBERG. *Asia Through the Back Door*. John Muir Publications, Santa Fe 1990.

Havelaar, or the Coffee Auctions of the Dutch Trading Company. University of Massachusetts Press, Amherst 1982.

NIEUWENHUYS, ROB. *Mirror of the Indes, A History of Dutch Colonial Literature*. University of Massachusetts Press, Amherst 1982.

SUTTON, ANNABEL. *The Islands in Between*. Impact Books, London 1989.

SZEKELY, LADISLAO. *Tropic Fever*. Oxford University Press 1979.

VAN SCHENDEL, ARTHUR. *John Company*. University of Massachusetts Press 1983.

ZACH, PAUL. *Indonesia, Paradise on the Equator*. St. Martin's Press, New York 1988.

Travel Guides

WINTERTON, BRADLEY. *Insider's Guide to Bali*. CFW Publications, Hong Kong.

Quick Reference A–Z Guide to Places and Topics of Interest with Listed Accommodation, Restaurants and Useful Telephone Numbers